Feminism
and
Anthropology

FEMINIST PERSPECTIVES
Series Editor: Michelle Stanworth

Published

Forthcoming

Feminism and Anthropology

HENRIETTA L. MOORE

Polity Press

Copyright © Henrietta L. Moore 1988

First published 1988 by Polity Press
in association with Blackwell Publishers Ltd.
Reprinted 1989, 1991, 1992, 1993, 1994, 1995

Editorial office:
Polity Press, 65 Bridge Street,
Cambridge CB2 1UR, UK

Marketing and production:
Blackwell Publishers Ltd
108 Cowley Road, Oxford, OX4 1JF, UK

CIP data for this book is available
from the British Library.

ISBN 0–7456–0114–6
ISBN 0–7456–0113–8 Pbk

Typeset in 10.5 on 12pt Malibu
by Times Graphics, Singapore
Printed in Great Britain by
T.J. Press (Padstow) Ltd., Padstow, Cornwall

CONTENTS

For My Mother

PREFACE AND ACKNOWLEDGEMENTS

The writing of this book has been punctuated for me by the expressions of dismay, amusement, support and envy with which my friends and colleagues have responded at different times to the news that I was engaged in such a task. It is undoubtedly both impertinent and foolhardy to write a book entitled 'Feminism and Anthropology'. There is no agreed way of defining or characterizing either of the key terms in question. There are many feminisms, just as there are many anthropologies. This book is not, and nor could it ever be, a comprehensive and definitive account either of feminism or of anthropology, let alone of their 'relations'.

It is commonly assumed that books about feminism are either 'women's books' or books 'about women'. This provides the unsympathetic reader with an excuse to avoid engaging with the issues raised, and can sometimes be seen as a justification for laying the book aside altogether. The identification of feminist concerns with women's concerns has been one of the many strategies employed in the social sciences to marginalize the feminist critique. This marginalization is quite unjustified, and one of the aims of this book is to demonstrate that the feminist critique in anthropology has been, and will continue to be, central to theoretical and methodological developments within the discipline as a whole. The basis for the feminist critique is not the study of women, but the analysis of gender relations, and of gender as a structuring principle in all human societies. It is for this reason that I can say that this book is not in any way concerned with the critique of male bias in the discipline of social anthropology, because it looks, not backwards to what we have already achieved, but forwards to the future of feminist anthropology, and to the contributions it will make to particular areas of the discipline in the future.

The structure of the book has a certain narrative historical form. Chapter 1 discusses the history of the relationship between feminism and anthropology. Chapter 2 deals with debates on gender, sexual asymmetry and male dominance, as well as with how these issues feed into problems of universalism and the future of comparative studies in anthropology. These debates were the 'first' ones to be dealt with by feminist anthropology, although they are by no means resolved, and the next few years are likely to see substantive new publications on gender symbolism – including new material on masculinity – and on sexual inequality. Chapter 3 discusses the relationship between Marxist and feminist anthropology, and considers the impact which feminist anthropology has had on traditional areas of anthropological enquiry, including property, inheritance and the sexual division of labour. These debates were extremely important in the late 1970s and early 1980s, and they are part of a more general shift in anthropological thinking which took place at that time. Chapter 4 deals with debates concerning the rise of capitalism, and the way in which forms of labour and the sexual division of labour have been transformed. The chapter goes on to discuss feminist theories of the relationship between productive and reproductive labour under capitalism, and shows how data from non-Western countries can provide new vantage points from which to view old debates. It concludes with a discussion of the changing 'family'. Chapter 5 presents material on women and the state which is arguably the 'newest' and most exciting area of feminist scholarship in anthropology; and it draws on perspectives developed in earlier chapters to outline the areas of the discipline in which feminist anthropology is likely to be making substantive contributions in the future. It also provides material on which to base a critique of feminist theorizing and feminist politics.

I am very aware that in writing this book I have given prominence to some areas of anthropological enquiry at the expense of others. My justification for doing this is simply one of space, as well as the fact that, in trying to demonstrate the value of the feminist critique in anthropology, I have been concerned to develop coherent themes rather than to catalogue the impact of feminist thought on all areas of the discipline. None the less, there is relatively little discussion of 'rites' and 'rituals', which have always been key areas of anthropological enquiry. Some anthropologists may feel that this is a significant omission, but I feel that the important developments in those fields with regard to the feminist critique in the discipline are adequately covered by the discussion of symbolic approaches to gender in chapter 2. I am also aware of the lack of discussion concerning the role of religion in human social life, and I can only hope that other authors may take on the formidable task of providing a comprehensive account of the impact of the feminist critique in this area.

Writing, as all authors acknowledge, is a collaborative exercise. However, this is most especially the case with regard to this book because most of the substantive content and the theoretical approaches are based directly on the work of other feminist scholars. It will be apparent to those already familiar with the anthropological material that I have drawn heavily on the work of a number of feminist anthropologists. It could not be otherwise: without the very brilliant work of these women it would not have been possible to write this book, because there would have been no feminist anthropology to write about. I have cited them extensively, and I only hope that, where I may have omitted to refer to them directly, they will understand that my debt to them is none the less for that. I also wish to acknowledge my debt to many anthropologists who do not think of themselves, and would not wish to be thought of, as feminists, and to many scholars from other disciplines who would certainly not want to be thought of as anthropologists!

I have depended enormously on the help and support of many friends and colleagues while I have been writing this book. I would especially like to thank Michelle Stanworth, who first encouraged me to write this book, and whose intellectual insight and fine editing skills have proved to be my saving. I would also like to thank Margaret Jolly and Megan Vaughan for commenting on the final draft of the manuscript and Anne Farmer for typing it, as well as many others who have provided support and advice.

1

FEMINISM AND ANTHROPOLOGY: THE STORY OF A RELATIONSHIP

Anthropology is the study of man embracing woman.
                                    Bronislaw Malinowski

The feminist critique in social anthropology, as in the other social sciences, grew out of a specific concern with the neglect of women in the discipline. However, unravelling the history of that neglect is difficult because of the ambiguous way in which social anthropology has always treated women. Women were not ignored in traditional anthropology.

> At the level of 'observation' in fieldwork, the behaviour of women has, of course, like that of men, been exhaustively plotted: their marriages, their economic activity, their rites and the rest. (Ardener, 1975a: 1)

Women have always been present in ethnographic accounts, primarily because of the traditional anthropological concern with kinship and marriage. The main problem was not, therefore, one of empirical study, but rather one of representation. In a famous study which discusses this problem, the authors analysed the different interpretations given by male and female ethnographers to the position and nature of Australian Aboriginal women. The male ethnographers spoke of the women as profane, economically unimportant and excluded from rituals. The female researchers, on the other hand, described the women's central role in subsistence, the importance of women's rituals and the respectful way in which they were treated by men (Rohrlich-Leavitt et al., 1975). Women were present in both sets of ethnographies, but in very different ways.

The new 'anthropology of women' thus began, in the early 1970s, by confronting the problem of how women were represented in anthropological writing. The initial problem was quickly identified as one of male bias, which was seen as having three layers or 'tiers'. The first layer consists of the bias imported by the anthropologist, who brings to the research various assumptions and expectations about the relationships between women and men, and about the significance of those relationships for an understanding of the wider society.

> Male bias is carried into field research. It is often claimed that men in other cultures are more accessible to outsiders (especially male outsiders) for questioning. A more serious and prior problem is that we think that men control the significant information in other cultures, as we are taught to believe they do in ours. We search them out and tend to pay little attention to the women. Believing that men are easier to talk to, more involved in the crucial cultural spheres, we fulfil our own prophecies in finding them to be better informants in the field. (Reiter, 1975: 14)

The second bias is one inherent in the society being studied. Women are considered as subordinate to men in many societies, and this view of gender relations is likely to be the one communicated to the enquiring anthropologist. The third and final layer is provided by the bias inherent in Western culture. The argument here is that, when researchers perceive the asymmetrical relations between women and men in other cultures, they assume such asymmetries to be analogous to their own cultural experience of the unequal and hierarchical nature of gender relations in Western society. A number of feminist anthropologists have now made the point that, even where more egalitarian relations between women and men exist, researchers are very often unable to understand this potential equality because they insist on interpreting difference and asymmetry as inequality and hierarchy (Rogers, 1975; Leacock, 1978; Dwyer, 1978; see chapter 2 for further discussion of this point).

It is hardly surprising, therefore, that feminist anthropologists saw their initial task as one of deconstructing this three-tiered structure of male bias. One way in which this could be done was by focusing on women, by studying and describing what women really do, as opposed to what men (ethnographers and informants) say they do, and by recording and analysing the statements, perceptions and attitudes of women themselves. However, correcting male bias in reporting, and building up new data on women and women's activities, could only be a first step – albeit a very necessary one – because the real problem about incorporating women into anthropology lies not at the level of empirical research but at the theoretical and analytical level. Feminist anthropology is, therefore, faced with the much larger task of reworking and redefining anthropology theory. 'Just as many feminists found that the goals of the women's movement could not be fulfilled by the "add-women-and-stir method", so women's studies scholars discovered that academic fields could not be cured of sexism simply by accretion' (Boxer, 1982: 258). Anthropologists quickly recognized themselves as 'heirs to a sociological tradition' that has always treated women as 'essentially uninteresting and irrelevant' (Rosaldo, 1974: 17). But they also recognized that simply 'adding' women to traditional anthropology would not resolve the problem of women's analytical 'invisibility': it would not make the issue of male bias go away.

Models and muting

Edwin Ardener was among the first to recognize the significance of 'male bias' for the development of models of explanation in social anthropology. He proposed a theory of 'muted groups', in which he argued that the dominant groups in society generate and control the dominant modes of expression. Muted groups are silenced by the structures of dominance, and if they wish to express themselves they are forced to do so through the dominant modes of expression, the dominant ideologies (Ardener, 1975b: 21–3). Any group which is silenced or rendered inarticulate in this way (gypsies, children, criminals) may be considered a 'muted' group, and women are only one such case. According to Ardener, 'mutedness' is the product of the relations of dominance which exist between dominant and sub-dominant groups in society. His theory does not imply that the 'mute' should actually be silent, nor does it necessarily imply that they are neglected at the level of empirical research. Women may speak a great deal, their activities and responsibilities may be minutely observed by the ethnographer, as Ardener points out, but they remain 'muted' because their model of reality, their view of the world, cannot be realized or expressed using the terms of the dominant male model. The dominant male structures of society inhibit the free expression of alternative models, and sub-dominant groups are forced to structure their understanding of the world through the model of the dominant group. As far as Ardener is concerned, the problem of muting is a problem of frustrated communication. The free expression of the 'female perspective' is blocked at the level of ordinary, direct language. Women cannot use the male-dominated structures of language to say what they want to say, to give an account of their view of the world. Their utterances are oblique, muffled, muted. Ardener, therefore, suggests that women and men have different 'world-views' or models of society (Ardener, 1975a: 5).[1] He goes on to link the existence of 'male' and 'female' models to the problem of male bias in ethnographic accounts.

Ardener argues that the kinds of models provided by male informants are the sort of models which are familiar and intelligible to anthropological researchers. This is because researchers are either men, or women trained in a male-oriented discipline. Anthropology itself orders the world in a male idiom. The fact that linguistic concepts and categories in Western culture equate 'man' with society as a whole – as in 'mankind', and as in the use of the male pronoun to mean both he and she – has led anthropologists to imagine that the 'male view' is also 'society's view'. Ardener's conclusion is that male bias exists not just because the majority of ethnographers and informants are male, but because anthropologists – women and men – have been using male models drawn from their own culture to explain male models present in other cultures. As a result, a series of homologies is established between the ethnographer's models and those of the people (men) who are being studied. Women's models are suppressed. The analytical and conceptual tools to hand actually prevent the anthropologist from hearing and/or understanding the views of women. It is not that women are silent; it is just that they cannot be heard. 'Those trained in ethnography evidently have a bias towards the kinds of models that men are ready to provide (or to concur in) rather than towards any that women might provide. If the men appear "articulate" compared with the women, it is a case of like speaking to like' (Ardener, 1975a: 2).

Ardener correctly identifies the problem as residing not just in the practice of anthropological fieldwork, but in the conceptual frameworks which underlie that practice. Theory always informs the way in which we collect, interpret and present data, and as such it can never be neutral. Feminist anthropology is not, therefore, about 'adding' women into the discipline, but is instead about confronting the conceptual and analytical inadequacies of disciplinary theory. The task itself is a formidable one, but the most immediate question is one of how it should be tackled.

Women studying women

Ardener's contention that men and women have different models of the world obviously applies as much to the anthropologist's society as it does to the society being studied by the anthropologist. This fact raises the interesting question of whether female anthropologists look at the world differently from their male colleagues and, if so, whether this gives them some special advantage when it comes to studying women. These kinds of issues were taken up very early on in the development of the 'anthropology of women', and fears were expressed that what had once been 'male bias' would be replaced by a corresponding 'female bias'. If the model of the world was inadequate when seen through the eyes of men, why should it be any less so when seen through the eyes of women? The issue of whether women anthropologists are more qualified than their male colleagues to study other women remains a contentious point. The privileging of the female ethnographer, as Shapiro points out, not only casts doubt on the ability of women to study men, but ultimately casts doubt on the whole project and purpose of anthropology: the comparative study of human societies.

> Implicit in many discussions of sex bias, and in much of the literature in women's studies . . . is the assumption that only women can or should study women – what we might call the it-takes-one-to-know-one position. This attitude, prompted by a feminist awareness of the distorting views of women held by the largely male social scientific establishment, also finds support in the practicalities of fieldwork; the division between men's and women's social worlds is sharply drawn in a large number of societies. Tendencies towards a sexual division of labour in our profession, however, require critical reflection more than they require epistemological justification or a new source of ideological support. After all, if it really took one to know one, the entire field of anthropology would be an aberration. (Shapiro, 1981: 124–5)

Women in the ghetto

Milton (1979), Shapiro (1981) and Strathern (1981a) have all pointed to problems concerning the assumption of a privileged status by women ethnographers with regard to the women they study. Critical reflection on this issue suggests that the problems are of three kinds. First, there is the argument about ghettoization and the possible formation of a sub-discipline. This argument is concerned with the position and status of women's anthropology within the discipline as a whole. The most salient fear is that, if an explicit focus on women or the 'female point of view' arises as an alternative to a focus on men and the 'male point of view', then much of the force of feminist research is lost through a segregation which consistently defines such work as the 'not male': the 'female anthropology'. This fear arises in part because the 'anthropology of women', unlike any other aspect of anthropology, consists of women studying women. The women who study women fear not ghettoization but marginalization, and this is a very well-grounded fear. However, to see the issues in these terms misses the point somewhat because it totally fails to take into account the very important distinction between the 'anthropology of women' and feminist anthropology. The 'anthropology of women' was the precursor to feminist anthropology; it was very successful in bringing women 'back into view' in the discipline, but in so doing it was more remedial than radical. Feminist anthropology is more than the study of women. It is the study of gender, of the interrelations between women and men, and of the role of gender in structuring human societies, their histories, ideologies, economic systems and political structures. Gender can no more be marginalized in the study of human societies than can the concept of 'human action', or the concept of 'society'. It would not be possible to pursue any sort of social science without a concept of gender.

This does not, of course, mean that efforts to marginalize feminist anthropology will cease. They will not. Anthropology has sometimes been praised for the way in which feminist critiques have found acceptance in mainstream anthropology, and for the way in which the study of gender has become an accepted part of the discipline (Stacey and Thorne, 1985). This praise may be deserved, at least in part, but we do need to heed those who point to the relatively small number of courses on gender, to the difficulty of getting research funds to work on gender issues, and to the relatively small number of employed women anthropologists. It is still abundantly clear that the political marginalization of feminist scholarship has much to do with the gender of its practitioners.

The accusation that the study of women has become a sub-discipline within social anthropology can also be tackled by reformulating our perception of what the study of gender involves. Anthropology is famous for a remarkable intellectual pluralism, as evidenced by the different specialist sub-divisions of the discipline, for example, economic anthropology, political anthropology, cognitive anthropology; the various specialist areas of enquiry, such as the anthropology of law, the anthropology of death, historical anthropology; and the different theoretical frameworks, such as Marxism, structuralism, symbolic anthropology.[2] It is true that there is considerable disagreement in anthropology about how such typologies of the discipline should be constructed. However, when we try to fit the study of gender relations into a typology of this kind, we immediately become aware of the irrelevance of the term 'sub-discipline' with regard to modern social anthropology. In what sense are any of the categories in such a typology sub-disciplinary? This question is one which is further complicated by the fact that the study of gender relations could potentially occupy a position in all three categories. Attempts to assign sub-disciplinary status to feminist anthropology have more to do with processes of political containment than with serious intellectual considerations.

The universal woman

Returning to the issue of women studying women, the second problem concerning the proposition that 'it takes one to know one' concerns the analytical status of the sociological category 'woman'. The anxieties about ghettoization and the formation of a sub-discipline of 'women's anthropology' are, of course, related to genuine fears about marginalization, but they are also connected to the ghettoization of 'women' as a category and/or object of study in the discipline. The privileged relationship between female ethnographer and female informant depends on the assumption of a universal category 'woman'. However, just as constructs like 'marriage', the 'family', and the 'household' require analysis, so too does the empirical category 'woman'. The images, attributes, activities and appropriate behaviour associated with women are always culturally and historically specific. What the category 'woman', or, for that matter, the category 'man', means in a given context has to be investigated and not assumed (MacCormack and Strathern, 1980; Ortner and Whitehead, 1981a). As Brown and Jordanova point out, biological differences do not provide a universal basis for social definitions. 'What cultures make of sex differences is almost infinitely variable, so that biology cannot be playing a determining role. Women and men are products of social relations, if we change the social relations we change the categories "woman" and "man"' (Brown and Jordanova, 1982: 393).

On the basis of this argument, the concept 'woman' cannot stand as an analytical category in anthropological enquiry, and consequently there can be no analytical meaning in such concepts as 'the position of women', the 'subordination of women' and 'male dominance' when applied universally. The inevitable fact of biological difference between the sexes tells us nothing about the general social significance of that difference. Anthropologists are well aware of this point, and they recognize that feminist anthropology must not claim that women cannot be confined to and defined by their biology while simultaneously refining female physiology into a cross-cultural, social category.

Ethnocentrism and racism

The third problem with regard to the theoretical and political complexities of women studying other women concerns the issues of race and ethnocentrism (bias in favour of one's own culture). Anthropology has been, and is still, critically involved in coming to terms with its colonial past, and with the power relationship which characterizes the encounter between those who study and those who are studied (Asad, 1973; Huizer and Mannheim, 1979). However, anthropology has yet to respond to the arguments of black anthropologists and black feminists who point to the racist assumptions which underlie much anthropological theorizing and writing (Lewis, 1973; Magubane, 1971; Owusu, 1979; Amos and Parmar, 1984; Bhavnani and Coulson, 1986). This is, in part, because anthropology has tended to approach the problem of Western cultural bias – which it recognizes and has analysed exhaustively – through the notion of ethnocentrism. The fundamental importance of the critique of ethnocentrism in anthropology is not in doubt (see chapter 2 for a demonstration of this point). Historically, anthropology has emerged out of, and been sustained by, a dominant Western discourse. Without a concept of ethnocentrism, it would be impossible to question the dominant categories of discipline thinking, to think outside the theoretical parameters those categories impose, and to interrogate the foundations of anthropological thought. The concept of ethnocentrism underlies anthropology's critique of anthropology. However, there are issues which cannot be contained in, or confronted under, the notion of ethnocentrism, because they are not engaged by the terms of this internal critique. Anthropology talks about the 'ethnocentric' assumptions of the discipline rather than the 'racist' assumptions. The concept of ethnocentrism, while immensely valuable, tends to sidestep the issue somewhat.[3] This can be demonstrated by looking afresh at some of the material already discussed in this chapter.

At the beginning of this chapter I discussed the debates which arose in the new 'anthropology of women' concerning male bias in the discipline. One sort or layer of male bias was correctly analysed as being inherent in Western cultural assumptions, and was seen as being imposed on other cultures through the process of anthropological interpretation. This argument is undoubtedly correct, but it must be seen itself as part of an emerging body of anthropological theory. It is quite clear that as a theoretical proposition it contains the assumption that anthropologists come from Western cultures, and that, by extension, they are white. Critics would, of course, be quite justified in saying that to assume that someone comes from a Western culture does not mean that it is also assumed that they are white; they might add that Western cultural biases will be evident in the work of Western-trained anthropologists whether they are Westerners or not. These are fairly standard responses, but to accept them uncritically also means accepting the argument that when the term 'anthropologist' is used it automatically refers to both black and white anthropologists. This is difficult because feminist anthropologists know only too well that the term 'anthropologist' has not always included women. Exclusion by omission is still exclusion.

However, the deconstruction of the sociological category 'woman', with the recognition that the experiences and activities of women always have to be analysed in their socially and historically specific contexts, provides a basis from which feminist anthropologists could begin to respond to the arguments concerning racism in the discipline. There are a number of reasons why this should be so. First, it forces us to reformulate the privileging of the woman ethnographer with regard to the women she studies, and to acknowledge that the power relations in the ethnographic encounter are not necessarily ones which are erased simply by commonalities of sex. Secondly, it brings into theoretical and political focus the fact that, while women in a variety of societies share similar experiences and problems, these similarities have to be set against the very different experiences of women worldwide, especially with regard to race, colonialism, the rise of industrial capitalism and the interventions of international develop-ment agencies.[4] Thirdly, it shifts the theoretical focus away from notions of 'sameness', from ideas about the 'shared experience of women' and the 'universal subordination of women', towards a critical rethinking of concepts of 'difference'. Anthropologists have always recognized and emphasized cultural difference; it has been the bedrock of the discipline. Furthermore, it has been the aspect of anthropology which feminists and many others outside the discipline have ap-plauded most. Anthropological data have been extensively used as the basis for a critique of Western culture and its assumptions. This is why it is necessary to say something about why the anthropological concept of 'cultural difference' is not the same thing as the notion of 'difference' which is beginning to emerge in feminist anthropology.

Anthropology has struggled long and hard to establish that 'cultural difference' is not about the peculiarities and oddities of 'other cultures', but rather about recognizing cultural uniqueness, while at the same time seeking out the similarities in human cultural life.[5] This is the basis for the comparative project in anthropology. Understanding cultural difference is essential, but the concept itself can no longer stand as the ruling concept of a modern anthropology, because it addresses only one form of difference among many. Anthropology has always investigated kinship, ritual, economics and gender in terms of the way in which these are organized, constructed and experienced through culture. The differences which have been observed have therefore been interpreted as cultural differences. But, once we agree that cultural difference is only one form of difference among many, this approach becomes insufficient. Feminist anthropology has recognized this insufficiency in so far as it formulates its theoretical questions in terms of how economics, kinship and ritual are experienced and structured through gender, rather than asking how gender is experienced and structured through culture. It has also gone on to ask how gender is structured and experienced through colonialism, through neo-imperialism and through the rise of capitalism. But it must be said that it has, for the most part, still to confront the question of how gender is constructed and experienced through race. This is largely because anthropology still has to unravel and take on board the difference between racism and ethnocentricism (see chapter 6).

Feminist anthropology is not alone, by any means, in its attempts to understand difference and to look at the complex ways in which gender, race and class intersect and cross-cut each other, as well as the way in which all three intersect with colonialism, the international division of labour and the rise of the modern state. Marxist anthropology, world systems theory, historians, economic anthropologists and many other practitioners in the social sciences are engaged in parallel projects. The question of difference, however, poses a particular problem for feminists.

Feminism and difference[6]

When we move away from the privileged status of the woman ethnographer with regard to the women she studies, and away from the concept of 'sameness' on which the notion of the universal 'woman' is based, we find ourselves questioning, not only the theoretical assumptions of social anthropology, but the aims and political cohesiveness of feminism. 'Feminism', like 'anthropology', is one of those words which everybody thinks they know the meaning of. In a minimalist definition, feminism could be taken to refer to the awareness of women's oppression and exploitation at work, in the home and in society as well as to the conscious political action taken by women to change this situation. Such a definition has a number of consequences. First, it implies that, at some fundamental level, there exists a unitary body of women's interests, which should be and can be fought for. Secondly, it is clear that although feminism recognizes differences in feminist politics – socialist feminists, Marxist feminists, radical separatists and so on – the underlying premise of feminist politics is that there is an actual, or potential, identity between women. This premise obviously exists because it is the basis on which or from which the unitary body of women's interests is derived. Thirdly, feminist politics further depends for its cohesion – whether potential or actual – on women's shared oppression. The recognition of shared oppression is the basis for 'sexual politics' premised on the notion that women as a social group are dominated by men as a social group (Delmar, 1986: 26). The end result is that feminism as a cultural critique, as a political critique and as a basis for political action is identified with women – not with women in their socially and historically distinct context, but with women as a sociological category. The problem for feminism is that the concept of difference threatens to deconstruct this isomorphism, this 'sameness', and with it the whole edifice on which feminist politics is based.

Both anthropology and feminism have to cope with difference. Looking at the relationship between feminism and anthropology, we can see that feminist anthropology began by criticizing male bias within the discipline, and the neglect and/or distortion of women and women's activities. This is the phase in the 'relationship' which we can refer to as the 'anthropology of women'. The next phase was based on a critical reworking of the universal category 'woman', which was accompanied by an equally critical look at the question of whether women were especially well equipped to study other women. This led, quite naturally, to anxieties about ghettoization and marginalization within the discipline of social anthropology. However, as a result of this phase, feminist anthropology began to establish new approaches, new areas of theoretical enquiry, and to redefine its project not as the 'study of women' but as the 'study of gender'. As we enter the third phase of this relationship, we see feminist anthropology begin to try to come to terms with the real differences between women, as opposed to contenting itself with demonstrations of the variety of women's experiences, situations and activities worldwide. This phase will involve the building of theoretical constructs which deal with difference, and will be crucially concerned with looking at how racial difference is constructed through gender, how racism divides gender identity and experience, and how class is shaped by gender and race. In the process of this, feminist anthropology will be involved not just in reformulating anthropological theory but in reformulating feminist theory. Anthropology is in a position to provide a critique of feminism based on the deconstruction of the category 'woman'. It is also able to provide cross-cultural data which demonstrate the Western bias in much mainstream feminist theorizing (see chapters 5 and 6 for further discussion of this point). The third, and current, phase of the relationship between feminism and anthropology is thus characterized by a move away from 'sameness' towards 'difference', and by an attempt to establish the theoretical and empirical grounds for a feminist anthropology based on difference.

2

GENDER AND STATUS: EXPLAINING THE POSITION OF WOMEN

This chapter is concerned with what it is to be a woman, how cultural understandings of the category 'woman' vary through space and time, and how those understandings relate to the position of women in different societies. Contemporary anthropologists who explore the position of women, whether in their own or another society, are inevitably drawn into the debate concerning the origins and universality of women's subordination. An interest in the hierarchical relations between men and women has been a feature of the discipline of anthropology since its earliest days. The emergence of theories of evolution in the nineteenth century gave new impetus to the study of social and political theory, and to the related question of the social organization of non-Western societies. Crucial to an understanding of social organization in such societies were such concepts as 'kinship', 'the family', 'the household' and 'sexual mores'. In the debates which ensued, relations between the sexes became central to the theories put forward by the so-called 'founding fathers of anthropology'.[1] As a result, a number of the concepts and assumptions which figure prominently in contemporary anthropology, including feminist anthropology, owe their origins to various nineteenth-century theorists. It is true, of course, that many of the claims of nineteenth-century thinkers have been challenged and found wanting. In anthropology, Malinowski and Radcliffe-Brown, among others, criticized the search for a hypostatized past – especially the emphasis on unilinear evolution and the transition from 'mother-right' to 'father-right'. The 1920s and 1930s saw the establishment of anthropology as a defined discipline, with an emphasis on empirical fieldwork. What took place was a rethinking of kinship, and an explicit emphasis on the function of social institutions in specific societies, rather than on their place in some putative historical schema. My aim in claiming that many of the theoretical assumptions of the nineteenth century are still with us is to show that the concerns confronted by the anthropology of women have a necessarily long history in the discipline.[2] Furthermore, the very fact that intellectual continuities and discontinuities exist is an important part of understanding the necessity for a contemporary feminist critique.

Any attempt to synthesize the various self-determined approaches in contemporary feminism is necessarily generalizing.[3] This is also the case with any attempt to formalize the different approaches which characterize the study of women in anthropology. The ways in which these different positions mirror fundamental intellectual disagreements in the social sciences as a whole will become clearer later in this chapter and in chapter 4. However, the different theoretical positions within feminist anthropology are best demonstrated through a consideration of the debate which dominates the subject: is sexual asymmetry universal or not?[4] In other words, are women always subordinate to men?

The analysis of women's subordination is dependent upon some consideration of gendered relations. Anthropological analyses approach the study of gender from two different, but not mutually exclusive, perspectives. Gender may be seen either as a symbolic construction or as a social relationship. The particular perspective taken by an individual researcher tends to determine, as we shall see, the types of explanation they provide to the question of the origins and nature of women's subordination. I begin, in the following section, by discussing gender as a symbolic construction.

The cultural construction of gender

One of the most outstanding contributions of the anthropology of women has been its sustained analysis of gender symbols and sexual stereotypes. The main problem facing researchers in this area is how to explain both the enormous observable variation in cultural understandings of what the categories 'man' and 'woman' mean, and the fact that certain notions about gender appear in a wide range of different societies. This is how Sherry Ortner expressed the problem at the beginning of her essay 'Is female to male as nature is to culture?':

> Much of the creativity of anthropology derives from the tension between two sets of demands: that we explain human universals, and that we explain cultural particulars. By this canon, woman provides us with one of the more challenging problems to be dealt with. The secondary status

of woman in society is one of the true universals, a pan-cultural fact. Yet within that universal fact, the specific cultural conceptions and symbolizations of woman are extraordinarily diverse and even mutually contradictory. Further, the actual treatment of women and their relative power and contribution vary enormously from culture to culture, and over different periods in the history of particular cultural traditions. Both of these points – the universal fact and the cultural variation – constitute problems to be explained. (Ortner, 1974: 67)

Ortner's essay, together with Edwin Ardener's article 'Belief and the problem of women', initiated an influential and powerful framework for studying the problem of women's subordination through an analysis of gender symbolism. Ortner began with the proposition that female subordination is universal, and, since this condition is not inherent in the biological differences between the sexes, an alternative explanation must be found. Starting from the idea that biological differences between men and women take on significance only within culturally defined value systems, she located the problem of sexual asymmetry at the level of cultural ideologies and symbols (Ortner, 1974: 71). The question she then posed was: what could be common to every culture such that all cultures place a lower value on women? Her answer was that women everywhere must be associated with something which every culture devalues. In Ortner's view there is only 'one thing that would fit that description, and that is "nature", in the most generalized sense' (Ortner, 1974: 72). All cultures recognize and make a distinction between human society and the natural world. Culture attempts to control and transcend nature, to use it for its own purposes. Culture is therefore superior to the natural world and seeks to mark out or 'socialize' nature, in order to regulate and maintain relations between society and the forces and conditions of the environment. Ortner suggests that women are identified, or symbolically associated, with nature, while men are associated with culture. Since culture seeks to control and transcend nature, then it is 'natural' that women, by virtue of their close association with 'nature', should also be controlled and contained.

It is worth setting out some of Ortner's argument in detail, because the grounds she asserts for associating women with nature – or for women being seen as closer to nature than men – raise a whole series of issues which form the foundations of the feminist critique, but which also threaten, at moments, to overwhelm it. The universality of Ortner's proposition forces her to provide equally generalized arguments to support her thesis. Her two main arguments may be summarized in the following way:

1 Woman's physiology and her specialized reproductive functions make her appear closer to nature. Men, unlike women, have to seek

cultural means of creation – technology, symbols – while women's creativity is naturally fulfilled through the process of giving birth. Men, therefore, are associated more directly with culture and with the creative power of culture, as opposed to nature. 'Woman creates naturally from within her own being, whereas man is free to, or forced to, create artificially, that is through cultural means, and in such a way as to sustain culture' (Ortner, 1974: 77).

2   Women's social roles are seen as closer to nature because their in-volvement in reproduction has tended to limit them to certain social functions which are also seen as closer to nature. Here, Ortner is referring to women's confinement within the domestic domain. In the context of the domestic family, women are primarily associated with the rearing of children, and thus with the pre-social or not yet culturally created person. Ortner points out than an implicit associ-ation between children and nature is a feature of a number of societies (Ortner, 1974: 78). The 'natural' association of women with children and the family provides an additional level of categorization. Since women are confined to the domestic context, their main sphere of activity becomes intra- and inter-familial relations, as opposed to men, who operate in the political and public domain of social life. Men thus become identified with society and the 'public interest', while women remain associated with family and, therefore, with particularistic or socially fragmenting concerns.

Ortner is careful in her presentation to emphasize that 'in reality' women are not any closer to, or further from, nature than men. Her aim is, rather, to identify and locate the cultural valuations which make women appear 'closer to nature'.

The formulation that 'nature is to culture as female is to male' provided social anthropology with a powerful analytical framework which had a wide impact on the discipline in the late 1970s and early 1980s. It was powerful because it offered a way of linking sexual ideologies and stereotypes both to the wider system of cultural symbols and to social roles and experience. Sexual ideologies and stereotypes vary greatly, but certain symbolic associations between gender and many other aspects of cultural life occur across a wide range of societies. The differences between men and women can be conceptualized as a set of opposed pairs which resonate with other sets of oppositions. Thus men may be associated with 'up', 'right', 'high', 'culture' and 'strength', while women are associated with their opposites, 'down', 'left', 'low', 'nature' and 'weakness'. These associ-ations are not inherent in the biological or social nature of the sexes, but are cultural constructs, which are powerfully reinforced by the social activities which both define and are defined by them. The value of analysing 'man' and 'woman' as symbolic categories or constructs lies in the identification of the expectations and values which individual cultures associate with being male or female. Such analysis provides some indication of the ideal behaviour of men and women in their different social roles, which can then be compared with the actual behaviour and responsibilities of the two sexes. It is in understanding how men and women are socially constructed, and how those constructions define and redefine social activities, that the value of a symbolic analysis of gender becomes apparent. There have, of course, been criticisms of the nature/culture–female/male opposition (Mathieu, 1978; MacCormack and Strathern, 1980), but it provides a useful starting point for discussing the cultural construction of gender, and for examining how the symbolic associations given to the categories 'man' and 'woman' can be understood as the result of cultural ideologies, rather than of inherent qualities or physiology.

'Male' and 'female'

One of the features of gender symbolism which has attracted a great deal of attention from scholars who wish to explain women's 'inferior status' is the concept of pollution. Behavioural taboos and restrictions, like those which many women experience after childbirth and during menstruation, provide clues as to how people categorize one another and thus structure their social world.[5] An analysis of pollution beliefs and their relationship to sexual ideologies is revealing, because such beliefs are frequently associated with the natural functions of the human body. Examples of societies which view women as polluting, either in general or at particular times, can be found all over the world. However, for the purposes of illustration, I concentrate here on Melanesian societies because of the richness of ethnographic material on pollution beliefs and sexual antagonism among such groups.[6]

The Kaulong

Among the Kaulong of New Britain, women are considered polluting from before puberty to after menopause, but they become particularly 'dangerous' during menstruation and childbirth. During these periods women must stay away from gardens, dwellings and water sources, and a woman must also be careful not to touch anything with which a man might come into contact (Goodale, 1980: 129). Female pollution is dangerous only to adult men, who may become ill by ingesting anything polluted or by placing themselves directly underneath a contaminated object or polluting woman. Normally, pollution is transmitted in a downward vertical direction, which does not necessitate the lateral separation of the sexes (Goodale, 1980: 130–1). However, during menstruation and childbirth, pollution spreads outwards from the woman and this necessitates her physical separation from all locations and objects used by both sexes. As a result, women are isolated during childbirth and menstruation, away from the main residential and gardening areas.

The fear of pollution among the Kaulong is important because it both characterizes the nature of gender relations and defines the qualities of men and women. According to Goodale, the Kaulong equate sexual intercourse with marriage, and 'men are quite literally scared to death of marriage (and sex)' (Goodale, 1980: 133). Sexual intercourse is considered polluting for men, and because it is also thought to be 'animal-like' it must take place in the forest, away from dwellings and gardens. Men and women marry to reproduce themselves, and this is the central meaning and purpose of a sexual relationship. This particular view of marriage is powerfully reinforced by the fact that suicide used to be an accepted way of ending an 'unproductive relationship'.

Since Kaulong men are afraid and reluctant to enter into a marriage partnership, it is therefore not surprising that it is the women who take the dominant role in courtship (Goodale, 1980: 135). Girls may offer food or tobacco to the man of their choice, or they may physically attack him. The man must either flee or stand his ground without retaliating until an agreement is reached concerning what items and valuables the girl may expect to receive from him. Goodale points out that from infancy girls are encouraged to behave aggressively towards males, and that men must either submit without retaliation or run away. If a man were to initiate an approach towards a woman it would be considered rape. Women have almost complete freedom in their choice of husband, although they do consult their close kin. A woman may deceive or lure a reluctant groom to his 'fate', often with the help of her brothers, while women themselves are only very rarely forced into undesired marriages (Goodale, 1980: 135).

From a consideration of these few facts concerning male–female relations among the Kaulong, a number of points can be raised concerning the cultural variability of definitions of gender, and the validity of seeing women as 'closer to nature' than men. First, it is clear that, if Kaulong ideas of the appropriate behaviour of men and women, and the nature of marriage, were to be compared with contemporary European or North American attitudes, a series of contrasts would appear. Women are not highly valued as 'initiators' in Western society, and this is especially true with regard to sexual relations. Furthermore, Western society encourages men to be active and 'stand up for themselves', while the Kaulong view apparently reverses the Western idea of the passive woman and the active man. The desire to have children is a potent reason for marriage in Western society, but marriage itself is conceived of as a partnership, with companionship and family life as key attributes. Kaulong marriage would seem to be a very different sort of institution. These points illustrate the kinds of cross-cultural variability which can exist not only in men's and women's behaviour but also in the kinds of individuals men and women are meant to be. It also raises the issue of the cross-cultural variability of institutions like marriage. However, variability is not the only issue at stake. The idea of the woman as 'seducer', the 'ensnarer of men', and the corresponding picture of the 'reluctant groom' are all images which find resonances in Western culture. The issue which the symbolic analysis of gender raises is how we use this complex and shifting imagery to arrive at an understanding of women's position. Kaulong women apparently have a considerable degree of economic independence, including control over resources and the products of their labour (Goodale, 1980: 128, 139). Yet the same women are considered dangerous and polluting to men. It is not necessarily clear how such contradictions are to be understood and balanced in any analysis.

Ortner's suggestion that women are seen as 'closer to nature' because of their physiology and reproductive roles could be applied to the Kaulong data. A chain of associations linking women–marriage–sexual intercourse–animal-like behaviour–the forest would seem to connect the physiology and reproductive roles of women, which are polluting, to the domain of the non-human, 'natural' forest. It is a short step from this to suggest that women are inferior because they are polluting, and they are polluting because of the 'natural' functions of their bodies, which in turn makes them seem bound to the natural world in some sense. This chain of associations is powerfully reinforced by the physical isolation of women in the forest during childbirth and menstruation. However, as Goodale points out in her article, there are certain deficiencies in this simple equation of women with nature, and men with culture. First, it is clear that both men and women are associated with the forest and the 'natural world' through their involvement in sexual relations. The central dwellings in each residential clearing are occupied by unmarried men and women, and it is the married couples who live in huts on the margins of the cultivated areas – the margins, in fact, of the cultural and natural worlds. Goodale (1980: 121) depicts the Kaulong model thus:

> Culture : Nature
> Clearing : Forest
> Unmarried : Married

In other words, both men and women become associated with nature through their involvement in reproduction, rather than just women (Goodale, 1980: 140). Furthermore, the Kaulong system of representation seems to provide no strong evidence for the singular association of culture with men. It is a notable feature of a number of analyses utilizing the nature/culture–female/male model that an association between women and nature is often taken to imply a similar association between men and culture. This assumption is not always valid.

Secondly, the formulation that women are seen as 'closer to nature' because of their reproductive functions raises a number of difficulties. If women are 'seen' as 'closer to nature', who sees them in this way? Do women see themselves as closer to nature, as polluting, or even as defined by their reproductive functions? It seems that Kaulong women might respond negatively to all these queries. The nature/culture–female/male model assumes a cultural unity which is unjustified, and leaves no room for the possibility that different groups in society might see and experience things in different ways.[7] Goodale (1980: 130–1) points out that Kaulong women are unconcerned, for the most part, about their potentially polluting effects on men – with the exception, however, of the fact that mothers may express concern about the harmful effects of pollution on their sons. This confirms a further difficulty in postulating a simple opposition between 'woman' and 'man' as symbolic categories, and that is that there is an undue focus on a single set of gendered relations. Opposition between the sexes is usually constructed, by implication, on the basis of opposition between spouses, and little mention is made, if any, of the other sets of gendered relations, brother/sister, mother/son, father/daughter, which are an equally important part of being a woman or a man. The fact that relations between spouses may not be appropriate as a model for other gendered relations is highlighted among the Kaulong by the fact that a brother may side with his sister to help her secure a marriage partner. This suggests that the potential anxiety which characterizes relations between spouses may not be a feature of relations between siblings.

The third point to be raised *vis-à-vis* the nature/culture–female/ male opposition is one concerning the culturally specific nature of analytical categories. 'Nature' and 'culture' are not value-free, unmediated categories; they are cultural constructs in exactly the same way as the categories 'woman' and 'man'. The notions of nature and culture, as they are used in anthropological analysis, derive from Western society, and, as such, they are the products of a particular intellectual tradition and of a specific historical trajectory.[8] Just as we cannot assume that the categories 'woman' and 'man' everywhere mean the same, so we must also be aware that other societies might not even perceive nature and culture as distinct and opposed categories in the way that Western culture does. Furthermore, even where such a distinction exists we must not assume that the Western terms 'nature'/'culture' are adequate or reasonable translations of the categories other cultures perceive (Goody, 1977: 64; Rogers, 1978: 134; Strathern, 1980: 175–6).

The Gimi

Among the Gimi of the highlands of Papua New Guinea, women are seen as polluting, but this cannot be attributed to the fact that they are associated with nature as opposed to culture (Gillison, 1980). The idea of the 'wild' exists in Gimi thought and refers to the plant and animal life which make up the rain forest. The forest is seen as a male realm, where the spirits of dead ancestors (embodied in birds and marsupials) reside and assert the abundance and creativity of the natural world, as well as the transcendent creativity of the male spirit in the world. 'Men's ambition, as expressed in their rituals, is to identify with the non-human world and to be revitalised by its limitless, masculine powers' (Gillison, 1980: 144). The settlement, in contrast, is associated with women.

Kore is the word in Gimi used to designate both the uncultivated and the after-life. *Dusa* is the opposite of *kore* and means 'this-worldly', and it stands for domesticated plants and animals, and for 'the constraints of human social existence' (Gillison, 1980: 144). Even if *kore* were to be translated as 'nature' and *dusa* as 'culture', these categories are not associated with women and men respectively. The Gimi set of oppositions would be closer to the following model:

Dusa	: *Kore*
Cultivated	: Uncultivated
Male/female relations	: Men

It is clear from Gillison's work that the nature/female–culture/male opposition does not hold for the Gimi. Furthermore, although a distinction between 'cultivated' and 'wild' is made, this is not analogous to the distinction in Western thought between culture and nature. In Western thinking 'nature' is something to be subdued and controlled by 'culture'; in Gimi thought the 'wild' is transcendent of human social life, and is certainly not subject to control or debasement. The concept of the superiority of culture over nature is a Western one, and is part of the conceptual apparatus of a society which sees civilization as the culmination of 'man's' triumph over nature. The experiences of industrialization, modern science and technology have all been fundamental to the development of the Western concepts of nature and culture. The most frightening and fallacious manifestation of this fantasy is the development of nuclear weapons, with the underlying implication that 'man can control the world' in all senses.

The ethnocentricity of analytical categories is an ever-present problem in anthropology. The dangers inherent in culture-bound assumptions were forcefully highlighted by the developing 'anthropology of women', which took a critique of male bias as one of its starting points (cf. Rosaldo and Lamphere, 1974; Reiter, 1975; and see chapter 1). However, as a discussion of the nature/culture model makes clear, the problem of 'analytical' bias is something which the 'anthropology of women', like all other aspects of the discipline, has to continue to face. This is partly because of the deeply rooted assumptions which lie behind anthropological theory in general, and which go far beyond a simple recognition of male bias in fieldwork methodology and practice (see chapter 1). Just how deeply rooted these assumptions can be is demonstrated by a discussion of women and the domestic sphere.

Domestic versus public

One of the reasons Ortner gives for why women are seen as 'closer to nature' is the fact that they are associated with the 'domestic' rather than the 'public' domain of social life. This idea begins a theme in the 'anthropology of women' which links the nature/culture dichotomy to a corresponding division between the 'domestic' and the 'public' – a framework which has similarly been advanced as a universal model for the explanation of women's subordination. Recently there have been a number of criticisms of the 'domestic' verus 'public' model (Burton, 1985: chs 2 and 3; Rapp, 1979; Rogers, 1978; Rosaldo, 1980; Strathern, 1984a; Tilly, 1978; Yanagisako, 1979), but it none the less remains a salient feature of many different types of analysis, and is frequently used as a way of ordering ethnographic data, and of marking out a clear domain for women within the material presented.

The 'domestic' versus 'public' model has been, and remains, a very powerful one in social anthropology because it provides a way of linking the cultural valuations given to the category 'woman' to the organization of women's activities in society. One of the earliest expositions of the model was contained in an article by Michelle Rosaldo, in which she made claims regarding its universal applicability: 'though this opposition ("domestic" versus "public") will be more or less salient in different social and ideological systems, it does provide a universal framework for conceptualizing the activities of the sexes' (Rosaldo, 1974: 23). Rosaldo, like Ortner, links the 'demeaning identification' of women with the domestic to women's reproductive role (Rosaldo, 1974: 30; 1980: 397). The 'domestic'/'public' opposition, like that of nature/culture, is ultimately derived from woman's role as mother and rearer of children. The categories 'domestic' and 'public' stand in a hierarchical relationship to each other. Rosaldo defines 'domestic' as those institutions and activities organized around mother–child groups, while 'public' 'refers to activities, institutions, and forms of association that link, rank, organize, or subsume particular mother–child groups' (Rosaldo, 1974: 23; 1980: 398). Women and the domestic sphere are thus subsumed by, and considered less important than, men and the public domain. However, both the categorical separation of the 'domestic' and the 'public', and their relative relationship are open to question.

A number of authors have pointed out that the rigid division of social life into 'domestic' and 'public' spheres owes much to the pervasive influence of nineteenth-century social theory (Coward, 1983; Rosaldo, 1980; Collier et al., 1982). The social theorists of the late nineteenth and early twentieth centuries saw transformations in the relations between the sexes – exemplified in changing family structures – as the clue to human historical development. The idea that human history could be conceived of in terms of a struggle between the sexes, where 'mother-right' eventually gave way to 'father-right', placed a considerable degree of emphasis on an understanding of the term 'rights'. What became clear was that women's rights in 'mother-right' societies were not comparable to those of men in 'father-right' societies (Coward, 1983: 52–6). No 'primitive' society could be found where men were systematically excluded from political rights and authority, in the way in which women were excluded from these domains in nineteenth-century Western society. The fight for women's suffrage merely highlighted the fact that men could represent women in the political sphere, but there was no apparent precedent for women representing men.[9] In contrast to the political realm of men, women's domain was the home. The exclusion of women from the vote defined them as lacking political rights, as less, therefore, than full citizens, and as dependent on men. The prevailing ideology of the day was that men were to govern society, and women would govern the home (Coward, 1983: 56). Western society in the late nineteenth and early twentieth centuries thus constructed an understanding of political rights based on a division by sex. The result was a model of social life which separated the 'domestic' from the 'public' sphere, and accorded different 'rights' to the gendered individuals within those separate spheres. The identification of these different 'rights' further constructed a specific cultural understanding of what women and men were meant to be, both within the home and outside it. This construction formed the basis for ideas about motherhood, fatherhood, the family and the home. These ideas have persisted in Western society in a variety of ways, and have been influential in maintaining the 'domestic'/'public' dichotomy as an analytical framework in social anthropology. One of the ways of exposing the arbitrary and culturally specific nature of the 'domestic'/'public' division is to examine some of the assumptions concerning mothering and the family on which it is based. (See also chapter 5.)

One of the reasons why the 'domestic'/'public' opposition is able to make strong claims for a genuine cross-cultural validity is that it presupposes a defined mother–child unit which seems 'naturally' universal. Whatever cultural elaborations may exist in family forms and gender roles, women everywhere give birth to children. The idea of mother–child units as the building blocks of society, as expressed by Rosaldo among many others, is a continuation of the debate in social anthropology about the origins and form of the family.

In an early work on the Australian Aborigines, Malinowski laid to rest earlier debates about whether all societies could be deemed to have families (Malinowski, 1913). Malinowski's argument was that the family was universal because it fulfilled a universal human need for the nurturance and care of children. He defined the family as consisting of (1) a bounded social unit which was distinguishable from other similar units; (2) a physical location (home) where the functions associated with child-rearing were performed; (3) a specific set of emotional bonds (love) between family members (Collier et al., 1982). This three-part definition of the family is compelling precisely because it accords well with Western ideas about the form and function of the family. 'The family', like any other comparative unit, raises problems of ethnocentricity, and Malinowski's characterization was clearly influenced by the prevailing nineteenth-century ideology of the home as a refuge and nurturant haven, separate from the vagaries of the public world (Thorne, 1982). In Western society, the family, the home and the 'domestic' are conceptualized as a single unit which is defined in juxtaposition to the 'public' sphere of work, business and politics: in other words, to the market relations of capitalism. Market relations involve relations of competition, negotiation and contract which Western society views as separate from and opposed to the relations of intimacy and nurturance which are associated with the family and the home (Rapp, 1979: 510). This particular view of the 'domestic' and 'public' spheres of social life, and of their relation to each other, cannot be considered as universal, and I shall return later in this chapter to the specific problems which are raised by the assumption that the concepts 'domestic' and 'public' are applicable to other cultures.

Malinowski's definition of the family has been very influential in anthropology. It is true that later anthropologists, including Fortes (1969), Fox (1967), Goodenough (1970), Gough (1959) and Smith (1956), challenged Malinowski's idea of the universal nuclear family. In contrast, they argued that the basic unit of society is not the nuclear

family consisting of father, mother and children, but rather the
mother–child unit. Thus the 'woman and her dependent children . . .
represent the nuclear family group in human societies' (Goodenough,
1970: 18). However, in spite of 'removing' the father from the family
unit, contemporary anthropology still retains Malinowski's basic
concept of the family. Mother–child units now provide the necessary
framework for the nurturing of children; they also form bounded units
distinguishable from other similar units, occupy a defined physical
location, and share deep emotional bonds of a particular kind. In
separating the father from the mother–child unit, contemporary
anthropology has stressed the difference between motherhood and
fatherhood, and has reinforced the idea that 'mother' is the kin
relationship most expressive of biological fact. The relationship
between mother and child is peculiarly 'natural', because of the
indisputable fact that the woman in question has given birth to the
child. Barnes (1973) makes the point that 'fathers are not self-evident
as mothers are.' He goes on to suggest that fatherhood ('genitor') is a
social status, unlike motherhood ('genetrix') which is more obviously
determined by natural processes. His general proposition is that,
because ' "genitor" is a social status, and societies vary greatly in the
rights and duties, privileges and obligations, if any, that they associate
with this status' (Barnes, 1973: 68), fatherhood is cross-culturally
extremely variable, while motherhood is more natural, more universal
and more constant.

> Whatever may be their ideas about physical parenthood, virtually all
> cultures attach symbolic significance to both fatherhood and mother-
> hood. I suggest that fatherhood is the freer symbol, able to take on a
> wider range of culturally assigned meanings, because it has a more
> exiguous link with the natural world. (Barnes, 1973: 71)

> The relations of nature to fatherhood and motherhood are different.
> (Barnes, 1973: 72)

In contemporary anthropology, the tendency to see mothers and
mothering as 'natural' is marked, and is directly inherited from a
Malinowskian view of the family (Collier et al., 1982: 28; Yanagisako,
1979: 199). It is the idea that mothers and mother–child units have a
universal function which maintains the easy separation of the 'domestic' from the 'public', and encourages the view that 'domestic' units
everywhere have the same form and function, which are dictated by
the biological facts of reproduction and the necessity of child maintenance (Yanagisako, 1979: 189). It is the self-evident quality, and most
particularly the 'naturalness', of mothers and motherhood and the
dependent concepts of the family and the domestic which recent
feminist critiques in anthropology address directly.

Mother and mothering

The idea that a 'domestic' domain as distinct from a 'public' arena is a universal feature of human societies effectively excludes the possibility of asking questions about those aspects of the 'domestic' which appear most natural, and through which the very notion of the 'domestic' is constructed: the intertwined concepts of 'mother' and 'mothering' (Harris, 1981). The concept of 'mother' is not merely given in natural processes (pregnancy, birth, lactation, nurturance), but is a cultural construction which different societies build up and elaborate in different ways. It is not just a matter of the cultural diversity in the way in which women perform their role as mother – in some cultures mothers are warm, caring and full-time, while in others they are authoritarian, distant and part-time (Drummond, 1978: 31; Collier and Rosaldo, 1981: 275–6). It is also a matter of how the category 'women' in each culture is linked to such attributes of motherhood as fertility, naturalness, maternal love, nurturance, life-giving and reproduction. There is a clear need to investigate the associations which link the idea of 'woman' to that of 'mother', especially for those writers who wish to connect women's universal subordination to the apparently universal role of women as mothers and rearers of children. In Western society, the categories 'women' and 'mother' overlap in substantial and clear-cut ways.[10] Ideas about and attitudes towards women are crucially linked to ideas about marriage, family, the home, children and work. The concept of 'women' is constructed through these different constellations of ideas, and individual women subsequently construct themselves through the culturally given definitions of womanhood which thereby emerge, even if that construction proceeds through conflict and contradiction. The result is a definition of 'woman' which is crucially dependent on the concept of 'mother', and on the activities and associations which that concept draws to itself. Other cultures do not, of course, define 'woman' in the same way, neither do they necessarily establish a close relationship between 'woman' and home or the domestic sphere, as Western culture does. The association between 'woman' and 'mother' is by no means as 'natural' as it might at first seem. The best way of demonstrating this point is perhaps to discuss what seem, in Western eyes, to be the most 'natural' features of motherhood itself: rearing children and giving birth.

Rearing children is an activity which is supposed to characterize domestic groups throughout the whole range of human societies (Goody, 1972). This is in spite of the wide range of observable variability both in the composition of domestic groups and in the assignment of particular individuals to the task of child-rearing. In her book on urban Americans, Carol Stack shows how variable household

formation is among urban black families, and makes the point that 20
per cent of the children in her study were being raised in a household
other than that which contained their biological mother – although in
most cases the household concerned was related to the mother's family
(Stack, 1974). However, it is a matter not just of claiming that mothers
may not be the only individuals who care for children, but of emphasizing (1) that domestic units may not necessarily be built around
biological mothers and their children, and (2) that the concept of
'mother' in any society may not be constructed through maternal love,
daily childcare or physical proximity. The biological facts of motherhood do not produce a universal and immutable mother–child
relationship or unit. This point can be illustrated with reference to
British society, and to changes in ideas about motherhood, childhood
and family life.

Philip Ariès (1973) has pointed out that childhood as we understand
it in Western culture today is a recent phenomenon.[11] The notion of
a separate child's world distinct from that of adults, with special
activities and diets, standards of behaviour and dress, is peculiar to a
specific historical period. The idea that mothers have always been
isolated in the home with their children, organizing their days around
the primary tasks of childcare, and acting as moral guardians of society
through their responsibility for socializing the young, is not generaliz-
able to all periods of Western life, let alone to all other cultures.[12]
Before the Factory Acts, women and children were important workers
and wage earners in some sections of British society (Olafson
Hellerstein et al., 1981: 44–6; Walvin, 1982). But, at the other end of
the spectrum in Victorian society, family life and the lives of women
were quite different. Middle- and upper-class women were responsible
for the running of their households and rarely worked outside the
domestic sphere. But the exclusion of such women from wage labour
did not necessarily mean that biological mothers were responsible for
the nurturance, daily care and upbringing of their children. Many
middle- and upper-class families relied extensively on nannies, not
only to care for small children, but also to run a whole section of the
household known as 'the nursery': 'over 2 million Nannies were a vital
index of and influence on the values and actions – the culture – of the
entire British upper classes and a large part of the middle class from
1850 to 1939' (Boon, 1974: 138).

The phenomenon of the nanny, as Drummond notes (1978: 32), is
an apt way of introducing the idea of 'motherhood' as socially
constructed. Both Boon and Drummond have suggested that the nanny
represents a theoretical erosion of the concept of a universal, biocul-
turally based family constructed on a mother–child unit. Boon draws

attention to the centuries-old tradition of mother surrogation in England before the nanny, through institutions such as wet-nursing, fosterage and apprenticeship. 'In post-eighteenth century upper class Britain genitrices briefly suckled, Nannies did the rest; in pre-eighteenth century aristocratic Britain genitrices did the rest and wet nurses suckled' (Boon, 1974: 138). British mothers were not considered 'bad mothers' because of this delegation of childcare. The point is not merely that mothers received help with childcare – a phenomenon well documented from many societies all over the world – but that the existence of 'nanny' in the mother–child complex obviously affects the way in which the concept of 'mother' is constructed. It also affects the relationship between the culturally given categories 'woman' and 'mother'.

Family life in upper-class Victorian households was not of the kind evoked by the use of the term 'family' today. Boon points out that the development of intra-domestic social sub-units raises the question whether high-class British 'families' were domestic units at all as understood in the contemporary twentieth-century sense (Boon, 1974: 319). He quotes Gathorne-Hardy on the existence of the separate units which went to make up the household: 'the kitchen under the head cook; the general household, bed linen etc., under the housekeeper; the pantry, dining room under the head butler; and the nursery under the Nanny' (Gathorne-Hardy, 1972: 191–2).

The existence of the nanny questions the exclusivity of mother–child love: 'many children, quite rightly, loved their nannies more than their mothers' (Gathorne-Hardy, 1972: 235); it also questions the boundedness of the domestic group based on the mother–child unit; and finally it questions the singular relationship between mother–child units and a defined physical location in which mothers carry out childcare activities, because the nursery was often separate from the rest of the household: 'It may have its own staircase, its own door out into the grounds, it may be in a separate wing, a separate corridor, a separate floor, cut off and even silenced from the rest of the house by a muffling, brass-studded, green baize door' (Gathorne-Hardy, 1972: 77). In short, the existence of the nanny questions the three-part definition of the family mentioned earlier. This is why both Boon and Drummond try to relate the 'nanny phenomenon' to the wider issues raised by the study of kinship in anthropology. Boon is particularly trenchant:

> were the Murdockian family and now Goodenough's mother–children family cases of ethnocentrism or pipe-dream . . . ? Have functional definitions of the Family been less ethnocentrism and more sheer romanticism . . . ? Premature universal functional definitions – first of

nuclear, now of matrifocal families – can distort cross-cultural perceptions. Why claim functional universalism at all, when heuristic problem-
posing would suffice? (Boon, 1972: 139)

At this point it could be argued that even if mothers do not always
care exclusively for their children, and even if they do not occupy a
defined physical location with them, or even love them, at least we can
be certain that they have given birth to them. The biological facts of
reproduction have an obvious 'naturalness', and their clearly universal
status accounts for the pervasive tendency to see women's lives as
indissolubly linked with their physiology: 'biology is destiny'. However, as I have argued, the category 'mother', like that of 'woman', is a
cultural construction. Drummond makes the point well:

> far from being 'the most natural thing in the world' motherhood is in fact
> one of the most unnatural . . . rather than going on about the universal,
> biocultural innateness of something called a 'mother–child bond', the
> process of conceiving, bearing and rearing a child should be viewed
> rather as a dilemma that strikes at the core of human understanding and
> evokes a heightened, not a diminished, cultural interpretation. (Drum-
> mond, 1978: 31)

Drummond's intention is not just to increase the appreciation of the
role cultural factors play in defining the status of mother, but rather to
insist that culture constitutes the possibilities of human experience,
including those of giving birth and motherhood. This point is not well
appreciated in Western culture, although it undoubtably is in other
societies. There are cultures where the processes of life-giving, including menstruation, pregnancy and birth, are social concerns of
society as a whole, and not confined to women or the 'domestic'
domain alone. In such cultures, men often believe that they have an
important part to play in social reproduction and in the process of
life-creation. Women in such cultures are not defined, therefore, by
an exclusive emphasis on their biological 'abilities' or on their control
over key areas of life – notably reproduction – from which men are
excluded. It has been noted that in a wide range of different societies
the concept of 'woman' is not elaborated through ideas about
motherhood, fertility, nurturance and reproduction.

> Readings on Australian Aborigines, American, Asian and African
> hunter-gatherers and hunter-horticulturalists led to the discovery that
> themes of motherhood and sexual reproduction are far less central to
> such people's conceptions of 'woman' than we had assumed. Contrary
> to our expectations that motherhood provides women everywhere with
> a natural source of emotional satisfaction and cultural value, we found
> that neither women nor men in very simple societies celebrate women as
> nurturers or women's unique capacity to give life. . . . Woman the

Fertile, Woman the Mother and Source of All Life was, quite remarkably, absent from all available accounts. (Collier and Rosaldo, 1981: 275–6)

Collier and Rosaldo go on to give examples from the !Kung bushmen of the Kalahari, the Murngin Aborigines of Australia and the Ilongots of the Philippines. The fact that they draw all their examples from what they call 'simple societies' is not insignificant. It is often argued that such societies are more egalitarian, and that women's greater control over resources and labour improves their status. This is an argument I return to later in the chapter, when I consider the case against the universal subordination of women. However, it should be noted here that there is some evidence from small-scale societies to support the argument that when women are not exclusively defined as mothers and child-rearers their status and cultural 'value' appear to improve. But it must be borne in mind that this is *not* the same thing as saying that women's status is a function of their role as mother and child-rearer. Women everywhere give birth to children, but this fact receives varying degrees of cultural recognition and elaboration. What 'woman' means culturally cannot be straightforwardly read off from what women do in society.

In some societies, male participation in reproduction and life-creation is organized around a ritual concern with the physiological functions of the female body, a practice known in anthropology as the couvade. Couvade is a broad term, but is usually taken to mean 'a husband's observance of food taboos, restriction of ordinary practices, and in some cases seclusion during his wife's delivery and postpartum period' (Paige and Paige, 1981: 189). The explanations for this practice have been varied,[13] and it has sometimes been seen as an affirmation of social paternity (Douglas, 1968; Malinowski, 1960 [1927]: 214–15). However, other writers, I think much more plausibly, have seen the practice as an acknowledgement of the husband's role in giving birth. Mauss is reported to have explained the couvade by saying 'birth is no unimportant event, and it is perfectly natural for both parents to do it' (Dumont, quoted in Rivière, 1974: 430). This is close to Drummond's argument concerning the social 'nature' of biological reproduction cited above, and to that of Beatrice Blackwood, who worked on the couvade practices of the Kurtatchi of the Pacific. During the delivery and for six days afterwards, Kurtatchi husbands remain in seclusion, practising certain food taboos and refraining from normal subsistence activities (Blackwood, 1934: 150–60). Blackwood interprets these activities as an acknowledgement of the husband's role in the birth of the child (Paige and Paige, 1981: 190).

The couvade is only one set of practices associated with male participation in reproduction. Anna Meigs's work on the Hua of Papua

New Guinea provides a rather different example of male concern with reproduction. She notes the following in the case of the Hua: (1) males imitate menstruation, 'a process they supposedly loathe in women'; (2) males believe that they can become pregnant.

> The status of the Hua belief in male pregnancy is difficult to describe. Most informants if asked 'can a male become pregnant?' would answer 'no'.... Nevertheless, this belief is implicit in informants' discussions of many of the food prohibitions and sexual avoidances. In these contexts, the belief is openly acknowledged. Some informants even claim to have seen fetuses after their removal from males' bodies. (Meigs, 1976: 393)

Meigs attributes the imitation of menstruation through blood-letting, and the belief in male pregnancy, to men's desire to imitate women's reproductive abilities. It is a vexed question whether such beliefs indicate that men covet the reproductive capacity of women, or even, as Bettelheim (1962: 109–13) suggests, that the couvade and other 'imitative' practices reflect men's desire to acknowledge the female aspects of their nature. However, the important point is that physiology presents possibilities; it does not determine cultural elaboration.

Gender as a social role

In the previous section, I argued that the categories 'woman' and 'man' are culturally constructed, and that even the most apparently natural of functions, 'mothering', is a culturally defined activity. The contribution of feminist scholarship has been to demonstrate the complexity and variability of these formerly taken-for-granted categories, and to emphasize that sets of analytical distinctions, like nature/culture, domestic/public, which are premised on the cross-cultural homo-geneity of such categories, are problematic and potentially distorting. However, there is no easy consensus among feminist anthropologists themselves on these issues, and different scholars take up different positions with regard to the utility and appropriateness of cross-cultural frameworks of analysis. This will become clearer in the following section, where I turn to a consideration of those writers who do not see women's subordination as universal.

It is an interesting fact that scholars who maintain that women's subordination is not universal tend to approach the problem of gender relations through a consideration of what women and men *do*, rather than through an analysis of the symbolic valuations given to women and men in any society. They are usually concerned, therefore, with more sociological explanations of gender, that is with gender as a social relationship. As I argued at the beginning of this chapter, symbolic and sociological approaches to the study of gender are not mutually exclusive, but the lack of any sustained analysis of cultural valuations and ideologies is a frequent flaw in many of the more sociologically oriented analyses. However, an emphasis on what women and men *do* inevitably raises questions about the sexual division of labour, and about the related division of social life into 'domestic' and 'public' domains, the former comprising women's activities and the latter those of men.

Eleanor Leacock is one Marxist anthropologist who has criticized the assumption of the universal subordination of women. She views such an assumption as arising from a basically ahistorical mode of analysis (Leacock, 1978: 254), which fails to take into account the effects of colonization and the rise of a world capitalist economy (Leacock, 1972, 1978: 253–5; Etienne and Leacock, 1980), and which suffers from ethnocentric and male-centred bias (Leacock 1978: 247–8; Etienne and Leacock, 1980: 4). Leacock does not exempt some early feminist texts from these criticisms, notably Ernestine Friedl's book (1975), *Women and Men*, and Rosaldo and Lamphere's collection (1974), *Women, Culture and Society*.

In her writing, Leacock rejects two of the arguments which have been put forward by other feminist writers, (1) that woman's status is directly related to the functions of giving birth and rearing children, and (2) that the 'domestic'/'public' distinction is a cross-culturally valid framework for the analysis of gendered relations. Using material from hunter-gatherer societies, she follows Engels (1972) in arguing that women's subordination to men, the development of the family as an autonomous economic unit and monogamous marriage are all related to the development of private ownership of the means of production. The relevance of Engels's argument for feminist anthropology is discussed in chapter 3, but the important point to note in relation to Leacock's work is her argument that in 'pre-class' societies women and men were autonomous individuals, who held positions of equal value and prestige. These positions were different, but that difference in no way implied inferiority or superiority. Talking of the position of women in such societies, Leacock says that:

> [when] the range of decisions made by women is considered, women's autonomous and public role emerges. Their status was not as literal 'equals' of men (a point that has caused much confusion), but as what they were – female persons, with their own rights, duties, and responsibilities, which were complementary to and in no way secondary to those of men. (Leacock, 1978: 252)

Leacock's argument is that, contrary to earlier accounts by male ethnographers, women in all societies make a substantial economic contribution; and that, contrary to the assertions of some feminist anthropologists, women's status is dependent, not on their role as mothers nor on their confinement to a 'domestic' sphere, but on whether or not they control (1) access to resources, (2) the conditions of their work and (3) the distribution of the products of their labour. This is a point which has been made by a number of researchers (for example, Brown, 1970; Sanday, 1974; Sanday, 1981: ch. 6; Schlegel, 1977). In her review of Iroquois Indian ethnography, Leacock points out that the separation of social life into 'domestic' and 'public' spheres makes no sense in small-scale communities where household production and management are simultaneously 'public', economic and political life.

> Iroquois matrons preserved, stored, and dispensed the corn, meat, fish, berries, squashes, and fats that were buried in special pits or kept in the long house. . . . women's control over the dispensation of the foods they produced, and meat as well, gave them de facto power to veto declarations of war and to intervene to bring about peace. Women also guarded the 'tribal public treasure' kept in the long house, the wampum, quill and feather work, and furs. . . . The point to be stressed is that this was 'household management' of an altogether different order from management of the nuclear or extended family in patriarchal societies. In the latter, women may cajole, manipulate, or browbeat men, but always behind the public facade; in the former case, 'household management' was itself the management of the 'public' economy. (Leacock, 1978: 253)

A similar argument has been made with regard to a number of hunter-gatherer societies. The autonomous status of Australian Aboriginal women, and their lack of subordination to men, was recorded by Phyllis Kaberry in the 1930s. Kaberry attributed women's position to the importance of, and their control over, their economic contribution (1939: 142–3), and to their participation in women's rituals, which were valued by both men and women (1939: 277). Comparable points have been made by Diane Bell in her recent ethnography of Aboriginal women, where she notes that men's and women's worlds are substantially independent of each other in economic and ritual terms (Bell, 1983: 23). The result of this is that men and women have separate, gender-specific, but equal power bases. Bell echoes Leacock when she argues that separateness and difference do not necessarily have to imply inferiority or subordination. However, Aboriginal ethnography also contains many references to male–female relations which are hard to fit in with this picture of autonomous complementarity, especially accounts of male violence towards women. Both Bell (1980, 1983) and Leacock seem to attribute such events to changes in gender relations which have occurred as a result of increased contact with the 'white man', the institution of reservations, and incorporation into the wider Australian economy.

It is now a well-documented and widely accepted fact that gender relations in many parts of the world have been transformed under the successive impact of colonization, 'Westernization' and international capitalism. A number of studies have noted that development and wage labour make women more dependent on men by undermining traditional systems where women have had a certain amount of control over production and reproduction (see chapters 3 and 4).[14] In her own research on the Montagnais Indians, hunters of the Labrador Peninsula, Leacock is able to show that gender relations changed significantly under the impact of the fur trade, and other European influences, including the Jesuit missionaries, and that women's previous autonomous status was undermined in consequence (Leacock, 1972, 1980).

Karen Sacks is another Marxist anthropology who takes issue with the assumption of women's universal subordination. In an early article (Sacks, 1974), she attempted to modify Engels's thesis that women's subordination began with the development of private property, by arguing that there is 'too much data showing that women are not the complete equals of men in most non-class societies lacking private property' (Sacks, 1974: 213). However, in spite of this assertion, she is in broad agreement with Engels's position because (1) it provides an account of the conditions under which women do become subordinate to men, and (2) it supports ethnographic and historical data collected since the publication of Engels's work which show that 'women's social position has not always, everywhere, or in most respects been subordinate to that of men' (Sacks, 1974: 207). Sacks's work is useful because it does not assume the equal and autonomous status of women in 'pre-class' societies, as Leacock seems to do, and it therefore allows for the possibility of examining variability in women's position in these societies.

In a recent work, *Sisters and Wives* (1979), Sacks has set out a framework for examining the variability in women's status cross-culturally. She begins by reiterating an earlier criticism (Sacks, 1976) about the ways in which anthropologists have tended to assume that the existence of a sexual division of labour in non-class societies necessarily implies asymmetry in male–female relations. She continues by criticizing feminists and non-feminists alike for presuming that women's subordinate status is related to their role as mothers. Sacks argues that this presumption is ethnocentric in that it projects Western concepts of the family and socio-sexual relations on to other cultures. She goes on to propose a framework for the analysis of women's position based on a consideration of women's differing relations to the means of production. Sacks identifies two modes of production in non-class societies: a communal mode and a kin corporate mode. In the first type, all people, whether men or women, 'have the same relationship to the means of production, and hence they stand to each other as equal members of a community of "owners"' (Sacks, 1979: 113). In the second type, kin groups collectively control the means of production, and women's status varies according to whether they are primarily defined as (a) sisters, in which case they are considered to be members of the controlling kin group,

or (b) wives, whose rights are derived through marriage into the controlling kin group rather than through their relationship to their own (natal) kin group. The point of Sacks's argument is that where women are able to exercise their rights as sisters their status is improved in comparison to those societies where their rights are more narrowly defined as those of a wife. This issue does not arise in a communal mode of production, where, according to Sacks, no clear distinctions are made between the differing rights of sisters or wives.

> I have been struck by the counterpoint between sister and wife in a number of preclass or protoclass African societies with corporate patrilineages – for example, the Lovedu, Mpondo, and Igbo. I have also been impressed with the obliteration of the sister relationship in class societies by the relationship of wife, as in Buganda. Further, in foraging bands, I do not see either wives or sisters clearly, as among Mbuti. Wife and sister have similar contrastive meanings in a variety of patrilineal societies with reference to a woman's relations to productive means, to other adults, to power, and to their own sexuality. I do not think I do much violence to the data by interpreting sister in situations of corporate patrilineages to mean one who is an owner, a decision maker among others of the corporation, and a person who controls her own sexuality. By contrast, a wife is a subordinate in much the way Engels asserted for the family based on private property. (Sacks, 1979: 110)

The underlying assumption in Sacks's work would seem to be that if women and men share equal access to productive means then there will necessarily be sexual egalitarianism.

Burton (1985: 23–30) makes a number of telling criticisms of Sacks's work based on an analysis of an earlier article (Sacks, 1976), but they are nevertheless relevant to a critique of *Sisters and Wives*. Two points are particularly important here: the first relates to the use of a domestic/public dichotomy, and the second concerns the problem of gender ideologies and their relationship to economic conditions. Sacks's use of a sister/wife distinction is based on an implicit assumption that the rights and activities of the one may be easily distinguishable from those of the other. This may be an unwarranted assumption in the context of societies where families are presumably not yet autonomous economic units. In other words, it may not be possible to distinguish a bounded 'domestic' sphere where women have rights as wives from a bounded 'public' or corporate sphere where women have rights as sisters. Sacks has elsewhere (Sacks, 1976) pointed out the analytical flaw in dichotomizing 'domestic' and 'public' domains in non-class societies, but she does not seem to link this realization to her own distinction between sisters and wives.[15]

The second criticism relates to the issue of cultural ideologies. Most feminist scholars would now agree, I think, that the cultural valuations given to women and men in society arise from something more than just their respective positions in the relations of production. It is a well-recognized feature of cultural representations of gender that they 'rarely accurately reflect male–female relations, men's and women's activities, and men's and women's contributions in any given society' (Ortner and Whitehead, 1981a: 10). This was an early realization in feminist anthropology, and it produced a large body of work which demonstrated conclusively that, although men were represented as dominant in many societies, women actually possessed and wielded a considerable amount of power.[16] The troubling point about this research was not just that it showed how anthropology, as a discipline, had neglected key aspects of women's lives and experiences, but that it also produced accounts of societies where women were represented as subordinate to men while not in fact being so as regards their ability to act, speak out and make decisions in the world of day-to-day interaction and living. This situation is sometimes referred to as the 'myth of male dominance' (Rogers, 1975), and is part of the debate discussed in chapter 1 concerning the possible existence of separate 'male' and 'female' models of the world. The problem it presents with regard to Sacks's work is that if women are thought of as subordinate to men, while actually possessing certain degrees of economic and political autonomy, then it is difficult to see how the status of women in any society could be straightforwardly read off from their position in the relations of production. Cultural representations of the sexes clearly have a determining influence on the status and position of women in society, and, if women are represented as subordinate while simultaneously maintaining considerable economic and political power, then this is a feature of social life which requires explanation. Sacks does not seem to deal with the issue of gender ideologies in any systematic way, and she makes little attempt to explain why the cultural valuations given to women and men often fail to reflect their respective access to and control over resources.

The symbolic and the sociological combined[17]

A number of feminist scholars have attempted to combine symbolic and sociological approaches to the study of gender, because of a realization that ideas about women and men are neither wholly independent of, nor directly derived from, economic relations of production. Jane Collier and Michelle Rosaldo, in their article 'Politics and gender in simple societies' (1981), develop a model for the analysis of gender systems in small-scale societies, of a type broadly comparable to Sacks's 'communal mode of production'. Collier and Rosaldo argue that productive and political processes cannot be understood in isolation from the cultural perceptions which people have of those processes, and that any analysis must focus both on what people do and on the cultural understandings which underlie their actions (Collier and Rosaldo, 1981: 276). Their aim is to provide some way of linking cultural ideas about gender to the actual social relations in which gendered individuals live, think and act.

Collier and Rosaldo focus on brideservice societies, where sons-in-law establish long-term relationships with their wife's parents through gifts of labour and food. Their argument is that these gifts, which both precede and continue after marriage, create sets of obligations and social relationships which are quite distinct from those developed in bridewealth societies. In the latter type of society, a son-in-law gives goods at the time of his marriage to his wife's kin in payment for rights in his wife's labour, sexuality and offspring. Here, the authors are suggesting that the analysis of gender in small-scale societies should be based on how marriage works in such groups. They argue that anthropologists have long recognized that kinship and marriage organize productive relationships and the structure of rights and obligations in non-class societies. As a result, the organization of marriage, and of the relationships which are built up around it, should provide clues to the organization of gender-based productive relationships.

> In marrying, people 'make families', but they also contract debts, change residence, stir enmities, and establish cooperative bonds. A typology of nonclass societies in terms of the organisation of marriage would seem, then, an important first step for the analysis of gender. The different ways in which tribal peoples 'make marriages' are likely to correspond, on the one hand, to important differences in economic and political organisation, and, on the other, to salient variations in the ways that gender is construed. (Collier and Rosaldo, 1981: 278)

This position is essentially a development of an earlier argument made by Janet Siskind (1973, 1978) and Gayle Rubin (1975) that kinship and marriage are powerful determinants of the way in which ideas about gender are constructed. This is where Collier and Rosaldo go beyond the kind of argument put forward by Sacks. Instead of seeing gender constructs as the direct reflection of social or productive relationships, they interpret these constructs as highly 'ritualized statements' which elaborate on what individual women and men perceive as particularly salient political concerns. In brideservice societies, marriage is a highly political relationship because it is the primary means through which women and men establish relationships with other individuals. It is also the mechanism through which productive relationships and rights and obligations are established. Thus Collier and Rosaldo argue that gender relationships receive symbolic emphasis because they are the social arena in which individuals are enabled to make political claims and initiate personal strategies. It is through the competing claims that women and men make on one another, in the context of particular sets of social and economic relations, that the cultural conceptions of gender are constructed.

This argument is broadly comparable to one I have made with regard to my own research on the Marakwet people of Kenya (Moore, 1986). In my discussion of gender relations, I demonstrate that the Marakwet draw on the different social and economic situations of women and men in society, and use those differences as a symbolizing mechanism. Cultural ideas about the different qualities, attitudes and behaviour of women and men are generated and expressed through the conflicts and tensions which arise between conjugal partners regarding claims over, and access to, land, animals and other resources (Moore, 1986: 64–71). Cultural ideas about gender do not directly reflect the social and economic positions of women and men, although it is true that they originate within the context of those conditions. This is because gender stereotypes are developed and used in the strategies which individuals of both sexes employ to advance their interests in various social contexts. Take, as an example, a phrase often to be found on the lips of Marakwet men: 'women are like children, they speak before they think.' In a society which lays great store on the seniority which age and experience brings, this statement obviously has nothing to do with whether women are actually child-like or not. Instead, it is a gender stereotype of great power, which is little influenced by the fact that many men can count strong and influential women among the people known to them. As a stereotype it is certainly related to the fact that within this patrilineal society women are jural minors with regard to certain areas of life, but its power and pervasiveness have to be accounted for in terms of its strategic use in the day-to-day context of interaction between women and men. The power of this stereotype derives, in part, from its wide applicability: it would characterize an individual woman's motives in a case of marital conflict, as well as indicating an attribute of women as a group distinct from men. However, both women and men know that stereotypes of this kind are contradicted by experience, and yet this has little to do with their substantial and continuing rhetorical and material power. Such statements not only provide a strategic reason why women should be excluded from certain activities, but also ensure that women will be excluded in many cases. The power of gender stereotypes is not just in the mind, for they have a perfect material reality, which helps to reinforce the social and economic conditions within which they are developed and employed.

Women as persons

In recent years, anthropology as a whole has seen a reorientation towards theories concerning thinking social actors and the strategies they employ in day-to-day living. This theoretical shift is, in part, a reaction to the influence of structuralism in anthropology, and it lays particular emphasis on actors' models of the way the world is, and on how they influence social action, rather than on the models of the analyst or anthropologist. Feminist anthropologists have found this particularly stimulating, because of the central role which feminist analysis of all kinds gives to women's actual experience (cf. Strathern, 1987b; Keohane et al., 1982; Register, 1980; Rapp, 1979).[18] This emphasis on experience necessarily involves some consideration of the 'experiencing self' or 'person'. An enquiry into the cultural construction of self or person, through an analysis of gender identity, is an area where feminist anthropology continues to make a significant and substantial contribution to theoretical development within the discipline. The analysis of women as persons inevitably leads us back to debates concerning the 'domestic'/'public' division, and to issues about power, autonomy and authority. In an early article, 'Women as persons', Elizabeth Faithorn (1976) argues forcefully for an analysis of male–female relations which sees women as individuals with power in their own right. As we have noted, the revaluation of women's activities was a notable feature of the 'anthropology of women' in the late 1970s, but it was particularly important in Melanesian ethnography, where it was accompanied by a specific emphasis on women as individuals or persons. Annette Weiner's well-known reanalysis of Trobriand women makes much of the importance of seeing women as individuals. 'Whether women are publicly valued or privately secluded, whether they control politics, a range of economic commodities, or merely magic spells, they function within that society, not as objects but as individuals with some measure of control' (Weiner, 1976: 228). Weiner's argument is that certain cultural activities are the domain of women, and that within this domain women exercise considerable power, and thus construct for themselves an arena of social action which demonstrates their value in Trobriand society.

Daryl Feil has analysed male–female relations among the Enga, and he lays corresponding emphasis on women as persons: 'Women are "persons" in New Guinea whatever the received notion and whether or not they appear so in the literature' (Feil, 1978: 268). However, Feil's position differs somewhat from Weiner's in two respects. First, he argues that to treat women as persons it is necessary to demonstrate that they participate in those socio-political affairs of life usually presented as the domain of men. Weiner, on the other hand, suggests that women have power in a domain which is specifically theirs, while none the less being equal in value to men. Secondly, Feil locates women's power in day-to-day social affairs, while Weiner stresses the cultural power of the symbolic encoding of femaleness, dramatized in activities and objects which are specifically female (cf. Strathern, 1984a). The central issue is an old one: if we want to see women as effective social adults in their own right, is it enough to say that they have power within a specifically female domain, or must we argue that they have power in those areas of social life which have so often been presented as the public, political domain of men? This issue is essentially a transposition of the 'domestic'/'public' debate, in that it uses the 'domestic'/'public' distinction as a means of constructing the problem which it seeks to resolve.

Marilyn Strathern has indicated a number of potential pitfalls with the much-needed, but sometimes rather uncritical, re-evaluation of women as persons or powerful individuals. Her own work on concepts of gender, identity and self among the Hagen in the Papua New Guinea highlands (1980, 1981b, 1984a) seeks to establish grounds for the analysis of these concepts, while critically reviewing many of the ethnocentric Western assumptions which can underpin analytical frameworks. Conceptions of the 'individual' or 'person' are cross-culturally as variable as the concepts 'woman' and 'man'. Strathern points out that there is an extraordinary power behind the demand that anthropologists should treat women as individuals or persons in their own right. However, there is a danger that in formulating such a demand we are merely appealing to Western assumptions about the nature of personhood and the relationship between individuals and society: 'we can usefully talk of Hagen ideas of the person, in an analytic sense, provided we do not conflate the construct with the ideological "individual" of Western culture. This latter is best seen as a particular cultural type (of person) rather than as a self-evident analytical category itself' (Strathern, 1981b: 168).

The concept of the individual in Western thought is a very specific constellation of ideas, which combines theories of autonomy, action and moral worth with a particular view of the way in which individuals both make up and stand apart from society. It seems clear that, because conceptions of the 'individual' or 'person' contain ideas about action, choice and moral behaviour, they necessarily involve problems of expectation. In other words, views about the appropriate behaviour of social individuals always impinge on the way in which people assess the motivation, behaviour and social worth of others. To assume that Western notions of the acting 'individual' or 'person' are appropriate to other contexts is to ignore the differing cultural mechanisms and expectation through which this process of evaluation proceeds.

The second point that Strathern makes in relation to our analysis of women as individuals or persons is to emphasize the ways in which the Western concept of the autonomous individual implies a division between the 'domestic' and 'public' spheres of social life. Strathern points out that in Western culture women may be conceived of as being rather less than persons, because of their association with the natural, with children, and with the 'domestic' sphere, rather than with culture and the 'social world of public affairs' which are usually seen as the domain of men (Strathern, 1984a: 17). As Strathern argues, these are precisely the criteria which Ortner uses to account for women's universal subordination, and they are thus open to the same criticisms as those made earlier against Ortner's work (Ortner, 1974; and see above). Strathern emphasizes that the demeaning nature of domestic involvement is a Western construct, and, as has already been argued, should not be confused with some cross-culturally valid quality of the 'domestic' sphere, or indeed of women. It is clear that Hageners do make both a symbolic and a social connection between 'femaleness' and 'domesticity', but, as Strathern has demonstrated, these associations cannot be explained by the Western distinctions between nature/culture and domestic/public (Strathern, 1980; Strathern 1984a: 17–18). In order for us to value Hagen women it is not necessary to revalue the 'domestic' or to demonstrate that these women are active in a 'public' sphere. The association of the 'domestic' with something demeaning or less than social is not a feature of Hagen thought.

> In Hagen social theory, however, women's identity as persons does not have to rest on proof that they are powerful in some domain created by themselves, nor in an ability to break free from domestic confines constructed by men. . . . Through both symbol and convention female-ness is associated with domesticity, and in turn this domesticity may symbolise interests opposed to the public and collective interests of men. Yet Hagen women are not thereby overshadowed by the possibility, so

denigrating in our own system, that they are somehow less than proper persons. (Strathern, 1984a: 18)

The male–female distinction in Hagen thought has a metaphoric value, and it is used to order other contrasts or distinctions, like domestic/public, rubbish/prestige, individual interests/social good, which are idioms for expressing social worth (Strathern, 1981b: 169–70). However, these contrasts are moral distinctions which apply to men, as well as to women, and Hagen women are not permanently or indissolubly associated with their negative poles. What these contrasts express is not just a 'problem of women' but a 'problem of people' (Strathern, 1981b: 170). The point Strathern stresses is that the actions of female individuals are to some extent separable from the values and associations given to the concept of 'femaleness' in Hagen culture (Strathern, 1981b: 168, 184; Strathern 1984a: 23).[19] Women, like men, may be thought of as acting for the social good or following their individual interests; they can be considered prestigious individuals or rubbish ones (Strathern, 1981b: 181–2). 'An individual Hagen woman is not entirely identified with the stereotypes of her sex. In using gender to structure other values . . . Hageners detach posited qualities of maleness and femaleness from actual men and women. A person of either sex can behave in a male or female way' (Strathern, 1981b: 178). Hagen women are closely associated with the domestic sphere, but understanding exactly what that association means is a matter for analysis. The desire to revalue women as 'persons in their own right' is undermined if it turns out to be little more than a reflection of Western cultural concerns. The contribution which Marilyn Strathern's work makes is to remind us that gender constructs are linked to concepts of self, personhood and autonomy. Any analysis of such concepts necessarily involves some consideration of choice, strategy, moral worth and social value as they relate to the actions of individual social actors. These are the areas of social analysis where the connections between the symbolic or cultural aspects of social life and the social and economic conditions under which life is lived can be most clearly recognized and investigated. It is here that the study of gender continues to make a significant contribution to the development of anthropological theory.

3

KINSHIP, LABOUR AND HOUSEHOLD: UNDERSTANDING WOMEN'S WORK

This chapter is about women's work, and about the social, economic and political contexts of that work. It examines some of the important themes which have emerged in debates concerning the sexual division of labour and the organization of gender relations within the family and the household. These issues are a complex but important area of social science scholarship, and this is reflected in the huge body of literature which has appeared in recent years. Scholars with a variety of approaches (Marxist, feminist, neo-classicist) have converged from different disciplines (anthropology, sociology, history and economics) to focus on a wide range of related issues. However, much of this work is characterized by a set of dominant concerns: what is the sexual division of labour and how is it changing; what is the relationship between the sexual division of labour and the status of women in society; what is the relationship between the organization of gender relations in the household and the entry of women into wage labour; and how is women's unpaid work in the home related to the reproduction of the capitalist labour force?[1] These are questions which clearly have to be analysed in historically and geographically specific terms. In anthropology, these questions have tended to be formulated through a concern with how the changing division of labour by gender is related to the organization of marriage and kinship relations, and to the variation in household forms. The changing nature of the 'family' has been the subject of much debate in anthropology, and this will be a predominant theme in the discussion which follows because of the way in which 'familial' relations shape women's access to work and other resources, and also play a key role in producing and maintaining gender ideologies.

Women's work

About half of the women in the world live and work on farmlands in developing countries and are responsible for 40 to 80 per cent of all agricultural production, depending on the country. (Charlton, 1984: 61)

In almost any household where the men are involved in cultivation, the women will also contribute to agricultural production in some capacity, even if the women themselves (and indeed the men) look on this contribution as part of 'housework'. (Sharma, 1980: 132)

Women all over the world are engaged in productive work both inside and outside the home. The exact nature of this work varies from culture to culture, but generally speaking it can be classified under four headings: agricultural work, commerce, household work and wage labour. A number of commentators have noted that the actual extent of women's unwaged work, and their consequent contribution to household income, has been consistently underestimated (Beneria, 1981, 1982b; Boserup, 1970; Boulding, 1983; Deere, 1983; Dixon, 1985). There are several reasons for this, but the most important is clearly related to the definition of 'work' itself. Work is not just a matter of what people do because any definition must also include the conditions under which that work is performed, and its perceived social value or worth within a given cultural context (Burman, 1979; Wallman, 1979: 2). Recognizing the social value given to work, or to particular kinds of work, helps us to understand why some activities are thought to be more important than others, and why, for example, in British society, we are able to ask a non-salaried woman with five children 'Do you work?' and receive the answer 'No'. The apparent invisibility of women's work is a feature of the sexual division of labour in many societies, and it is reinforced by the ethnocentric assumptions of researchers and policy-makers, and by indigenous gender ideologies. If work is conventionally understood as 'paid work outside the home', then the value of women's subsistence and domestic labour goes unrecognized. This definition of work may persist even when it is clearly contradicted by people's experiences and expectations. The literature abounds with cautionary examples of women who are defined as 'housewives', when they are actually involved in agricultural labour and small-scale market production, in addition to their household maintenance and childcare tasks.[2] Through their activities, these women make a significant contribution to household income, both indirectly in terms of their unpaid agricultural and household labour, and directly through the money they earn in market-trading and petty commodity production. In her analysis of Cajamarcan peasant households in Peru, Carmen Diana Deere found that, while the most important form of income overall derived from male wage labour, women's contribution to household income was substantial. 'Across all strata of the peasantry, adult women are principally responsible for commerce and animal care, which generate approximately one-third of both the mean net income and the mean monetary income of the household' (Deere, 1983: 120). There is nothing in the available material from household income studies to suggest that these findings are unusual, although the actual amount women contribute to household income clearly varies from one society to another.

Esther Boserup was one of the first scholars to provide a comparative analysis of women's work, based on data from a wide range of societies. In her book, *Women's Role in Economic Development* (Boserup, 1970), she emphasized that, in spite of sex-role stereotyping and cross-cultural regularities in the sexual division of labour, women's work differed from society to society. Using material from African farming systems, she showed that it was not always the men who were the primary providers of food. In many societies in Africa, men clear the land for cultivation, but it is women who actually cultivate the crops. Boserup's comparative method enabled her to contrast the situation in Africa, where women play a fundamental role in subsistence agricultural production, with that in Asia and Latin America, where their role is less marked. She explained this difference by linking aspects of the sexual division of labour to population density, landholding systems and technology. Boserup also pointed out the negative effects that colonialism and the penetration of capitalism into subsistence economies had had on women. In some cases, colonial administrators introduced land reforms which dispossessed women of their rights to land. As Boserup makes clear, these reforms were not unconnected to the strongly held European view that cultivation should properly be the work of men. The impact of Western gender ideologies on the sexual division of labour in the developing world has already been discussed in chapter 2, and I shall return to it again later. Boserup stressed the underestimation of women's work, particularly in the spheres of subsistence agriculture and domestic labour. She pointed out that the ideological bias underlying statistical categories tends to undervalue women's work, and that 'subsistence activities usually omitted in the statistics of production and income are largely women's work' (Boserup, 1970: 163).

Boserup's book is an important starting point because it raises issues which have dominated discussion on women's status and their economic roles in society, and which have subsequently inspired much of the empirical work conducted over the last ten to fifteen years.[3] Boserup's perspective as an economist, and her comparative approach, led her to ask the right sorts of question.[4] A similar approach to these issues can be found in Jack Goody's book *Production and Reproduction*. Jack Goody discusses the relationship between his work and that of

Esther Boserup (Goody, 1976: ch. 4), and demonstrates a large degree of similarity between their findings. Goody is concerned to link forms of marriage and patterns of property transmission to types of agricultural production, and, to this end, he contrasts the African and Asian systems, just as Boserup does. The chief value of Goody's work is the specific linkages it suggests between kinship relations and economic organization.[5] He argues that the major difference between African and Eurasian inheritance systems is that Eurasian forms are characterized by diverging inheritance (where property goes to children of both sexes) and by dowry (where parental property is given to a daughter on her marriage), both of which are unusual in Africa (Goody, 1976: 6). Goody links the existence of diverging inheritance to 'relatively advanced' economies with intensive and plough agriculture. African hoe-agriculture societies, on the other hand, are characterized by homogenous inheritance, 'where a man's property is transmitted only to members of his own clan or lineage who belong to the same sex' (Goody, 1976: 7). In these African societies, women cannot inherit, and they receive no dowry when they marry. Instead, bridewealth (gifts of cattle or other goods) passes from the male kin of the groom to the male kin of the bride. This transfer of goods does not confer status on the bride, as dowry does, but acts instead as a means of compensating the bride's kin for the loss of her labour, while simultaneously transferring rights in the women's reproductive potential (i.e. in any children she may bear) from her kin group to that of her husband.

Boserup draws very similar conclusions regarding the relationships between the sexual division of labour, marriage systems and types of agricultural production. She argues that where hoe agriculture predominates and most agricultural work is done by women, as in the case of many African societies, there is a high incidence of polygyny (men having more than one wife) and bridewealth. In such systems, women only have limited rights of support from their husbands, but they may have some economic independence from the sale of their own crops. However, in areas where plough agriculture predominates, and women do less agricultural work than men, as in the Asian examples she cites, few marriages are polygynous and dowry is usually paid. In these communities, women are entirely dependent upon their husbands for economic support, and the husband has an obligation to provide for his wife and children (Boserup, 1970: 50).

Both authors are concerned to link changes in agricultural systems to changes in domestic institutions, including marriage and the sexual division of labour. The relevance of their work lies in the demonstrable links between women's status, the sexual division of labour, forms of marriage and inheritance, and the economic relations of production. It is these links which form the subject of much feminist scholarship in anthropology, as well as in related disciplines. In particular, it has been the way in which these relationships are changing as a result of political and economic developments in the contemporary world – an issue prefigured in Boserup's work – which has generated the most lively debate. In order to investigate how these debates have developed in anthropology, it is necessary to turn to Engels and to the arguments about the relations between productive and reproductive labour which attempt to explain the links between kinship and economics in human societies.

Production and reproduction

The sexual division of labour, the nature of kinship relations and the historical 'development' of the family are all themes which have a long history in social analysis. These themes were, of course, the concern of nineteenth-century social thinkers, and many of the issues which their analysis generated have continued into contemporary theorizing (see chapter 2). The best example of this continuity is undoubtedly the feminist debate concerning Friedrich Engels's book *The Origin of the Family, Private Property, and the State* (1972 [1884]). This is a nineteenth-century text, which draws on the anthropological studies of Lewis Henry Morgan, in an attempt to link the history of the family to the development of private property and the rise of the state.[6] Engels's interest in nineteenth-century evolutionary theories concerning the history of the family is clearly evident in his fulsome praise of Bachofen's theory of a universal matriarchal system prior to the development of patriarchy (Engels, 1972: 46–68 *passim*). Engels argued that the growth of male-owned private property and the development of the monogamous family transformed women's position in society and brought about 'the world-historical defeat of the female sex'. He characterized sexual relations prior to this 'defeat' as egalitarian and complementary.

> Division of labour was a pure and simple outgrowth of nature; it existed only between the sexes. The men went to war, hunted, fished, provided the raw material for food and the tools necessary for these pursuits. The women cared for the house, and prepared food and clothing; they cooked, weaved and sewed. Each was master in his or her own field of activity; the men in the forest, the women in the house. Each owned the tools he or she made and used: the men, the weapons and the hunting and fishing tackle, the women, the household goods and utensils. The household was communistic, comprising several, and often many families. Whatever was produced and used in common was common property: the house, the garden, the long boat. (Engels, 1972: 149)

Engels thus sees women and men as equal members of the 'tribe' or 'clan'; both sexes own tools, and both participate in political and economic decisions. In the society he envisages, all production is for use, and people work for the communal household rather than for themselves. His principal point is that in the absence of private property women's and men's work are of equal social value and worth: their domains might have been separate, but this did not mean that one was more highly valued than the other. Engels is primarily concerned to link changes in family form and gender relations to changes in material conditions. He argues that the domestication of animals – and, thereafter, the development of agriculture – led to the possibility of surplus, and to the necessity of controlling the 'productive property' which created that surplus (cf. Sacks, 1974: 213–17). This 'productive property' (initially domestic animals) was concentrated in the hands of men as a consequence of the 'natural' division of labour. In Engels's view, the final 'death' of the collective economic unit and the subsequent rise of the monogamous family were due to men's desire to transmit the wealth they had accumulated to their genetic offspring, and hence the importance of monogamous marriage, which guaranteed the paternity of children (Engels, 1972: 74).

Engels's thesis is a well-known one, and it has been very influential in Marxist and feminist analyses of the causes and origins of women's subordination. Early anthropological reformulations of Engels (Gough, 1972, 1975; Leacock, 1972; Brown, 1970; Sacks, 1974) produced points of criticism – including reservations about the reliability of the ethnographic data – but remained close to the original thesis.[7] However, recent feminist writers, while acknowledging the importance of Engels's contribution to debates on 'the woman question', have made a number of important criticisms. Rosalind Coward, for example, has argued that Engels's thesis is imbued with certain essentialist assumptions. First, she notes that he assumes a 'natural' division of labour, where men are primarily concerned with productive tasks and women with domestic ones. This 'natural' division appears to be assumed on the basis of given propensities. The existence of such propensities is reinforced in his discussion of the demise of group marriage, where he suggests that women will 'naturally' abominate promiscuity, while men, on the other hand, will always pursue their promiscuous inclinations whenever possible. In the same way, his argument concerning the relationship between property, paternity and legitimacy assumes that men will 'naturally' want to transmit property exclusively to genetic offspring (Coward, 1983: 146–7). These essentialist assumptions, which underlie what is actually a theory of the social construction of gender relations, are serious flaws.

Lise Vogel (1983) makes similar criticisms, but her main concern is with what she calls the 'dual systems perspective'.[8] Vogel sees this dualism as characteristic of socialist-feminist theory and she traces its origins to Engels (Vogel, 1983: 29–37).

> According to the materialist conception, the determining factor in history is, in the last resort, the production and reproduction of immediate life. But this itself is of a two-fold character. On the one hand, the production of the means of subsistence, of food, clothing and shelter and the tools requiste therefore; on the other, the production of human beings themselves, the propagation of the species. The social institutions under which men of a definite historical epoch and of a definite country live are conditioned by both kinds of reproduction: by the stage of development of labour on the one hand, and of the family on the other. (Engels, 1972: 25–6)

This much-quoted passage from Engels is open to a number of interpretations, and has been cited in support of various positions in recent years. However, Vogel is clearly correct in seeing it as opening the way for a dual perspective on 'the woman problem'. The possibility of dualism arises because women are both mothers and workers, reproducers and producers, and these two aspects of their lives can be seen as analytically separable.[9] The social relations of reproduction, or the 'sex gender system' as Rubin (1975) prefers it, are a set of arrangements which reproduce the human group from generation to generation, and which include ways of conceptualizing and organizing such things as sex, gender, procreation, and domestic labour and consumption. These social relations of reproduction are located in the family, and, although they clearly have an impact on the organization of production, they are to some extent distinct from the economic relations of production which are the subject of traditional Marxist analyses.

Vogel is critical of the tendency to separate reproduction from other productive relations, and thus to conceive of both sets of relations as distinct domains. She notes that Engels sees the origins of women's oppression as arising from a 'naturally' determined sexual division of labour, which in turn shapes the form of the family. Vogel argues that this conceptualization reifies the family as an analytical category, while, at the same time, it fails to specify how the family functions within the overall process of social reproduction.[10] The result is that, while the relations of production and the relations of reproduction are seen as coexisting systems, which influence and affect each other, an artificial separation is none the less maintained between 'the economy' and 'the family'. This separation has been criticized by writers from various disciplines, but it is particularly problematic in anthropology, where families, kinship and gender/age relations cannot be separated from economic and political relations. The feminist critique in anthropology makes it clear that the productive and reproductive roles of women cannot be separated out and analysed in isolation from each other.[11] In the final analysis, such a separation would be little more than a transformation of the domestic/public division, which, as I argued in chapter 2, is not only artificial but analytically constraining.

Theories of reproduction

Arguably the most significant anthropological text on the interrelationship between production and reproduction is Claude Meillassoux's *Maidens, Meal and Money* (1981). Meillassoux's book takes as its central theme the importance of the social relations of human reproduction (or the domestic domain), and asks what role these relations play in the reproduction of economic systems.[12] His work is obviously an important contribution to the debate on the relationship between productive and reproductive relations, but its starting point is rather different from that of Engels. The explicit connection which Engels makes between women's subordination and the rise of private property means that he sees women's inferior status as directly connected to their non-ownership of the means of production (first animals, and later land). Meillassoux, on the other hand, argues that the control of the means of production is less important than the control of the means of reproduction, i.e. women (1981: xii–xiii, 49). His argument harks back to an old debate in anthropology, put forward by Lévi-Strauss, about the exchange of women and the origins of human cultural behaviour (Lévi-Strauss, 1969, 1971).[13] Meillassoux acknowledges his engagement with Lévi-Strauss and with other writers on kinship, because kinship is the form in which anthropology has traditionally treated the relations of reproduction (Meillassoux, 1981: 10). His argument is thus carefully inserted into a series of complex debates in anthropology, which I cannot review here. However, aspects of his work are particularly relevant to the feminist critique of Marxist theory in anthropology, and so require some serious consideration.

The aim of *Maidens, Meal and Money* is to analyse the workings of the social relations of reproduction within what Meillassoux terms the 'domestic agricultural community'.[14] This community is engaged in subsistence agricultural production, and is made up of a number of separate 'domestic units' which form the basic working cells of society. These domestic units or cells are patrilineal (descent is traced through men) and patrilocal (married couples reside with the husband's kin group); and these facts have two important consequences.

The first is that marriage involves women moving from one community to another; and the second is that boys gain their social affiliation and their access to resources, including wives, through their father and his male kin. The result is that (1) women are dependent on their husbands because they are cut off from their original kin groups, and (2) young men are dependent on their fathers for access to resources. Both these sets of dependencies are crucial to understanding how the society reproduces itself.

Meillassoux argues that the main concern of the domestic community is, in fact, its self-reproduction, or, more simply, its continued existence over time (1981: 38). He argues that there are three key factors which determine social reproduction: food, seeds and women. Naturally enough, the male elders in each domestic community control these key factors. They control women because they control their wives and daughters. They control the young men and their labour because the young men want wives, and only the elders can supply both the wives and the goods necessary for bridewealth payments. In addition, the elders control the grain stores which contain not only the food supplies necessary for survival throughout the year but also the seed-grain which is essential to the reproduction of the agricultural cycle. Meillassoux terms the control of women and grain the 'means of reproduction', while the social relations which organize these means are the 'relations of reproduction' of the society. Meillassoux's argument is interesting because it appears to make women and the social relations of reproduction central to an understanding of social continuity and development. However, both his treatment of women and his conceptualization of the relations of reproduction have been extensively criticized by feminist anthropologists.

The most common criticism concerning Meillassoux's treatment of women is that, instead of analysing the form(s) of women's subordination, he assumes that this subordination is an established and unproblematic state of affairs which does not require further specification or analysis (Mackintosh, 1977; Harris and Young, 1981; Edholm et al., 1977). This is, in part, because Meillassoux's book offers a model of the relationship between productive and reproductive relations, and not an analysis of an empirically defined and historically located community, made up of women and men. As Mackintosh (1977: 122) points out, the reader is never given enough details to make sense of the society Meillassoux describes. Meillassoux's analysis thus raises a number of questions which he leaves unanswered. If the reproduction of society depends on the control of women's productive and reproductive potential by male elders, have the women not evolved strategies to deal with this control? If they have such an important role in agricultural production, what happens to the crops they produce?

Do they really surrender them all to their husbands, or do they retain control over them? According to Meillassoux, kinship relations are defined solely in terms of those relationships between men which give access to power and authority. But do women have no kin relations of their own, do they not retain links with their brothers, or with other kin networks outside those of their husband?[15]

The lack of historical and ethnographic detail means that women, and what they say, do and think, are quite invisible in Meillassoux's analysis, in spite of the fact that they are apparently central to it. It could be argued that all social actors are invisible to a degree in his analysis because he intends it to be a model and not an ethnographic monograph. This is a fair point, except that his treatment of women casts doubt on the validity of his model. For example, there is no discussion of the nature of the sexual division of labour. This is particularly problematic, given that one of the issues Meillassoux's work addresses is whether the ability of certain men to control women is a necessary condition for the reproduction of the social formation (Harris and Young, 1981: 120). In other words, if Meillassoux wants to argue that a particular position of women, or a particular relationship between the sexes, is necessary for a given social unit to be reproduced through time, this is impossible if that position or relationship is never specified.

A second, and related, criticism is that Meillassoux treats women as a homogeneous category. There is no sustained discussion of how the circumstances of women's lives change as they get older: a senior mother-in-law is not in the same position *vis-à-vis* her male kin, or indeed *vis-à-vis* other women, as a young bride. Meillassoux mentions, but does not adequately discuss, the possibility of social differentiation among women, and fails therefore to address a number of issues, including the particularly thorny one of why some women collaborate in the oppression of others (1981: 76).[16]

In addition to these points concerning his treatment of women, Meillassoux has also been criticized for the way in which he conceptualizes the relations of reproduction. In his analysis, he speaks of these relations in terms which conflate the biological reproduction of human beings with the reproduction of social units. The concept of reproduction has been very contentious in feminist-Marxist theory, and the debate is by no means resolved. I cannot review the twists and turns of the different arguments in this book, but a few brief points need to be mentioned. A number of feminist writers have argued that Meillassoux's concept of the relations of reproduction confuses three different reproductive processes which need to be kept analytically separate: social reproduction, the reproduction of the labour force, and human or biological reproduction (Edholm et al., 1977; Harris and

Young, 1981; Mackintosh, 1977, 1981). Meillassoux lumps these three types of reproduction together because in the pre-capitalist social formation he envisages the social reproduction of society is assured through the control of other people's labour. Labour, and the individuals who perform it, must be reproduced, and this in turn involves control over biological reproduction and the persons who are the means of that reproduction: women. Feminist critics agree with Meillassoux in seeing these reproductive processes as connected, but they argue that what is needed is an analysis of exactly how these connections operate. Such an analysis is, of course, impossible if different sorts of reproductive process are treated as a single set of relations.

Edholm, Harris and Young have argued that, in assuming 'that the reproduction of the labour force is synonymous with human reproduction', Meillassoux fails to confront the fact that the labour force is socially constituted (Edholm et al., 1977: 110). Not all members of society become part of the labour force: certain categories of person are prevented from entering it altogether, and others find themselves removed from it: witness the case of the British and North American women who were drawn into the labour force during World War II, as shipbuilders and armaments manufacturers, only to be unceremoniously returned to their homes when their 'menfolk' were demobbed and needed jobs. Feminist critics argue that Meillassoux's analysis is flawed because it is impossible to understand how the labour force is reproduced unless we can understand how individuals are allocated to it in the first place (Harris and Young, 1981: 128). The value of this argument is clear, because a simple theory of the social constitution of the labour force would have allowed Meillassoux to discuss the relationship between women's productive and reproductive roles. This relationship is one which eludes Meillassoux because he insists on seeing women predominantly as reproducers. This single-minded focus does not advance our understanding of the 'position of women', and it subsumes the problems of women's reproductive labour under the general concept of the reproduction of the labour force.

Women's reproductive labour, as we know, involves a great deal more than giving birth to children. It also involves all the activities – cooking, cleaning, childcare, looking after the old and the sick, running the household, etc. – which we usually refer to as domestic work. Meillassoux presents an analysis of the relations of reproduction in which the concept of the domestic community is absolutely crucial, and yet he does not even mention women's domestic work. We have returned again to the invisibility of women's domestic labour; an invisibility which operates at both the empirical and the theoretical level (see chapter 1 and above). Feminist critics have suggested that it is because domestic activities are closely associated with the physiological needs of the human body (sleeping, eating, shelter, etc.) that they appear 'natural' and are therefore not integrated into theoretical discourses concerning the relations of reproduction (Harris and Young, 1981: 131; Harris, 1981: 61–2; Mackintosh, 1979: 176–7). Since domestic work is considered natural, it is easy to make the mistake of seeing it as constant throughout history, as an unchanging set of necessities which do not need to be subjected to historical analysis (Harris and Young, 1981).

There are two obvious problems with this position. First, the relationship between domestic labour and non-domestic labour is not constant, but is subject to historical determination. Under capitalism, there is a rigid distinction between domestic labour in the home and productive labour in the workplace, but this marked separation between the two spheres of activity is not characteristic of other types of economy (see chapter 4). Secondly, there is the related question of the content of domestic labour. It is simplistic to imagine that domestic labour remains constant through time, and this is abundantly clear once we start to think about such things as technological change (hoovers and food processors), the availability of fuel (mains-supplied gas as opposed to collecting firewood), access to water, and so on. We also need to think about the consequences for domestic labour of increasing involvement in the capitalist economy (see also the arguments made about socialist economies in chapter 5) – for example, the ability to buy certain foodstuffs and clothes, or the necessity of increasing 'production' in the home (beer-brewing, weaving, etc.) in order to earn cash. Drawing boundaries around activities so as to give them the correct theoretical label is not easy. The sexual division of labour can differ greatly from one society to another, especially with regard to those tasks which are defined as 'domestic' and/or those which are defined as 'women's work'. The social relations within which these tasks are carried out vary enormously, as do the domestic units defined by those social relations (see chapter 2 and above). Furthermore, not all women perform domestic tasks: class and age differences exempt some groups of women from the more arduous and boring domestic activities.

The value of the feminist critique is that it stresses that women's domestic/reproductive labour cannot be assumed to be a set of naturally given tasks common to all societies at all times; nor can it be assumed that all women perform these tasks. Feminist writers emphasize that it is the relationship between women's reproductive and productive labour which is the crucial determinant of their position in society.[17] Meillassoux appears to address the question of the position of women, in so far as he sees it as connected to their role in the relations of reproduction. But, in fact, he is unable to approach the problem directly because he does not discuss the relationship between women's productive and reproductive labour, and because he sees women's reproductive labour as naturally defined and therefore not in need of further specification or analysis. The tendency to assume that the characteristics of women's lives are generally known, and that the same perspicuity applies to the social units, particularly 'the family' and 'the household', within which women are embedded, is an assumption which is strongly challenged by much feminist writing. In order to demonstrate this point more clearly, and to further our understanding of the relationship between women's productive and reproductive labour, it is necessary to turn to the analysis of the household.

The problem of the household

The major difficulty in talking about the 'domestic' is that we auto-matically find ourselves having to consider a range of amorphous concepts and entities, like 'the family', 'the household', 'the domestic sphere' and 'the sexual division of labour', which overlap and interact in complex ways to produce a sense of the domestic sphere. The family and the household are two terms which are particularly diffi-cult to separate clearly. In some societies, they may overlap quite substantially, as, for example, in contemporary British society; in others, like those of the Nayar (Gough, 1959) and the Tallensi (Fortes, 1949), they do not. The relationship between family and household is always something which requires detailed social and historical analysis. Anthropological research has long made clear the enormous cross-cultural variability in kinship systems and residential arrange-ments (Goody, 1972). More recent historical work has stressed varia-tion in household and family composition through time (Anderson, 1980; Creighton, 1980; Donzelot, 1980).[18] Flandrin has emphasized geographical variation in his study of French family forms, where he shows that a variety of family types existed simultaneously in differ-ent regions of the country (Flandrin, 1979). Family forms also vary with the life-stages and social strategies of their members, and a number of writers have demonstrated that individual families pass through a variety of different forms during the different stages of their development (Goody, 1971; Berkner, 1972; Hammel, 1961, 1972; Hareven, 1982).[19] In much of the anthropological literature, 'house-hold' is the term used to refer to the basic unit of society involved in production, reproduction, consumption and socialization. The exact nature and function of the household clearly varies from culture to culture, and from period to period, but the anthropological definition usually rests on what the people themselves regard as the significant unit of their society. However, it is important to recognize that, although recruitment to households is often through kinship and marriage, these units are not necessarily the same thing as families. Leaving aside the definitional difficulties, households are important in feminist analysis because they organize a large part of women's domestic/reproductive labour. As a result, both the composition and the organization of households have a direct impact on women's lives, and in particular on their ability to gain access to resources, to labour and to income.

In spite of arguments about the cultural and historical variability of households, and their relationship with or insertion into wider social configurations, feminist critics have demonstrated that we still have much to learn about what goes on inside households, and about what sort of links exist between them.[20] One obvious difficulty concerns the naturalistic assumptions which still imbue much of the writing on households and gender relations. The clear recognition of household variability has made little or no impact on the tendency to assume that the content of domestic life is generally known. Olivia Harris points out that the English term household implies co-residence, and that this carries with it connotations of intimacy and sharing which necessarily separate out internal household relations from other types of social relations. The latter, of course, appear accessible to analysis, while the former remain both private and obvious (Harris, 1981: 52). Harris cites Sahlins's work because in his discussion of the 'domestic mode of production' he clearly demonstrates how naturalistic assumptions influence analysis. He maintains that the distribution of goods and labour within the household is characterized by pooling and sharing, in contrast to the distribution which takes place between households which is based on exchange or balanced transactions (Sahlins, 1974).[21] Harris, on the other hand, argues that there are economies – those with generalized commodity circulation – where such a distinction might be justified, but that this is certainly not the case in all societies (Harris, 1981: 54–5). The more serious point, however, is that if we assume that pooling and sharing characterize all intra-household relations we obscure the real nature of those relations and preclude any possibility of enquiring into how they actually work.

Patricia Caplan's work in an Islamic village on the coast of Tanzania provides an example of a society where spouses do not share or pool their resources within the household. In the village she discusses, women retain their private property, including valuable coconut trees, after marriage. A woman's property and her income are hers to manage and dispose of as she pleases, and, although she may

contribute to the cash needs of the household, she is under no obligation to do so. She is also entitled to retain any crops she grows
on her own account. Furthermore, if a woman is wealthy and her
husband is not, he may 'borrow' from her, but he must repay her
(Caplan, 1984: 33). Caplan concludes: 'the household is a collection
of individuals engaged in productive activities, but retaining the fruits
of their own labour to a large extent. Relations within the household
are characterized by *exchange* rather than *pooling*' (Caplan, 1984: 34).

This case from Tanzania is not unusual; there are many documented
instances from East and West Africa of married women and men being
involved in exchange transactions with each other. According to
feminist critics, the inability to recognize the occurrence of these
transactions stems from two sources: (1) insufficient enquiry into
women's circumstances and the strategies they employ as social actors;
(2) the assumption that households are headed by men, who centralize
resources and control their allocation within the houshold. These two
points are connected because an overemphasis on men, and on male-
defined units and strategies, will inevitably lead to the invisibility of
women and to a general distortion in the representation of gender
relations. It is in this sense, as many feminist writers have pointed out,
that the analytical privileging of the 'male' produces inadequate
anthropology (see chapter 1).

The assumption that household resources are always controlled by
and through men is incorrect, because in many African societies, like
the Tanzanian case cited above, women and men maintain separate
income streams. In such cases, the right of husbands and wives to the
produce of the other's fields or to the income derived from the sale of
that produce is severely limited. However, questions of income have
to be seen in the context of labour utilization and the rights some
individuals have to the labour of others. Wives and, to some extent,
husbands have an obligation to work for each other. This is usually
referred to as 'family labour', and is a common feature of small-scale
agrarian societies, as it is of small business enterprises, like shopkeep-
ing.[22] Family labour is normally unremunerated, and conflicts often
emerge between spouses as they try to balance the demands of family
labour against the time and resources necessary for their individual
projects and enterprises (Whitehead, 1981). The control and allocation
of resources within the household is a complex process which always
has to be seen in relation to a web of rights and obligations. The
management of labour, income and resources is something which is
crucially bound up with household organization and the sexual
division of labour. The following case study illustrates some of these
points.

Labour and household organization: the Kusasi

Ann Whitehead discusses family labour and the income of individuals in a farming community in the Bawku district of north-eastern Ghana (1981; 1984). The predominant group in the area are the Kusasi. The staple crop is millet, which is produced mainly by men, but women contribute a significant amount of agricultural labour, especially during planting and harvesting. All households are involved in farming, some of them manage to produce a surplus, but a good proportion cannot produce all the food they need to keep them going from one year to the next. This is a patrilineal community, where households form significant production/consumption units, but can vary greatly in size and composition. Households are not based on conjugal partners nor on the nuclear family, but tend instead to be organized around agnatically (in the male line) related males, who may each have more than one wife (Whitehead, 1981: 92). Whitehead illustrates the complexity of household organization by describing the composition of the ideal Kusasi household: 'a male head, his junior brother, both of whom are married with two wives each, an unmarried adult male (brother or son) and able-bodied daughter or daughters, a woman given in pawn and one or more "mothers" ' (Whitehead, 1981: 95).

There are two types of farm associated with the household: private farms and household farms. Land for farming is allocated through chiefs and elders, but there is no absolute land scarcity, and the basic constraint on production is access to and control over the labour necessary to work the land (Whitehead, 1981: 94). The most important farms are the household farms, which are used for growing millet to feed the household members, and also for growing groundnuts which are sold for cash. The first obligation of household membership is to work to produce sufficient millet for household needs (i.e. to fill the granaries). It is encumbent upon the household head to make sure that this happens, and to make sure that millet is regularly distributed to all the married women of the household.

Household farms are worked by household members and by parties of 'exchange labour'. The former are unremunerated, but the latter are seasonal in nature and are 'paid' for with food and drink. In addition to the household farms, there are private farms, which are 'owned' by both male and female members of the household. These private farms are primarily used for growing cash crops (rice and groundnuts), although some supplementary subsistence crops are also grown on them. The produce from these farms is owned by the individual farmer and may be disposed of as she or he sees fit. The result is that women and men have access to separate resources and income which they do not pool or share with each other (Whitehead, 1981: 100).

However, women and men do not have equal access to the resources generated by private farming. The reason for this, as Whitehead makes clear, is that women and men are in different positions with regard to their ability to command the labour of others. Men can use the unremunerated labour of their wives and of the other women in the household, but the only way in which women can use the labour of male household members is by 'paying' for it with food and drink. In other words, women are obliged to work for the senior men of the household, but men work for women only if they can engage in exchange labour with them (Whitehead, 1981: 98). One result of this is that the acreages of women's private farms are smaller than those of men. Whitehead attributes this in part to women's 'weaker' claims to land, in a society where women live with their husband's kin group and land is allocated on the basis of agnatic links, and in part to women's restricted access to labour. Most women, therefore, profit less from their private farms than do men.

The fact that wives and husbands have 'separate purses' and do not operate a joint conjugal fund does not necessarily mean that there is greater equality between women and men. There are two reasons why this may not be the case. The first is the factor of marriage and kinship. It is clear that much agricultural labour is recruited through 'non-market' relations based on kinship, household membership and social status. The interlocking nature of these networks is demonstrated by the fact that Kusasi household heads are able to mobilize both unremunerated male and female household labour, as well as 'exchange parties' to work on their private farms (Whitehead, 1981: 98). Women work for men, juniors work for seniors, the poor work for the rich, and all these relationships are inserted into a web of social relations woven largely, in the case of small-scale agrarian communities, through kinship, residence and patronage. However, women mobilize these social relations of production primarily through marriage. It is as wives that women gain most of their access to land, labour (both male and female) and capital. Furthermore, women's access to extra-household male labour is frequently mediated through their husbands; and their access to other forms of labour ('exchange parties' and wage labour) is dependent upon their overall ability to command resources, especially income. Women's dependence on the conjugal relationship for access to resources is linked, in complex but historically changing ways, to their labour obligations to their husbands (Guyer, 1984).[23]

The second reason why separate income streams do not necessarily mean that there is greater equality between women and men is linked to the first and concerns the problem of social status or power. Intra-household relations among the Kusasi are clearly hierarchical, with gender and age operating as cross-cutting variables. Senior wives are obviously not subordinate to junior men, and such women may occasionally call on the junior men of their compound and other agnatically related compounds to form a communal work party. However, even senior women lack the real 'social power to command labour', and, although some of them are wealthy enough to do so, they could not mobilize a 'community-wide' exchange labour party. The most that they could do would be to 'beg a household head or husband to direct labour onto their farms' (Whitehead, 1984: 39). Men, on the other hand, provided they have the resources, are able to mobilize these community-wide exchange parties, both for work on the household fields and for work on their own private farms. Women's inability to call on the labour of others is a function of their lack of social power, and is clearly related to their position both in the household and within a wider set of social relations outside the household. This is a point I return to below in my discussion of property relations.

Extra-household relations

It is clear that the nature of household organization and relations cannot be assumed, but must be empirically and historically investigated. A number of feminist writers have pointed out that it is not enough to revise our ideas about internal household relations; we must also revise our views about the nature of extra-or inter-household relations. The main point at issue is whether the household is the most satisfactory unit of analysis. Feminist critics have argued that an overemphasis on the bounded household leads to a misleading conceptualization of households as autonomous units, where marriage is the defining relationship between the genders and conjugal relations are privileged over other types of relations and strategies (Guyer, 1981; Whitehead, 1984; Harris, 1981). Olivia Harris (1981) has pointed out that relationships between household members are not defined by the nature of the household itself, but by social, economic and ideological relations outside the unit. In her discussion of the authority invested in the household head, she argues that in small-scale agrarian societies this authority is derived from the control of male elders within the community at large, and in state-dominated societies it is derived from the state. 'To understand how the position of the household head is defined and reproduced takes us beyond the confines of the domestic unit itself' (Harris, 1981: 59).

The relationship of the household to the groups, institutions and networks beyond its boundaries has long formed the subject of contentious debate in anthropology. It is generally held that in many, if not most, societies kinship relations provide the basic links beyond the household through which a wide variety of things may be activated, from succession to public office and the inheritance of goods and titles, to more diverse forms of loyalty, support and mutual aid.[24] In small-scale societies, kinship structures are simultaneously political and economic structures.[25] However, in state-dominated societies, kin relations may be used to subvert or 'get round' institutionalized economic and political structures. The 'role' of kinship varies enormously through time and space, a fact which is further complicated by the ideological aspects of kinship. The anthropological literature is full of examples of kin relations being claimed or created or invoked, quite independently of any biological relationship, in order to cement or legitimize certain social relations. This is hardly surprising, since kinship systems by their nature classify people, and thus create differences between them: kin are not the same as non-kin, for example. However, not all systems create difference in the same way, with the result that certain kinds of relationships get emphasized and others do not.

These facts are well-known to anthropologists, but they have not informed the analysis of women and kinship systems as much as they should. The main reason for this is that, following Fortes, anthropology tended to divide kinship systems into two domains: the domestic and the politico-jural. It goes without saying that women were seen as involved in the domestic domain. The domestic and the politico-jural domains were viewed as mutually determining, but this did not alter the fact that kinship systems were essentially about the ways in which men could gain access, or arrange for other men to gain access, to resources, including women. Women certainly have rights in kinship systems, but systems of marriage, residence, descent and inheritance are rarely organized in such a way as to guarantee women's access to resources and/or to allow them to secure access for other women. It has long been argued that matrilineal systems are no different in this respect from patrilineal ones. If patriliny creates ties between the 'father' and his wife's sons, then matriliny creates ties between the mother's brother and the sister's sons (Meillassoux, 1981: 23).[26] It is sometimes thought that matrilineal systems necessarily involve a more equal relationship between spouses, but as Audrey Richards said of the matrilineal Bemba: 'This is a male dominant society and, even though descent is reckoned through the mother, the wife is very much under the control of her husband even while he is an outsider in his wife's village' (Richards, 1950: 225).

The traditional analysis of kinship systems in anthropology largely ignored women, especially as independent social actors or initiators.

The overt focus on men and male concerns was no doubt reinforced by indigenous ideologies. However, the neglect of women's kinship links, and of their involvement in kin and non-kin networks outside the household, was also due to a general view that the content of the domestic domain was known, and to the conceptualization of the household as a bounded unit. The implicit assumption was that women operated within the domestic sphere, while men utilized their links with other men to operate in the public/political domain, where links between households were created and maintained.[27]

This view of the household and its links with the wider kinship system tends to obscure many of the important activities and relationships which women are engaged in. As Olivia Harris has pointed out, there is a great deal of co-operation and collectivity in domestic work between households (1981: 63). Such tasks as cooking, childcare and generally 'covering' for other women constitute types of 'domestic' labour which can be crucial with regard to women's involvement in 'productive' work. Help with childcare, for example, can leave other women free to engage in wage labour, or to increase the number of hours spent in the fields during periods of peak labour demand. Help with cooking will make a substantial difference where it involves assistance with food processing or the carrying of firewood. Women all over the world have to perform domestic labour tasks in addition to their work 'outside the home'.[28] A number of writers have suggested that women who are isolated from strong support networks may find themselves more dependent on men and more subject to male authority within the household (Caplan and Bujra, 1978; Rosaldo, 1974; Sanday, 1974; Moore, 1986).

Women may also use kinship and non-kinship links to gain access to resources outside the household. In her study of rural women in a matrilineal community in southern Malawi, Megan Vaughan discusses two ways in which women manage to do this. In the first case, women utilize close kinship links outside the household. In the community Megan Vaughan describes, an adult woman is supposed to grow sufficient food on her land to feed her husband and her children. The ideal of 'family' self-sufficiency is so strong that even a group of sisters living in adjacent huts would not take grain from one another's grain-bins. Not owning a grain-bin, which you fill yourself, is tantamount to 'admitting destitution' (Vaughan, 1983: 277). However, in reality, the poorest households are frequently headed by women, and they are 'heavily dependent' on food transfers from other households. These food transfers are disguised as much as possible. A group of sisters, or sisters and their matrilineal kin, may eat communally, and when this happens each woman cooks her food and brings it to be shared with the others in the group. The result is that food is transferred at the point of consumption, but because the transfer is 'masked' and is therefore not seen as a redistributive mechanism the ideal of 'family' self-sufficiency remains intact (Vaughan, 1983: 278). Vaughan points out that, as economic differentiation between households increases, this 'covert' distribution at the stage of consumption becomes more and more 'central to the economic organisation and welfare of certain groups' (Vaughan, 1983: 278).

The second way in which women may gain access to resources is by utilizing non-kinship links. *Chinjira* is a special friendship between two women, involving social, economic and ritual obligations. However, it is not formed between kinswomen, and, in fact, a woman would not form such a relationship with any woman whom she thought might be remotely related to her. *Chinjira* is a relationship based on confidentiality, and a woman should be able to tell her *anjira* things she could not tell members of her kin group (Vaughan, 1983: 282). Vaughan argues that *Chinjira* not only supplements kinship ties but also modifies a woman's dependence on conjugal ties. *Chinjira* is always formed between women whose households have 'complementary economic resources', and most commonly between women who live with their husbands on tea estates and those who live in the villages nearby.

> Whenever a woman visits her *anjira* she is obliged to take a present with her. Women from the 'lines' [estates] take small manufactured goods purchased from local shops. Women from the villages take foodstuffs from their gardens. It would be ridiculous, said informants, for a woman from the 'lines' to bring her *anjira* grain, or the woman from the village to bring her *anjira* soap. Women in this area thus use the relationship to help them complement their household resources and to escape some of the constraints of their economic circumstances. (Vaughan, 1983: 283)

The importance of links between women draws attention to the insufficiency of the household as the sole unit of analysis, and also questions the ways in which anthropologists have tended, particularly in the past, to conceive of the links between households.

Female-headed households

Female-headed and female-centred domestic groups have been identified in a wide range of communities all over the world (Smith, 1973; Tanner, 1974), and – in spite of conceptual differences in the use of terms like 'matrifocality' – it is clear that attempts to reconceptualize the 'household' face one of their severest tests in connection with such households.[29]

In the first place, researchers working in the Caribbean and among the black populations of the Americas have long realized the insufficiency of the household as a unit of analysis, possibly because the 'unusual' prominence of women in these social systems forced a rethinking of traditional categories and modes of analysis. Carol Stack discusses the fluidity of domestic arrangements in her study of a black American urban community (1974). In her work, she develops a notion of the domestic network. She argues that the basis of domestic life is a cluster of kinspeople related predominantly through children, but also through friendship and marriage. This cluster or domestic network is spread over several kin-based households. Stack notes that households form around women because of their role in childcare, and that ties between women are the basis of domestic networks. The important point is that the material and moral support needed to care for and socialize community members is provided by the domestic network, and not by a 'bounded' household or nuclear family. Individual households – as defined by residence and communality – have a shifting membership, but this does not affect the composition of the domestic network. Household boundaries may be 'elastic', but kin ties are strong and enduring (Stack, 1974).

A second point concerns the way in which researchers have been analysing the female-headed households which are emerging, in apparently increasing numbers, in a variety of communities around the world. It is important to consider under what conditions – social, economic, political and ideological – female-headed households become a significant proportion of the total number. The evidence is complex, but it seems that female-headed households are common in situations of urban poverty; in societies with a high level of male labour migration; and in situations where general insecurity and vulnerability prevail (Youssef and Hefler, 1983; Merrick and Schmink, 1983). For example, female-headed households are on the increase in many rural areas in Africa. The prevailing view in the literature is that this is due to male labour migration. It is clear that in some rural economies the strain placed on conjugal relations by the exploitation of rural areas as labour reserves is producing an enormously high proportion of female-headed households (Murray, 1981; Bush et al., 1986).

However, in addition to male labour migration, there is also the suggestion that increasing socio-economic differentiation in rural communities is producing a group of female-headed households (Cliffe, 1978). Changes in kinship systems and in the organization of agricultural production have meant that many poorer women have lost the security provided by former kin networks and relationships. It is true that many female-headed households are very poor, but, as Peters points out, this is not the case for all of them, and we have to be very careful to avoid any analytical elision which suggests: lack of males = female-headed = marginal = poor (Peters, 1983). The situation is more complex than this and requires more research.[30] For one thing, there is a certain amount of evidence from Africa, as there is from many other parts of the world, that some women are choosing not to marry (Allison, 1985; Nelson, 1978; Obbo, 1980) and that significant numbers of married women are choosing to live separately from their husbands (Bukh, 1979; Abbott, 1976). This process is perhaps more of a feature of urban than of rural life, but it highlights the dangers of easy generalization and reinforces the importance of historically and socially grounded research.

Changing household forms and changes in the sexual division of labour within the household are related to broader processes of social, economic and political transformation. In order to specify the parameters of the observable changes in the sexual division of labour, and the consequences of such changes for women's status, it is necessary to turn to an examination of the social relations which create and sustain kinship and household forms: marriage and property.

Women, property and marriage

> This investigation of women's role in the process of production . . . has to include more than just a description of the kinds of work which women do. It must include an account of familial authority relations according to which this work is organized, and of the property relations which this authority structure realizes and maintains. (Sharma, 1980: 15)

This quotation from Ursula Sharma indicates that work and property are crucially linked, and that both are ordered by the kinship relations which constitute the productive and reproductive domains of women's lives. Anthropologists have long recognized the important connections between property and marriage (Bloch, 1975; Goody, 1976; Goody and Tambiah, 1973), and in an analysis of women's relationship to 'property' these connections take on a strange duality, as we come to consider both women's *access to* property and women as a *type of* property. The long-running debate in anthropology about the exchange of women through marriage is itself an example of this dualism.[31] Anthropology has traditionally defined the institution of marriage as a legal transfer of rights in property and people which works both to perpetuate descent groups and to create ties of alliance through exogamy (marrying out). Radcliffe-Brown characterized marriage as the means through which the husband and his kin group acquire rights in the wife. These rights can be of two kind: *in personam* (rights in the wife's labour and domestic duties) and *in rem* (rights of sexual access) (Radcliffe-Brown, 1950: 50).[32] In patrilineal societies, the husband and his kin will also acquire rights in the children born to the marriage. The rights that a man acquires in his wife and her children are related to the obligations he will have to his wife, and to her kin group. A man's obligations to his wife are usually focused on the question of economic support, while his obligations to her kin group may involve the transfer of goods or labour, which are considered as some form of recompense for the loss of a daughter. Women and men bring different things to a marriage, and they acquire different things through marriage. Marriage systems are themselves variable, and in order to consider the relationship between women, property and marriage it is necessary to examine some of the features of different systems.

Marriage transactions and the rural economy in China

In her work on women and marriage in post-revolutionary China, Elizabeth Croll discusses the state's attempt to change the nature of marriage, as well as the negotiations and transactions (betrothal gifts and dowry payments) concerning women and property which were the crux of martial arrangements (Croll, 1981a, 1984). In 1950 the government of China promulgated a Marriage Law which sought to abolish arranged marriage, the exchange of women through marriage, the negotiations and transactions accompanying marriage and the subordination of women to men. The new Marriage Law supported the right of young people to choose their own marriage partners ('free-choice' marriage), and to handle their affairs without interference from family and relatives. The state followed the promulgation of this law with a series of educational campaigns which explicitly linked the redefinition of marriage 'with the rejection of male kinship rights in women's labour, fertility and person, and the exchange of women between kin groups' (Croll, 1984: 46–7). However, Croll's study of contemporary marriage in rural China has revealed that marriage is still thought of as a contract negotiated between senior kin (although the young have much more say than they used to), and that financial transactions are still connected to the transfer of rights over women. Elizabeth Croll accounts for what the state interprets as the 'conservatism' or 'backwardness' of rural peasants by drawing out the links between marriage and the role of the peasant household in the rural economy of contemporary China. In post-revolutionary China, the aim in the rural areas was to collectivize production and to allow the communes to provide the basic services necessary for the local populations. Ideally, this would involve radical changes in the peasant household as the basic unit of production and consumption, where households would no longer be landholding units, where much production and consumption would take place outside the household, and where the corporate interests of the household would be weakened by the payment of wages to individual household members for their work in the collective labour force. Changes did, of course, take place, but certain socio-economic features of contemporary peasant households have actually served to reinforce particular marriage strategies.

Croll describes the rural economy as being made up of three sectors: the collective waged labour force, certain private subsidiary activities, and the domestic labour which involves running and maintaining the household. All three sectors add to the income of the household, either in cash or in kind, and the last two sectors reduce the cost of maintaining the household as an economic unit. Under the system Croll describes, the peasant household is still a unit of production, albeit somewhat reduced in the range of productive activities it organizes, and it also remains the basic unit of consumption (Croll, 1984: 51). Croll argues, therefore, that if individual households are to continue to exist as units of production and consumption they must organize their labour resources and distribute them effectively throughout the three sectors of the rural economy. This turns out to have particularly important consequences for marriage strategies and for women, because women's labour is crucial to all three sectors. Young married women work in the collective labour force, but they may also run the private subsidiary sector and provide domestic labour in the household. Women distribute their labour across the three sectors in ways which can vary with an individual's life-cycle. For example, in joint households, an older woman may 'retire' from the collective sector to run the household and manage the subsidiary activities, while a new daughter-in-law is brought in to take her place in the collective labour force. The result is that women's labour is crucial to the efficient functioning of the peasant household, and that the exchange of women between households (through marriage) is something which concerns the corporate interests of household members. The acquisition of the labour of daughters-in-law and the reproduction of the family's labour force are essential to the continued existence of the peasant household, and this situation accounts for the continuing importance of marriage, and for the necessity to control marriage negotiations and transactions. The private hiring of labour is prohibited by law in China, and marriage is therefore the only means of reproduction and the direct recruitment of labour.[33] Marriage takes on an even more important role when it is realized that control over labour is a form of wealth in a system where the success of the household is dependent on the efficient use of labour resources. Labour in this system has become a form of property (Croll, 1984: 57).

The value of women's labour in the rural economy has had an effect on the financial arrangements relating to marriage. In one sense the mass entry of women into the waged labour force in the last three decades has given a new 'value' to daughters. This value is recognized, in part, by the increase in the amount or cost of the betrothal gift which the bride's household receives from the groom's household as compensation for the loss of a daughter. As the cost of these betrothal gifts has risen, so it has become more difficult for households to amass sufficient resources to marry off their sons. But, although the increase in the value of the betrothal gift may have caused difficulties for the groom's family, it has also had important consequences for daughters in terms of their ability to make claims on family funds and property. In the past, the bride's family would have returned the betrothal gift to the groom's family in the form of a dowry, which would also have provided the bride with a potential source of independence. However, the incidence of dowry is declining because the bride's family may now wish to use the resources they gain through betrothal to marry off their own sons, rather than using them to endow their daughters.[34] Daughters are therefore less likely to be given a dowry, even though they may have been contributing their wages to the family fund for some years before marriage (agricultural wages are often paid in a single wage-packet direct to the head of the household). This means that, although the bride's family may be able to claim a large betrothal gift in 'compensation' for the loss of their 'valuable' daughter, the woman herself receives no recognition of or benefit from her contribution to family funds.

The rise in the cost of betrothal gifts also has consequences for daughters-in-law as well as for daughters. After marriage, a woman's earnings may be viewed by the husband's household as compensation for the expense involved in 'acquiring' her, and her wages will be incorporated into family funds. 'At present then a woman may not only be deprived of a dowry that once formed a potential basis of any independence, but furthermore her earnings may not be recognized as hers by right after her marriage' (Croll, 1984: 59). This is, of course, in spite of the fact that the law gives women equal inheritance and equal rights to family property. As Elizabeth Croll points out, it is the increase in the value of women's labour which has paradoxically undermined their access to dowry and other property (Croll, 1984: 61).

Dowry systems

The issue of marriage payments and their relationship to women's economic security and independence has always been a difficult one to unravel. One simple reason is that superficially similar types of marriage systems and practices may mean very different things and thus have very different consequences.[35] Dowry, for example, is often thought to indicate a woman's right to inherit a share of the patri-monial property (Goody, 1976) and to give her greater economic security, status and independence within the marriage. In her analysis of a Greek village, Ernestine Friedl argues that women have consider-able power within the domestic sphere because of the land they bring to their marriage as dowry. In the community studied by Friedl, women maintain control over this land which cannot be alienated by their husbands without their consent, and, in some cases, not without the consent of their father's brothers or guardians (Friedl, 1967: 105).[36] Dowry has traditionally been seen in anthropology as a form of pre-mortem inheritance for women (Goody and Tambiah, 1973; Goody, 1976).

However, recent feminist writing on the subject has not only shown how variable is the institution of dowry, but has also strongly questioned this view. Previous anthropological discussions of mar-riage payments have tended to look at them in terms of the relation-ships they establish between kinship groups, property-holding units or households – entities which may or may not overlap, depending on circumstances. Women are, however, frequently subordinate with-in such systems, and their concerns and interests with regard to mar-riage payments and the inheritance of property have not had sufficient analytical attention. Feminist writers have pointed out that treating dowry simply as a form of pre-mortem inheritance fails to specify many of the critical questions: what kinds of property women inherit; how much control or what kinds of control they actually have over this property; what their status is as property owners/controllers compared with other members of their natal and marital families; and at what point in a woman's life-cycle she actually gets control over property (marriage, death of parents, death of husband). A considera-tion of questions such as these has allowed feminist writers to look at women's relationships to marriage payments, and to reconsider the connections between property, inheritance, marriage and produc-tion.[37]

In her discussion of women work and property in north-west India, Ursula Sharma produces evidence for a very different sort of dowry system from that described by Ernestine Friedl, and she does so by concentrating on the kinds of questions I have just raised (Sharma, 1980, 1984). According to Sharma, customary Hindu and Sikh practice in the states of Himachal Pradesh and Punjab prevents women from inheriting land as daughters, except in the absence of sons, because they inherit their shares in the patrimony at the time of their marriage in the form of dowry. In spite of the fact that the Hindu

Succession Act of 1956 allows daughters, widows and mothers to inherit land equally with sons, few women apparently exercise this right (Sharma, 1980: 47). Sharma criticizes anthropologists who see dowry as a form of pre-mortem inheritance. She maintains that dowries are not actually conceived of as shares in a specific and divisible patrimony, and that the kinds of movable goods which daughters inherit cannot be considered as comparable to the immovable or landed property which sons receive (Sharma, 1980: 48).

> The gifts subsumed by the term dowry . . . are given at the time of the wedding or very soon after. They usually include household goods (furniture, utensils, bedding, perhaps electrical appliances) and clothes (most of which are destined to be redistributed among the groom's kin). There may also be certain goods designated more or less as personal gifts for the groom. Some cash may be given but in North India, land, agricultural equipment or cattle are never included to my knowledge, in spite of their central importance to the rural economy. (Sharma, 1984: 63)

It is usual for the bride herself to prepare some of the items for her dowry, and nowadays wage-earning women might buy something from their wages (Sharma, 1980: 109). It is also important to realize that, when the dowry is transferred, the bride does not gain control over it in the way that a son gains control over his inheritance. The dowry is transferred to the'groom's parents, and will be distributed by them to other kin. Normally, some of the dowry is allocated to the bride and groom, but it is allocated to them as a couple, and not to the bride as an individual (Sharma, 1980: 48).[38] Even the husband's control of his wife's dowry is circumscribed by his parents while they live. Sharma makes the point that, in the north-west Indian case, dowry enhances a woman's position in the household only because it makes her family respected; it does not actually give her any power or autonomy within her husband's household (Sharma, 1980: 50).

Taking into account the nature of the property a daughter receives on her marriage, and her degree of control over it, Sharma concludes that it is imprecise, if not actually incorrect, to regard dowry as a form of inheritance (Sharma, 1980: 48; Sharma, 1984: 70). Her contention is that anthropologists who consider dowry as a form of pre-mortem inheritance have uncritically accepted the fiction that women inherit movable property at marriage in lieu of the immovable property which their brothers inherit at a later date. This fiction, she says, helps to obscure a very real difference in women's and men's relationships to property (Sharma, 1980: 47). Daughters are now legally entitled to inherit land along with sons, but few exercise this right, and, as Sharma points out, in the light of this fact, it would be more accurate to say that dowry serves to 'purchase the cancellation of the daughter's automatic right to inherit when she has brothers to whom her hypothetical share can be made over' (Sharma, 1980: 48). In this case, dowry is less an endowment for daughters, a recognition of their share in the patrimony, than it is a mechanism for maintaining the rights of sons in the patrimonial property. What Sharma's work makes clear is that it is important not to see dowry as something which necessarily gives women power or control within the household.[39]

Bridewealth transactions

In contrast to dowry, which is a transfer of goods from the kin of the bride to the kin of the groom, bridewealth is a form of marriage payment where valuables are transferred in the opposite direction. In bridewealth transactions, groups of men exchange goods for women, or rights in women, between themselves. Women would appear to have very little say in these transactions, and also appear to profit very little by them as individuals. The rights transferred with the bridewealth valuables often involve the transfer of rights over children. David Parkin makes this point very clearly in his discussion of marriage payments among the Giriama and Chonyi peoples of Kenya (Parkin, 1980). Both the Giriama and the Chonyi make a distinction between the two types of payment which together make up bridewealth. These two types of payment are the uxorial payments (sexual and domestic rights) and the genetricial (childbirth) payments. Issues concerning the social recognition of children become particularly crucial when divorce occurs, and in bridewealth societies fathers frequently retain rights of control over their children. Custody of children and rights to property are associated features of social life.

Sandra Burman discusses women and divorce in urban South Africa, where, under customary law, bridewealth or *lobola* must be transferred to the woman's family by the husband. (Women and men can also marry by civil law, and many urban African women appear to be opting for civil marriages.) Once *lobola* is paid, the children of the marriage belong to the husband's family. On divorce, part of the *lobola* should be repaid, less a certain amount if the woman has borne children for the husband's family (Burman, 1984: 122). (Nowadays, however, there is an increasing breakdown in urban areas of the institution of returning *lobola*.) As Burman makes clear, the exact nature and determinants of marriage strategies and payments are difficult to unravel because of the 'legislated disruption of African family life' which forms a part of the apartheid system.[40] However, Burman's work suggests that controls on housing are particularly important in divorce cases because housing is in short supply, and the authorities tend to award the house to whichever parent has custody of the children (Burman, 1984: 131). Disputes over divorce settlements can, therefore, be bitter. According to Burman, many men believe that payment of the *lobola* should give the husband custody of the older children, at least, and should also preclude him from having to pay maintenance. The reluctance to give custody to the mother and/or to provide maintenance is strongly reinforced by the difficulties of paying maintenance on very low wages, and by the possibility of losing the house to the mother (Burman, 1984: 132). South Africa is clearly a special case, but Burman's work does make the point that rights over children and rights over property are not to be considered in isolation from one another, and that the institution of bridewealth has a determining effect on women's ability to gain custody and maintenance.

Bridewealth as a social institution has been extensively written about in social anthropology, but there is almost no work which considers bridewealth from the woman's point of view.[41] This is an area which feminist anthropologists have yet to address themselves to in a sustained way, and it is an area which is very much in need of new ethnography. Ursula Sharma, in her discussion of the changeover from bridewealth to dowry in some areas of north-west India, has argued that, when looked at from the woman's point of view, the differences between bridewealth and dowry are not nearly so significant as the question of how much control the woman herself exerts over these transactions and their outcomes.

> Looking at the matter from a feminist point of view, therefore, the opposition which anthropologists have traditionally drawn between dowry and bridewealth may not be so important as other distinctions made on the basis of the degree and kind of control which brides can exert over their own marital fortunes and over the property which is transferred at the time of marriage. (Sharma, 1984: 73)

It is clear from the above discussion that the question of a woman's control over property and her 'marital fortunes' has to be considered in the light of the kinship relations within which marriage, labour and property are all embedded. Ann Whitehead has suggested that our understanding of this is enhanced if we look at how kinship systems help to construct women and men in different ways, as different sorts of persons. Concepts of property are ultimately bound up with concepts of the person. One example of this is the way in which the legal definition of property rights designates what is appropriate and permissible for certain sorts of persons to do with certain sorts of property. Another example is the way in which one person may have rights in another who then becomes in some way the property of the first: marriage is precisely this sort of institution in many instances. Whitehead argues that whatever the nature of the economic system, in terms of productive and exchange relations, women's ability to act as fully operative individuals in relation to property and/or in relation to those aspects of persons which can be treated as property (i.e. rights in people) is always less than that of men (Whitehead, 1984: 180). In her view, it is the kinship/family system which constructs women in such a way that they are less able to act as fully operative subjects than men are in any particular society.

> A woman's capacity to 'own' things depends on the extent to which she is legally and actually separable from other people . . . the issue raised is the extent to which forms of conjugal, familial and kinship relations allow her an independent existence so that she can assert rights as an individual against individuals. In many societies a woman's capacity to act in this way may be severaly curtailed compared to a man's. Conjugal, familial and kinship systems appear often to operate so as to construct women as a subordinate gender, such that by virtue of carrying kinship (or familial or conjugal) status women are less free to act as full subjects in relation to things, and sometimes people. (Whitehead, 1984: 189–90)

This is a powerful argument, and although it has some continuities with the old anthropological approach that women are powerless because they are associated with the 'domestic', and with the socio-logical argument that 'the family is the site of women's oppression', it is actually a sophisticated theoretical development of both those arguments (see also Strathern, 1984b), as well as an indication of where the best feminist research in kinship and economics is now leading us.

4

KINSHIP, LABOUR AND HOUSEHOLD: THE CHANGING NATURE OF WOMEN'S LIVES

As we saw in the previous chapter, the sexual division of labour is constantly being transformed and re-created as social and economic change takes place. In anthropology, the recognition that social and economic change is a continuous process owes much to the Marxist anthropology of the last two decades. The great strength of this approach, and of the work it has inspired, has been the final determination by anthropology to link micro-processes with macro-processes, to link the household and the family with the wider regional, national and international processes – social, economic and political – within which they are embedded. The task is a large one and it has only just begun. In the last twenty years, anthropology has moved from talking about lineages, chiefs and tribes to discussing the incorporation of pre-capitalist social formations into the world capitalist economy.[1] In the determination of this transition, Claude Meillassoux has been an influential figure. He has argued that capitalism does not destroy the pre-capitalist modes of production it encounters in the developing world, but instead maintains them in articulation with the capitalist mode of production. He asserts that the pre-capitalist modes of production are beneficial to capital because they provide capitalism with cheap labour. This is possible for two reasons: first, because the food produced in the pre-capitalist sector covers part of the subsistence costs of the worker's household; and, secondly, because the pre-capitalist sector pays the costs of the reproduction of the labour force, which includes raising children, caring for the sick and the elderly, and maintaining women. Both these 'benefits' allow capitalists to pay workers lower wages, because their wages do not have to cover all the costs of household subsistence, nor the costs of the reproduction of labour. And cheap labour leads to larger profits (Meillassoux, 1981).[2]

There have, of course, been various criticisms of Meillassoux, and of other French Marxist scholars, like Terray, Rey, Suret-Canale and Coquéry-Vidrovitch, writing in the same tradition.[3] I cannot go into the details of this very important debate here, but it is worth noting that the concept of articulation (between the capitalist and pre-capitalist modes of production) has at least emphasized that what capitalism encountered in the developing world was a series of specific social formations with their own institutions and sets of relations. These indigenous social formations had a determining influence on the way in which capitalism affected rural production systems.[4] This emphasis on the specificity of social formations highlights the necessity for historical analysis, and some of the most insightful research, at least with regard to Africa, has focused on analysing kinship systems in their political and historical contexts (e.g. Murray, 1981; Beinart, 1982). The value of a historical approach is clear, because it demonstrates that the processes of capitalist transformation have been very uneven in their geographical spread and in their effects, and that they are manifest in a variety of situations all over the world which always require concrete investigation. It is therefore not possible to generalize about the consequences of capitalist transformation for women. Women are not a homogeneous category, and the circumstances and conditions of their lives in the varying regions of the world are very different.

The differential effects of capitalism on women

All scholars agree that colonialism and capitalism restructured traditional economies in a way which had a profound impact on women's economic activities, on the nature of the sexual division of labour, and on the kinds of social and political options which remained open to women. However, there is, rather unsurprisingly, a considerable amount of debate about the exact nature of the effects of these processes on women's lives. Scholars like Boserup (1970) and Rogers (1980) have suggested that capitalist exploitation combined with Eurocentric ideas about the roles and activities proper to women led to the destruction of women's traditional rights in society, and undermined their economic autonomy. Other writers have pointed out that it may be wrong to imagine that the pre-colonial/pre-capitalist world was one where women had a significant degree of independence (Huntingdon, 1975; Afonja, 1981). However, the penetration of capitalism into subsistence economies, through the growth of commercial agriculture and wage labour, is acknowledged as having a generally deleterious effect on rural women. A number of authors have stressed that the development of intensive agriculture and the introduction of new forms of technology discriminated against women (Wright, 1983; Ahmed, 1985; Chaney and Schmink, 1976; Dauber and Cain, 1981). An increasing market in land and labour, together with changes in land tenure systems and developing migrant labour, also worked against the interests of women (Brain, 1976; Remy, 1975; Okeyo, 1980; Mueller, 1977; Jones, 1982). The overall result of this literature on the disadvantaged position of women with regard to the processes of capitalist transformation has been an emerging theory of the 'feminization' of subsistence agriculture – particularly with regard to Africa and parts of Latin America.

The 'feminization' of subsistence agriculture is thought to come about through two mechanisms or processes, which are sometimes combined. The first is the process of the commercialization of smallholder agriculture, where men engage in growing cash crops while the burden of providing for 'family' consumption needs falls on women, who find themselves contributing increasing amounts of labour time to subsistence agriculture. The heavy demands of subsistence production often prevent women from engaging in cash crop production themselves, and the frequent bias of government schemes and incentives in favour of male farmers (and the cash crops they produce) leads to further discrimination and disadvantage for women (Staudt, 1982; Lewis, 1984). The second mechanism or process which leads to the 'feminization' of subsistence agriculture is male migration, where men leave an area in search of work and the women remain behind and continue supporting the subsistence sector (Murray, 1981; Bush et al., 1986; Hay, 1976; Bukh, 1979).

> Growing the subsistence crop has been increasingly left to African women as men migrate to cities. Statistics show that one-third of farm managers in Africa south of the Sahara are women, with even higher percentages recorded in some countries: 54 per cent in Tanzania and 41 per cent in Ghana. Algeria reported female participation in agriculture had more than doubled between 1966 and 1973. (Tinker, 1981: 60)

The picture Irene Tinker paints is a familiar one, but the 'feminization' of agriculture thesis is not a generalization which holds good for all regions of Africa, let alone for the rest of the world. There are plenty of examples, particularly in societies practising female seclusion, where women's contribution to agricultural labour in the fields is still very small compared to that of men (Longhurst, 1982; Hill, 1969); there are also many instances where the overall effect of commercialization has been dramatically to increase both male and female labour in smallholder agricultural production. The point is not that the 'feminization' thesis is incorrect (it is clearly supported by overwhelming empirical evidence), nor that scholars wish to use it as a way of generalizing about global responses to capitalist transformation, but that the thesis itself is now so commonplace in the 'women in development' literature and has achieved such orthodoxy within the social sciences that it is perhaps worth considering some of the conceptual limitations which might underlie it.

The first difficulty with the thesis of the 'feminization' of subsistence agriculture is the dichotomy it sets up between subsistence and commercial farming. Commercialization, particularly in African agriculture, is often seen as involving a process whereby women are forced into working longer hours in the subsistence sector, in order to provide for the 'family', while men become involved in cash-cropping. There are, of course, many instances where this is exactly what happens. For example, Jette Bukh describes a situation in southern Ghana, where during the boom in cocoa production men took over the job of producing the cocoa, while women took on responsibility for cultivating the basic food for the household. When the price of cocoa fell in the 1970s, many men migrated to look for work, and the women and children remained behind on the land. Many women found it difficult to cover their household and personal expenses, so they supplemented their incomes by combining farming with petty trading, wage labour, craft work and food processing. When the time taken to perform domestic tasks is taken into account, it is clear that these Ghanaian women have an enormous workload: more like a triple burden than the frequently mentioned double one (Bukh, 1979).

However, in spite of the fact that aspects of what Bukh describes are often the result of the integration of export crops into rural production systems, we should be cautious about setting up a straightforward equation between women and subsistence agriculture, and men and cash crops. First, it may encourage a stereotyped view of the position of women in developing economies. The easy dichotomy of women/men and subsistence/cash mirrors other conceptual dualisms in social-scientific thinking, most notably the domestic/public distinction. There is a danger in portraying rural women as engaged in subsistence agriculture for domestic consumption, using basic/traditional technologies, and men, on the other hand, as having access to new technology, new seed varieties and extension services (agricultural advice) as a result of their involvement in commercial farming, including the production of cash crops for export. In equating women with subsistence production, we should be careful that we are not merely replicating Western ideologies, seeing women's work as concerned with sustenance and the feeding of the family, while regarding men as somehow associated with the cut-and-thrust of the market and the outside/non-domestic world.

The second reason for caution is that simplistic equations between women and subsistence and between men and cash crops run the risk of caricaturing women's work and their contribution to rural production. Women's involvement in the modern agricultural sector is more diverse and complex than this uncritical dichotomy suggests. There are plenty of examples of women growing cash crops, working as wage labourers and engaging in a wide variety of other market-oriented activities, as Bukh herself suggests (Bukh, 1979; Stoler, 1977). The third reason for caution is that, on balance, any simple equation between women and subsistence agriculture and between men and cash crops presents a rather inaccurate view of the relations between women and men in rural production systems. The overall effect of the penetration of capitalism into such systems has frequently been the impoverishment of the peasant agricultural sector as a whole, rather than a simple gain for men (Deere and Léon de Léal, 1981). Men as well as women suffer, and the changing nature of gender relations and of the sexual division of labour need to be studied in the light of the contradictions and conflicts which arise from the uneven and contradictory process of capitalist transformation.

Maila Stivens has demonstrated just how difficult it is to analyse the changing nature of gender relations and of women's access to resources under capitalism, in her study of the matrilineal Negeri Sembilan people of Malaysia (Stivens, 1985). Some early feminist accounts argued that Negeri Sembilan women lost much of their land to men as a result of colonial and capitalist development (Boserup, 1970: 61; Rogers, 1980: 140). Stivens challenges this view, and she asserts that women, in the villages she studied, actually hold title to almost all the ancestral rice lands and orchards and to half the smallholder rubber land (Stivens, 1985: 3). Stivens's refutation of earlier writers' accounts of the fate of Negeri Sembilan women and of *adat perpatih* (matrilineal customary law) is detailed and complex. However, she begins by pointing out that, although the colonial authorities were ambivalent about Negeri Sembilan matriliny, the desire to create a rice-growing peasantry in the region actually resulted in a series of legislative practices and policies which served to codify and preserve matrilineal customary law (Stivens, 1985: 9). It is true that the rubber boom of the early twentieth century brought about further changes in the economy, as peasant farmers became involved in petty-commodity rubber production. But Stivens makes it clear that cash-crop rubber production did not lead directly to a loss of female property rights over land (Stivens, 1985: 12). Many new rubber land titles were registered *initially* in men's names, because rubber land was associated with men who did most of the heavy work involved in clearing the jungle for planting. However, as Stivens argues, 'the real issue is not the initial registration of land in male names, but whether this implied the creation of a permanently "male" sector of ownership and a form of dual inheritance – subsistence land to women, rubber land to men' (Stivens, 1985: 13). In Stivens's view, the evidence for such dualism is lacking because, in research conducted in the 1970s, she was able to demonstrate a considerable 'feminization' of land – rubber land (women own 61 per cent of the rubber acreage), as well as traditional rice lands and orchards.

Stivens outlines the transfer mechanisms through which this process of feminization comes about, but she makes it clear that the overall process is to be accounted for in terms of the decline in the rural economy and not in terms of the maintenance of traditional matrilineal inheritance arrangements. For example, much of the village rubber land remains untapped: this may be partly related to the absence of male labour (out-migration from the area has increased substantially), but it is probably better accounted for in terms of the decline in the profitability of smallholder rubber production overall. This interpretation appears to be strongly reinforced by Stivens's informants, who see rubber land as a form of 'insurance' rather than as a directly profitable enterprise (Stivens, 1985: 22). It is the idea of land as a form of 'insurance' which provides the key to the present situation. Clearly, matrilineal ideology and the colonial codification of matrilineal customary law have served partially to protect women's interests over the years, but the obvious trend in the feminization of land cannot be accounted for merely in terms of the continuity of matrilineal inheritance practices. Stivens is able to cite many cases where a couple's jointly acquired land was subsequently registered in the wife's name (Stivens, 1985: 24). Other cases are clear examples of daughters receiving land from their fathers; in some instances land was handed over directly, while in others the land was first bought for the wife and then inherited by the daughter (Stivens, 1985: 24–6). Why should men give land to women in a matrilineal system? Informants' responses to this question all seem to focus on women's more vulnerable position within the declining rural economy, the need to provide women with independent economic resources in case of divorce, and a certain desire (albeit somewhat contradictory) to protect tradition/family values associated with women and the matrilineal system. Informants even cited women's disadvantaged position in the labour market as a reason for transferring land to them, while sons are regarded as better able to look after themselves by earning their living through other means (Stivens, 1985: 26–8).

The case which Stivens describes for Negeri Sembilan is extremely complex. One of the most useful parts of her argument is her challenge to earlier accounts which 'reduced the impact of colonialism and capitalist development on women's land rights to a picture of men gaining individually and personally at the expense of women, through misogynist colonial ideology' (Stivens, 1985: 28). Stivens makes it clear that the significance of women's property relations and their access to resources within the rural economy can only be understood by analysing such relations historically, and by showing how gender relations and other social relations inform, and are affected by, the complex, contradictory and uneven processes of capitalist transformation. This kind of analysis is undoubtedly an advance on earlier feminist analyses, which sometimes tended, rather uncritically, to portray women as the victims of processes of transformation.

In spite of criticisms concerning earlier feminist analyses, and although the necessity of questioning conceptual orthodoxies must be recognized, it is still abundantly clear that women are differentially affected by capitalist development, and that their overall position is one of extreme vulnerability.

However, we must be wary of simplistically portraying men as the winners and women as the losers. A simple picture of this kind may distort the complexity of the real nature of gender relations, and it also works to obscure two very important dimensions of analysis. The first concerns women's response to processes of social transformation. If women are portrayed merely as losers and victims, then there is a danger that they might be represented simply as passive recipients of social change rather than as active participants. A view of women as confined or pushed back into subsistence agriculture, for example, may lead to insufficient attention being given to all the ways in which women struggle against the situation they find themselves in. There is a long history of resistance to forced cultivation of cash crops in many Third World regions (Nzula et al., 1979; Taussig, 1979; Cooper, 1981: 31–9), and there is a growing body of feminist literature in the social sciences which demonstrates how women struggle against the demands made on their labour, time and resources by their husbands and other male kin. Early feminist writing produced examples of women's resistance to government policies (Van Allen, 1972), while more recent studies have emphasized women's roles in labour struggles (Robertson and Berger, 1986: section III). (These issues are discussed more fully in chapter 5.)

The second difficulty with any simple characterization of women's disadvantaged position in developing economies is that it tends to reinforce the treatment of women as a homogeneous category. The rejection of such homogeneity is now taken for granted in the social sciences, and I argued in chapter 1 that the category 'woman' cannot stand as a sociologically relevant category of analysis. However, it is also the case that, until very recently, feminist anthropology was much better at analysing gender difference – the difference between the culturally and sociologically constructed categories 'woman' and 'man' – than it was at analysing the differences between women.

It is certainly true that social anthropology has always recognized 'women' as culturally distinct, and that it has always stressed the importance of understanding the differences which occur between women as a result of variation in age and in marital and kinship status. But the issue of emerging social differentiation between women – the issue of class – has only recently become a mainstream subject of study within social anthropology. This probably reflects two trends. First, anthropology has traditionally tended to analyse social difference in terms of stratification and hierarchy within societies, as opposed to looking at the uneven and contradictory processes of social differentiation and class formation.[5] Secondly, early feminist anthropology was initially much concerned with exploring the similarities of women's position cross-culturally, and it has been somewhat slow to come round to a more critical position which not only examines the exploitation of women by women (Caplan and Bujra, 1978), but also looks at emerging class differences between women, and at the crucial problem of analysing the intersections of class and gender difference (Bossen, 1984; Nash and Safa, 1976; Robertson and Berger, 1986). The recognition of class and gender as mutually determining systems, and of the fact that gender differences find very different expression within different class levels, has not only helped anthropology's understanding of the changing nature of gender relations, but has also contributed directly to the development of new areas of enquiry within the discipline of social anthropology as a whole.

Women in rural production systems

The connections between male migration, wage labour, the commercialization of agriculture and increasing social differentiation within the rural agricultural sector are often difficult to unravel, and always require historical and social specification. Gavin Kitching's analysis of class and economic change in Kenya shows the relationships between male migrant labour, women's wage labour in agriculture and the processes of social differentiation among peasant producers (Kitching, 1980). In a situation of male labour migration, as described by Kitching, access to women's labour becomes the basis for emerging social differentiation within the agricultural sector. Where the male migrant associated with the household earns little and can only send very small remittances home to his wife, she cannot pay for labour on the farm, and she may therefore be unable to produce crops for sale, thus having little or no cash income. In such circumstances, the woman concerned may have to engage in part-time agricultural labour for others in order to make ends meet. However, wives of men who are able to send regular remittances home may be in a position to purchase extra land and to employ other women to help work the enlarged farm. Not only may this result in increased income from the sale of cash crops, but it may also release the woman concerned from part of her agricultural labour, thus giving her more time for other entrepreneurial/income-generating activities (Kitching, 1980: 106, 241, 338).

Ann Stoler describes a situation in rural Java where increasing incorporation of the peasant agricultural sector into the colonial state did not result in the extraction of male labour and the confinement of female agricultural labour to the subsistence sector. In Java, both female and male labour were required for the commercial production of sugar, and decreasing access to arable land for subsistence production required increased intensification of female, male and child labour in wet rice production for household consumption. In pre-colonial Java, landholdings were apparently relatively homogeneous, but during the colonial period increases in population and developing land scarcity led to variations in the amounts of land held by individual households. As land became less available, differential access to land became 'differential access to all strategic resources' and formed the basis for increasing social differentiation (Stoler, 1977: 78).

Ethnographic writings have frequently emphasized the 'unusually high status' of Javanese women, who control family finances and play a dominant role in decision-making processes within the household (Geertz, 1961; Stoler, 1977: 85). In the light of this observation, it is interesting that Stoler's research demonstrates that capitalist penetration into the Javanese rural economy has not led, as has been argued for many other situations, to an increased dichotomization of the sexual division of labour, resulting in increased inequalities between women and men (Stoler, 1977: 75–6). Stoler accounts for this situation in terms of the sexual division of labour in pre-colonial and colonial Java, where both men and women were involved in agriculture and in forms of extracted/wage labour (Stoler, 1977: 76–8). The crucial role that women play, and have played, in both subsistence agriculture and wage labour has meant that processes of transformation have not exacerbated differences between women and men within the household, but have instead increased differentiation between households, and thus between individual women. Stoler goes on to demonstrate that, since household income is related overall to access to land, women from landless and small landholding households are dependent on employment opportunities generated by large landholding households. One of Stoler's conclusions is that 'Among poor households, the woman's earnings provide her with an important position *within* the household economy; among wealthier households, such earnings provide her with the material basis for social power' (Stoler, 1977: 84). A final and very interesting point that Stoler makes is that women are 'better equipped' to deal with increasing impoverishment through landlessness than men. Javanese women from small landholding and landless households have traditionally been involved in alternative income-generating activities outside subsistence rice production, and it is in fact men, rather than women, who have a smaller set of viable alternatives to agricultural labour (Stoler, 1977: 88).

The studies by Kitching and Stoler both demonstrate that women in rural production systems cannot be considered as a homogeneous group. They also provide contrasting situations which illustrate the complexity of response to capitalist processes of transformation, and which show that we cannot assume that such transformations will necessarily lead primarily to increasing differentiation along gender lines and/or to women's confinement to subsistence agriculture. Stoler's study emphasizes that the overall effect of the penetration of capitalist relations into the rural economy is frequently the impoverishment of part, or all, of the peasant agricultural sector as a whole. Our understanding of the changing nature of gender relations and of the sexual division of labour under capitalism is much improved by considering such processes in the light of increasing social differentiation within the rural economy, and in the light of the overall economic fortunes of the peasant agricultural sector.

Women and 'domestic labour'[6]

The responses of women to the processes of capitalist transformation are clearly very varied, and are, in part, determined by their ability to control, utilize and dispose of economic resources, and the products of those resources. These factors are in turn determined by the sexual division of labour, the organization of the household, and by kinship, marital and inheritance patterns. Analysing the processes of change at work in the transition from a subsistence economy to a market economy based on wage labour raises the kinds of questions which we began to address in the last section. What is the impact of economic development on women's status and work? How is the sexual division of labour changing? Are women increasingly relegated to a 'domestic' sphere? Does women's entry into wage labour give them greater personal autonomy and control? How are all these factors to be correlated with class, with cultural differences, and with the different types of work which women are involved in? So far these issues have been raised with regard to women's agricultural labour; now it is necessary to look at women's involvement in other types of work. The first areas to be considered are forms of income generation and wage labour which take place within the 'home' and which raise again, albeit in a slightly different form, the problem of the 'invisibility' of women's work.

One of the most interesting studies to focus on a form of income generation within the 'home' is Maria Mies's study of the Indian women lacemakers of Narsapur, in Andhra Pradesh (Mies, 1982). Mies conducted her field research in the late 1970s, and she discovered that more than 100,000 women were involved in the cottage industry of lacemaking, that their wages were extremely low, that the industry had been in existence for about 100 years, and that nearly all the lace made was exported to Europe, Australia and the USA. Furthermore, a number of private exporters had made large fortunes from the industry, which provided the largest share of foreign exchange earned from the export of handicrafts for the state of Andhra Pradesh (Mies, 1982: 6–7). In spite of the scale of the industry, no systematic survey or census of the lacemakers had ever been carried out. Lacemaking seems to have been started in the area in the 1870s–1880s by Christian missionaries who wanted to provide poor women with a means for generating income (Mies, 1982: 30–3). The sale of the lace was organized through the mission, and later developed on commercial lines. The production of lace was organized then, as it is now, on a putting-out system, where thread is distributed to women in their homes by an agent, who returns at a later date to collect the finished product and to pay the women for their work on a piece-rate basis. The agent then hands the lace on to an exporter. This production system is very advantageous for the capitalist exporter, who does not have to invest in buildings or machines – in effect, all the costs of production are borne by the workers. In addition, the cost of wages is easily regulated because when demand is slack there is no need to lay off anyone; the exporter merely hands out less thread to fewer women. When demand is high, more women are simply drawn into the production process (Mies, 1982: 34). Since 1970, the lace industry has undergone a period of very rapid expansion, largely due to an increase in demand from markets in India and abroad (Mies, 1982: 47–9).

Mies makes two points about the 'invisibility' of the women

involved in this large industry. The first is that in India, as elsewhere, the occupational status of a household is defined by the occupation of the male head of household, and, in this instance, these are mainly farmers, fishermen or workers. The second, and more interesting, point is that these women are invisible as workers because of the prevailing and overriding ideology that they are really only 'house-wives' who happen to be using their leisure time in a profitable way (Mies, 1982: 54). The invisibility of the women is compounded by the organizational features of the putting-out system, where individual women make individual components which are then assembled by the agents and given to another woman to put together. This 'splitting up' of the production process means that individual women have no sense of the overall production process or of a final product with which they could identify. Mies also argues that splitting up the production process is a strategy on the part of exporters to prevent the autonomous marketing of lace products by the women producers (Mies, 1982: 59). Furthermore, the fact that individual women work in their homes makes it difficult for the women to get together as a group of workers and confront the exporters. It is not surprising, of course, that the exporting/marketing sphere of the industry is handled almost exclu-sively by men. The organization of the lace industry as a cottage/domestic industry and the ideology of the laceworkers as 'housewives' must be understood in terms of a specific interconnection between the productive and reproductive spheres of social and economic life.

The main links or sets of productive relations within the lace industry are obviously those between exporters, traders, agents and lacemakers. However, Mies shows that lacemaking is also connected with the growing impoverishment of the peasant agricultural sector, where increasing social differentiation has led women in poorer agricultural households to take up lacemaking as a way of generating supplementary income. However, the question of the class of the women lacemakers is further complicated by differences based on caste, and by the fact of the sexual segregation and seclusion of women. Given the connection between lacemaking and poverty, it is interesting to note that the poorest women from the lowest caste, the *harijans*, are not lacemakers, but work mainly in agricultural labour or in other manual jobs (Mies, 1982: 101). Mies found that the majority of lacemakers in her sample (66 per cent) came from the *kapu* caste, where female seclusion is closely related to caste status, and a further 9 per cent of women lacemakers were Christian. Mies points out that these figures are significant because in India a rise in class status is associated with a rejection of manual labour, and in particular with the removal of women from labour outside the home (Mies, 1982: 111). The relationship of household and individual status to the domestication of women – that is to their ideological and material definition as 'housewives' – is something which can be noted in many societies in different parts of the world. In the case of the lacemakers, the Christian ideology of women as housewives and the *kapu* caste ideology of female seclusion have worked together with a particular set of productive relations to assure a cheap supply of female labour to the lace industry. This particular conjunction of productive and reproductive relations has permitted women to generate supplementary income for the household without altering the sexual division of labour or the nature of gender relations. If anything, women's insertion into the capitalist relations of market production has merely served to reinforce existing gender relations.

Maria Mies's study is interesting because it provides an example of how women's work is defined by a particular set of interconnections between reproductive and productive relations. It also provides an example of women's insertion into capitalist relations of production in a way which does not depend on a separation between the home and the workplace. Lacemaking appears to offer women the opportunity to combine their roles as housewives and workers. In reality, of course, the exploitation of these women is a function of this combination or conjunction. Another example of a conjunction between productive and reproductive relations, of women entering wage labour within the home, is of course domestic service.

Domestic servants work in private families, performing tasks which are usually done by the housewife/mother without compensation. Writing of domestic servants in the United States, David Katzman notes the following:

> Females predominated overwhelmingly among paid household workers, and throughout the late nineteenth and early twentieth centuries it was the single most important class of women's gainful employment. As a low-status occupation without any educational, experiential, or skill requisites for entry, it tended to be shunned by the native-born, and thus it was work performed disproportionately by immigrants and blacks. (Katzman, 1978: 44)

Domestic service is an area of waged employment which is very much under-researched, and indeed its importance as a sector of employment in developing/industrializing economies has only recently been fully appreciated. Speaking of contemporary Zambia, Karen Tranberg Hansen has noted that 'three major economic sectors dominate the Zambian labour market: mining, agriculture and domestic work' (Hansen, 1986a: 75). 'Today, paid domestic service forms the largest single segment of the urban wage-labouring population in Zambia' (Hansen, 1986a: 76). Given the scale and importance of the domestic service sector, it is surprising that more has not been written about it. Probably the most important reason for looking at domestic service is the opportunity it provides for analysing the interconnections between gender, class and race. Gaitskell et al. make this point in their discussion of domestic workers in South Africa:

> In South Africa it is often said that African women are oppressed in three ways: oppressed as blacks, oppressed as women, and oppressed as workers. Domestic service comprises one of the major sources of wage employment for African women in South Africa, and it is an important nexus of this triple oppression. The meaning of triple oppression is complex. It does not simply represent a convergence or 'coalescence' of three distinct types of oppression, seen as variables which can be analysed in isolation from each other and then superimposed. Sexual subordination when one is racially subordinate is one thing. Sexual subordination when one is a wage labourer in a racist society is quite another. (Gaitskell et al., 1983: 86)

The complexity of the interconnections between gender, race and class can perhaps best be grasped by looking at the history of the development of domestic service in different contexts. At a certain stage in the development of domestic service it is men rather than women who predominate in this sector of employment. Karen Tranberg Hansen's study of Zambia, where men still predominate in domestic service, shows that in the emerging colonial economy men were drawn into domestic service because it offered unique opportunities for wage employment and because the ideology of black/white relations found no contradiction in the subservience of black men. Several studies have argued that changes in the gender and race composition of domestic service employment can be explained with reference to industrialization and the expansion of the economy under capitalism. For example, Katzman shows in his work on the United States that in 1880 the majority of domestic servants in California and Washington were Chinese men. As urbanization and industrialization increased, and Chinese migration fell, the number of women servants grew to fill the urban demand and to replace the 'disappearing' men servants (Katzman, 1978: 55–6). Jacklyn Cock notes that in Britain women had not always dominated in domestic service, and that the employment of men as servants gradually gave way to the employment of women, so that by the nineteenth century the employment of male domestic servants had become 'a badge of high social status' (Cock, 1980: 179).

In a similar vein, Cock's history of the development of domestic service in South Africa illustrates the process whereby immigrating European servants were gradually displaced by black servants as colonization and urbanization progressed. During the first half of the nineteenth century, domestic service appears to have been a very 'mixed' institution, where men and women, black and white, were employed (Cock, 1980: 183–5). However, Cock demonstrates that 'there was a clear hierarchy of wages structured on racial and sexual status so that "Non-European" women were paid the lowest wages' (Cock, 1980: 213). By the end of the nineteenth century, the majority of domestic servants were African women. Both Katzman and Cock argue that expanding employment opportunities and increasing urbanization result in a certain amount of job mobility: as more individuals enter the labour market, those already employed move into other sectors of employment, vacating the lowest-paid and most insecure jobs for the 'newcomers'. Cock demonstrates this point with reference to the ways in which the occupational structure of South Africa is segregated by both gender and race. For example, in 1970 domestic service was the second-largest occupational category for African women – after agriculture – engaging 38 per cent of all employed black women. White women, on the other hand, have generally left the agricultural and service sectors, and are increasingly employed in industry, mostly in clerical capacities. A comparison of figures relating to white employment in the professions provides a familiar picture, where white women are 65 per cent of teachers, but only 18 per cent of Inspectors of Education; and 85 per cent of social workers, but only 10 per cent of doctors (Cock, 1980: 250–1). As Cock makes clear, black women are at the bottom of the sexual and racial hierarchy in South Africa, and this is reflected in their predominance in domestic service; a predominance which is maintained through poverty, educational disadvantage and state policies.[7]

There is, however, no easy generalization to be made about the interconnections of gender, race and class under capitalism, as a contrast between South Africa and Zambia, where men still predominate in domestic service, clearly shows. There is some evidence for a trend towards the 'feminization' of domestic service in Zambia, but at present men still predominate in this sector of employment (Hansen, 1986a: 77–8). The reasons for this predominance would appear to be related to stagnation in the economy (since the decline in export earnings from copper in the 1970s), resulting in a lack of alternative wage opportunities for men, a situation which is combined with rapid urbanization, migration to the towns and the impoverishment of rural areas. The result of these processes is an increasing number of individuals seeking employment in the towns who have few 'marketable' skills and who need somewhere to live. Domestic service provides an obvious opening (Hansen, 1986a: 75).

The issue of domestic service is an interesting one, and there is much more that could be said about it. However, there are a few points which are particularly relevant to an understanding of women's work, and to how the content and form of that work may be changing as a result of the penetration of capitalist relations. One point concerns the necessity of distinguishing domestic workers from housewives (Gaitskell et al., 1983: 91–3). Domestic workers may carry out those tasks usually done by housewives, but there is nothing pre-eminently 'female' about such tasks; it is not a matter of women being particularly suited for this type of work, as an examination of the situation in Zambia clearly shows. Under *emerging* capitalism, domestic service has a class nature, drawing its labour from unskilled migrants who turn to this work in conditions of extreme economic insecurity. However, contemporary urban South Africa is a *developed* capitalist economy where domestic service still forms a significant sector of employment – by contrast with other developed capitalist economies in, for example, Europe or North America, where full-time, live-in domestic service has declined in significance. The persistence of domestic service in South Africa is basically to be explained, as Cock makes clear, with reference to the particular circumstances generated by the intersection of race, class and gender; a configuration of class and gender alone would be insufficient.

Focusing on the intersections of race, class and gender is also crucial when we look at the particular connections between productive and reproductive relations which characterize domestic service. I have already argued that it is insufficient to suggest that women go into domestic service because it is an extension of their work in the 'home'. Hansen has argued that domestic service in Zambia, far from being considered women's work, is thought of as being quite the opposite, 'for it is not considered "natural" for a woman with small children to leave her own household to attend to someone else's' (Hansen, 1986b: 22). This appeal to cultural ideology could, of course, be interpreted as part of a mechanism to keep women out of a sector of employment where they would be directly competing with men for work. However, in South Africa this kind of ideology is clearly not operating, or not operating in the same way, because women are employed in domestic service under conditions which actually make it impossible for them to lead any kind of 'family' life. They are usually resident at their place of work, they work long hours and have little holiday, with the result that their own children, who are resident elsewhere, have to be looked after by others.

It is instructive at this point to compare the situation of black women domestic workers in South Africa with that of the lacemakers of Narsapur, because both groups of women are apparently working for wages in the 'home', and both groups are underpaid, 'invisible' and largely non-organized. However, one difference that stands out immediately is that, although both groups work in the 'home', the black women of South Africa are actually leaving their homes to go and work in other people's. This, of course, raises interesting questions about the functions of women's domestic labour for capitalism, but it also highlights one of the key areas in the analysis of domestic service, which is the relationship between employer and employee. The availability of domestic workers actually serves to free other women from domestic chores. However, the functions of this relationship for capitalism are not at all clear. In theory, the availability of domestic service may mean that higher-class/white women can continue working outside the home, and thus it can be argued that domestic workers release other women for work in the labour force. But, in reality, this is often not the case, because the aim of employing domestic workers is actually for some women to gain more leisure, more choice about time allocation, more autonomy and more control within the household (Jelin, 1977: 140). Women are divided by class and race, and their positions as housewives under capitalism are not the same. This point becomes particularly clear when we consider the fact that women domestic workers, far from being housewives, are actually primary wage earners, with their own households – for whatever reason – often solely dependent on their wage.

Women in petty commodity production and commerce

Having considered some of the ways in which women may earn a wage within the 'home', let us now turn to some of the opportunities which are open to women in the 'market-place'. I have already suggested earlier in this chapter that, where capitalism begins by drawing on male wage labour, women's labour in peasant agriculture is intensified, but at the same time, in order to meet personal and household expenses, women are drawn into petty commodity production or petty commerce.[8] Some women begin by growing crops for sale on the market, as well as the subsistence crops necessary for household consumption, but they may also be involved in brewing beer, making baskets or mats, and selling processed food. However, it is clear that such activities rarely lead to capital accumulation or to any form of personal 'enrichment' (Mintz, 1971). Mueller makes this point in her study of women in Lesotho, where it is startlingly clear that women brew beer, and sell a variety of agricultural products, just to provide basic daily necessities, as well as to meet occasional medical expenses and shortfalls of staple foodstuffs. There is no question of saving or investment or improvement of living standard (Mueller, 1977: 157–8, 161). In such instances the effects of capital on women are uneven and contradictory; while one strategy for survival is undermined (agriculture), another is opened up (the 'market-place'). Overall, however, women are, if anything, worse off.

The precarious nature of women's involvement in petty commodity production and commerce is very forcefully illustrated with regard to women's activities in the urban 'informal' economy. The 'informal' economy, sometimes called the 'second' economy, is a series of income-generating activities which are distinguished from formal, contractual wage labour. Such activities are small-scale and require little or no capital to set them up; they are often itinerant and seasonal, and are also frequently illegal. Business is risky, both because profits are small and insecure, and because participants run the risk of being arrested and fined. Informal activities may take place 'at home' or 'on the street', and they can include the sale of cooked food, seasonal fruits, sweets, shoe-shine services, beer, sexual services, tourist items and various kinds of 'repair' services. Of course, both men and women are involved in the 'informal' sector, but women's involvement is of a particular kind.[9] Lourdes Arizpe discusses the case of women in the informal labour sector in Mexico City. A wide range of activities is involved, and interestingly enough these activities are stratified by class, for it is not only poor women who engage in the informal economy. According to Arizpe, Mexican middle-class women generally consider work outside the home to be undesirable, and only a minority engaged in outside wage labour. However, many women whose husbands do not earn enough undertake part-time activities within the home in order to supplement household income. These activities include language tuition, embroidery, baking, sewing, leather work, etc. 'Interestingly, all of these activities are normally done freely for friends and relatives; the only difference between such informal jobs and domestic or family tasks is wages' (Arizpe, 1977: 33). The situation of middle-class women contrasts with that of lower-class women, who carry out their informal economic activities in the streets or in other women's homes. These activities involve petty commerce, personal services and domestic service. Arizpe points out that female petty trade usually involves edibles, such as fruit, sweets, chewing gum and cooked food, and that many of the unauthorized street sellers are rural migrants (Arizpe, 1977: 34).

The informal economy provides middle-class women with supplementary income, while it provides lower-class women with the minimum amount of cash necessary for survival in the urban economy. Clearly the function of this work in the context of a capitalist economy is rather different in the two cases. In the case of middle-class women, their informal activities are obviously subsidizing the wages paid to men in the formal sectors of employment. However, the circumstances of their productive activities raise new questions about the Marxist argument concerning the creation of privatized domestic labour for women as a precondition of capitalist production. These women are clearly not just housewives in the generally accepted meaning of the term, but it would be a mistake to assume that their situation is characteristic of a particular stage of capitalist development or that it is connected to a specific, pre-existing form of the sexual division of labour. In the long run their position may not be very different from that of many middle-class women in contemporary Britain who find themselves teaching English, typing or doing piece-work at home in order to supplement household income. In the case of the lower-class women in Mexico City, their informal activities are clearly providing, in many instances, the sole support for themselves and their dependants. These women are engaging in the capitalist economy in a way which does not depend on a rigid separation of the 'home' from the 'workplace', and yet they still have to contend with the problem of managing the domestic labour of the household as well as earning a living. They are neither housewives nor wage labourers, and as such Marxist-feminist analysis has very little to say about them. This is an area which requires much more research, but it is one in which anthropology could make a substantial contribution, both theoretically and empirically.

It is important, of course, to remember that women's involvement in petty commodity production and trade was not something which only began with the advent of colonialism and/or the penetration of capitalism. This is particularly the case in West Africa, and anthropologists have made much of the famous women traders of this part of the world. Robertson discusses the Ga women of Accra, Ghana, who are reported as being involved in trade as early as 1600 (Robertson, 1976: 114). Some writers have argued that women's trading activities and economic autonomy were adversely affected by colonialism and capitalism (Etienne, 1980). However, it is clear that in the later colonial period, at least, some women were making money, as Little points out.

> Business women in the larger West African towns who have shops and stores of their own . . . are not nearly so numerous as male buyers of produce and retailers. Nevertheless, some of them conduct their business on an extensive scale and in Nigeria, for example, they trade chiefly in textiles bought wholesale from European firms, a thousand pounds' worth at a time, and sell retail, through their own employees in bush markets as well as in town. Others trade in fish or palm oil, own lorries, build themselves European-type houses, and have their sons educated overseas. (Little, 1973: 44)

Little is sensibly cautious about such success stories, and he notes that 'the great majority of these West African market women and others in commerce are petty traders' (Little, 1973: 45). However, it is clear that in the past and in the present trading is a viable option open to women, not only to supplement household income, but also to provide for the household under the very difficult conditions of urban life, and that it can under certain conditions provide opportunities for capital accumulation, political influence and economic autonomy.

Janet MacGaffey discusses the success of some women entrepreneurs in Kisangani, Zaïre.[10] MacGaffey argues that Zaïre is a male-dominated society, where women in urban situations suffer both social and legal discrimination. Women have low levels of education compared to men, and they are therefore under-represented in the professions and in government. They also suffer economic discrimination: for example, the rule that a woman may not open a bank account without her husband's consent (MacGaffey, 1986: 161, 165). In spite of these restrictions, since the 1960s some women have managed to develop and manage successful business enterprises. The emerging commercial middle class have been helped in this period by political upheaval, by the Zaïreanization of foreign businesses and capital, and by the deepening economic crisis since 1976, all of which have contributed to the provision of business opportunities in a situation of scarcity and confusion in which huge profits can be made (MacGaffey, 1986: 164–5). In this situation, some women have managed to become part of the emerging commercial middle class individually and not just as dependants of men.

However, as MacGaffey makes clear, the processes of class formation are gender-specific, because women have different problems from men and are forced to enter economic activities in a different way (MacGaffey, 1986: 165). This is borne out by the fact that it is through the activities of the informal economy that women have largely found opportunities for capital accumulation. According to MacGaffey, by 1979 women were famous for their success in business and some were known to be millionaires; by 1980 women were 'specializing in long-distance retail and semi-wholesale trade, exporting and importing goods to and from Kinshasa or to the interior by boat, plane and truck' (MacGaffey, 1986: 166). The most profitable business is shipping fish, rice and beans down to Kinshasa, but even if a woman has a commercial licence, she will not necessarily use the bank, keep accounts or declare all her commerce, even though it may be on a very large scale. It is in this sense that even the large-scale commercial enterprises run by women can be considered as part of the informal or second economy. For the women concerned this is particularly important because it is through operating in the second economy that women have been able to bypass the state controls and the specific restrictions imposed on them by men. For example, the new Civil Code specifies that the management of the wife's goods is presumed to be in the husband's hands, even though the marriage contract records separate ownership of goods by each spouse. 'Hence the importance for women of second-economy activities which are undocumented, not governed by law, and thus outside the control of men' (MacGaffey, 1986: 171). However, commerce is risky, and once again it is clear that, although a few do very well, the majority fail or only have some small success.

Women and wage labour: migration and proletarianization

Proletarianization is the process through which a working class is created whose members have no choice but to sell their ability to work. It is therefore linked to the process through which people become separated from the means of production, notably land. Proletarianization and migration are very frequently linked in developing economies, where individuals move away from the land in search of work. Such migration may be permanent, seasonal or temporary, and, to the extent that individuals continue to rely on subsistence production activities in addition to their wages in order to maintain themselves and their dependants, we can say that they are partially or incompletely proletarianized. This partial or incomplete proletarianization is a marked feature of developing economies under capitalism. Proletarianization, both as a theoretical concept and as an empirical object of research, is not a process which has been extensively studied in social anthropology until quite recently, although migration, wage labour, urbanization and emerging worker protest were all issues in the social anthropology of Africa in the 1930s, 1940s and 1950s. Feminist anthropology, however, has been much concerned with conflict and contradiction in gender relations, and this has led to consideration of the different ways in which women and men are affected by social change, economic opportunity and the emergence of capitalist relations of production and reproduction. These are, of course, the concerns of feminist scholars in a wide variety of other disciplines, but within social anthropology itself feminist scholars have made and continue to make a significant and distinctive contribution in these areas.

The processes through which women are drawn into wage labour in developing economies are yet to be investigated adequately, and this is an area which requires more substantive research. At the present time in the Third World women are being drawn into wage labour in the agricultural sector at all levels. In some areas women work on the farms of wealthier neighbours; sometimes this work is remunerated in cash, but in other instances women may only receive food or labour services or a share of the crop in return (Stoler, 1977; Kitching, 1980).[11] Other women work as seasonal agricultural labourers for commercial farmers, an activity which may or may not involve women in seasonal migration to the place of work. Women's seasonal work of this kind used to be very common in some parts of Europe, and it is still practised in contemporary Britain with regard to picking potatoes, hops and soft fruit. In some instances, women are employed full-time as agricultural labourers, as on some South African farms. Women's labour in plantation economies is also extremely important in many parts of the world, possibly more so in Asia (Kurian, 1982), Latin America and the Caribbean than in Africa (Mackintosh, 1979). This work may be seasonal (Bossen, 1984: ch. 3) or it may involve residence on the plantation.

The question of women's migration has recently undergone some revision in the social science literature. A number of writers have now challenged the received idea of the migrant as young, male and single (Izzard, 1985; Sharma, 1986: ch. 4; Bozzoli, 1983; Jelin, 1977: 131–2). These writers have also challenged the view that either women are left behind in the rural areas of out-migration, or they migrate merely to follow their husbands. Sharma, in her study of Shimla, North India, has pointed out that the assumption that women migrate to cities only as the dependants of men results in insufficient attention being given to the economics of female migration itself. The idea that female migration is due to marriage or 'other non-economic factors' means that the rural–urban migration of women remains unanalysed because it is seen as 'belonging to the domestic sphere rather than to the sphere of production and the economy' (Sharma, 1986: 42). Sharma also argues that it is a mistake to assume that if a wife comes to town to join her husband this is 'social' migration. The woman may have come precisely because the town offers better employment opportunities for her than the village, in which case such migration is clearly 'economic'.[12] She points out that 'studies of rural–urban migration among men have shown that men usually migrate to a particular city because they have kin or friends there, but this does not lead sociologists to term their migration "social"' (Sharma, 1986: 44). Of the 58 women interviewed by Sharma, 13 of them had originally come to Shimla to study, to train for a job or to take up a job. She agrees that this means that many more of her female respondents had come to Shimla at or after marriage solely because their husband worked in the city. But she demonstrates that this obscures the fact that a number of these women took up waged employment after arriving in Shimla, never having done any paid work before (Sharma, 1986: 44).

Jelin summarizes the data on migration to Latin American cities, and argues that women migrate to cities more often than men, in spite of the apparent importance of such cultural traditions as machismo, a high degree of male control over women and women's lack of autonomy outside the family (Jelin, 1977: 131). Part of this revision of the literature on migration is clearly due to the fact that patterns of migration have been changing since World War II. Increasing urbanization and industrialization have coincided with a decline in economic opportunities in the countryside, and consequently many more women are migrating to the cities than before. This process has been aided, at least in Africa, by changes in government policy. In some parts of colonial Africa, there were restrictions on the movement of women, who were prevented from joining their husbands on plantations or in the mines, and they were also sometimes prohibited from moving to cities. But colonial policies were shifting and contradictory, and in other circumstances they encouraged the movement of women into certain areas in order to provide sexual services for the male workers, and/or to 'stabilize' the workforce (Parpart, 1986; MacGaffey, 1986; Little, 1973: 16–19). In addition to the restrictions imposed by the colonial government, there were also cultural restrictions based on ideas about women's roles in society. Caldwell (writing a few years after the end of colonial rule in Ghana) found that many of the Ghanaian men he interviewed supported the idea of young men going to town to learn a skill or earn money, but that a large number disapproved of women doing the same thing because they feared that they might become prostitutes (Caldwell, 1969: 106–7). Christine Obbo discusses the fact that contemporary stereotypes of African women indicate fears and doubts about women's changing roles, and in particular their increased participation in economic and political life. Rapid social change apparently raises fears about controlling women, fears which are often expressed through a concern with controlling women's morality and sexual behaviour. Women who are, or who seek to be, economically independent run the risk of being characterized as sexually or morally loose.[13] Thus, according to the dominant male ideology, female migration to towns is not something to be encouraged (Obbo, 1980: 6–16).

Recent feminist research has concentrated on asking women why they migrate, and on analysing the social and economic reasons for their decision. One very interesting point to emerge is that gender relations, and in particular conflict between men and women, are absolutely central to any understanding of why women migrate, and of how and why women experience changing social and economic pressures differently from men. Bryceson suggests that women often migrate as a result of divorce or the death of a parent. In the latter case, women seek jobs in town in order to send money home to support the widowed parent. In the case of divorce, women may lose their usufruct rights to land (rights which will have been conditional on their marital status), and consequently they may be unable to support themselves unless aided by a brother or father, some of whom will not be willing to help (Bryceson, 1985: 144–5). Obbo also notes the importance of divorce as a 'push' factor for women, but in addition she mentions widowhood, premarital pregnancy and barrenness as deciding factors. Thus women may migrate because they have lost access to the means of production and other resources, and/or because they are trying to escape from some sort of social stigma or disagreement between kin. However, Obbo draws attention to conflict between men and women: out of 51 women she interviewed who had migrated alone, 16 of them said they had moved to town to 'escape unsatisfactory marriages' (Obbo, 1980: 75–9). This is not a new idea: several anthropologists writing in the 1960s mentioned the large number of 'husbandless' women living in African towns who were apparently economically independent, and they attributed this situation to increasing marital instability (Southall, 1961: 51; Gugler, 1969: 139). Recent feminist research, however, has taken these empirical findings a stage further, and, instead of treating them merely as evidence of the deleterious effects of urbanization and modernization on 'traditional' family life, has sought to place the changing nature of gender relations and the evidence of gender conflict at the centre of an understanding of emerging class divisions and their consequences for women.

However, it is important to note that migration is often not a single, discrete event, but part of a strategy for coping with economic change and opportunity which depends on multiplex links being established between rural and urban areas. Izzard, in her study of women migrants in Botswana, makes the point that women migrate to towns because they need money, and towns provide a greater diversity of formal and informal income-earning activities than are available in the rural areas. The importance of recognizing women's migration as an economic strategy becomes clear when viewed in the context of familial responsibilities and household survival strategies. Many women interviewed by Izzard in the towns could be considered as belonging 'to a wider family group whose permanent residential base was in the rural areas' (Izzard, 1985: 272). Wages from migrant workers are important to the survival of rural households in Botswana, as they are in many parts of southern Africa, and this is particularly true for female-headed households. Links between rural and urban areas are of various kinds. Women 'left behind' in the rural areas are often dependent on the money which their children earn in the town. In other instances, women working in the town may send their children back to the rural areas to live with their mother. This has advantages for both mother and daughter. Women in formal employment find it expensive to get childminders, and they may have to be absent from their children for long periods (Fapohunda, 1982). Some kinds of work, particularly residential domestic service, make it impossible for a woman to keep her children with her. Women engaged in informal activities, particularly beer-brewing and prostitution, sometimes do not wish their children to become involved in the 'life' these activities involve, and prefer them to be brought up in the rural areas, where they can be supported more easily and more cheaply (Nelson, 1986). As far as women in the rural areas are concerned, over a third of women interviewed by Izzard received money, goods or food from their daughters working in the towns, mostly because they were looking after the daughter's children. This money is essential to the survival of the rural household, and there is the added advantage that the children contribute labour to the production activities of the rural household, thereby increasing its chances of survival still further (Izzard, 1985: 272–5). Rural–urban links of various kinds have, of course, been widely discussed in social anthropology. A number of authors have noted that women from the rural areas visit their husbands in town during slack periods in the agricultural cycle to collect money and purchase necessary items; these women might also bring food from the countryside for consumption by the urban household (Obbo, 1980: 74–5). In polygynous societies, the household might be 'split' between the rural and urban areas, with one wife resident on the farm and one resident in town (Parkin, 1978). The practice of sending children to live with relatives in town is also very common. Young female children provide town dwellers with a cheap source of domestic labour and childcare, and this strategy relieves the rural household of the responsibility of feeding, clothing and educating a child (Nelson, 1986). These kinds of links are well known, but the significance of recent research on female migrants, in Africa, is the emphasis on the importance of mother–daughter links across the rural–urban divide, as part of strategies of household survival.

Women and wage labour: factories and the formal sector

There has been a rapid increase in the number of women engaged in non-agricultural employment in the countries of the Third World in the last twenty-five years. Obviously, not all these increases are of the same magnitude, and not all of them have occurred in the same sectors of employment. Some of these 'new' women workers have gone into the industrial labour force, and most especially into light industrial manufacturing: electronics, textiles and clothing. Food processing is another area where women find employment, perhaps (as more than one writer has mentioned) because it is an area which resembles women's traditional activities in the home. In some countries, a significant proportion of women have gone into the tertiary sector of employment, where they are employed in personal services and government occupations, as well as in the professions. However, women's labour-force participation rates vary from one region to another. For example, the Arab region has the lowest female labour-force participation rates in the world, even though it has been affected by the trend towards increasing formal employment for women (Azzam, 1979; Abu Nasr et al., 1985), while in comparison some Caribbean and Latin American countries have rates of female non-agricultural employment which are comparable to those of Western, industrial nations. The determinants of female participation rates in non-agricultural employment are both complex and very varied in their effects, but it is possible to outline a number of influential factors. Broadly, they include the structure of the economy, the level of industrialization, opportunities for education, the legal position of women, cultural values concerning the appropriate behaviour of women, the demographic structure of the population, and age at marriage. None of these factors acting alone can provide a sufficient explanation for women's participation rates in formal employment, but they all need to be considered in any discussion of what determines women's entry into non-agricultural employment.

Women's participation rates in non-agricultural employment show enormous variation around the world. Two questions need to be considered. First, why is this variation so great, and what determines it? Secondly, are the theories which have been developed to explain women's labour-force participation in developed countries appropriate or useful in analysing the situation in the developing countries of the world? I cannot survey here the enormous body of literature which has been produced on these issues in anthropology, sociology and economics, but a brief discussion of a few points will allow us to examine the ways in which changing socio-economic circumstances and changing gender relations are shaping women's access to non-agricultural employment, and how all these factors work together to produce and maintain gender ideologies.

Industrialization and the structure of the economy

One of the major determinants of women's participation in non-agricultural employment is the level of industrialization of the country concerned. Industrialization alters patterns of work, it changes the relationship between the workplace and the home, and it reorganizes the distribution of employment opportunities within the different sectors of the economy, creating new forms of employment – particularly in bureaucratic and clerical capacities – and destroying others. A simple comparison of industrialized and developing countries (classified according to per capita income and the activity rate of adult males in non-agricultural work) shows that women's participation rates in non-agricultural sectors of employment are higher in the industrialized economies: the mean activity rate for women in industrialized countries, according to a study conducted by Youssef in 1974, is 28.1 per cent, compared to 12.3 per cent in developing countries (Youssef, 1976: 10–11).[14] However, Youssef demonstrates that a straightforward comparison of this kind is extremely misleading, because closer examination of the data reveals the considerable variation which exists in women's non-agricultural participation rates between countries which apparently have very similar levels of economic development. For example, Youssef compares Jamaica, Chile, Egypt and Iraq, which apparently have very similar levels of economic development, but female participation rates in non-agricultural activities vary from 36 per cent in Jamaica, to 22 per cent in Chile, to 3 per cent in Egypt and Iraq (Youssef, 1976: 18). The inappropriateness of explaining female labour-force participation rates with reference solely to industrialization is further reinforced by the similarities which exist in some cases between industrialized and non-industrialized/developing countries. For example, female employment in non-agricultural sectors in Nicaragua and Ecuador is nearly as high as in the industrialized nations of the Netherlands, Norway and Israel; and the female activity rates for the developing nation of Jamaica are comparable to those reported for Switzerland, Sweden and Denmark (Youssef, 1976: 21).

There is every reason to be extremely sceptical about the validity of the data available on female participation, but it is clear that a simple reference to the level of industrialization is not enough to explain women's participation in non-agricultural employment. One possibility, however, is that countries at similar levels of economic development may differ with regard to the specific structure or organization of their economy, thus offering different sorts of opportunities to women and men within the labour market. An analysis of occupational structure can be very revealing, especially when considered in historical perspective. In her analysis of women's work in Guatemala, Norma Chinchilla shows how increasing industrialization has actually decreased women's participation in non-agricultural employment because of the kinds of changes which have taken place in the organization of the Guatemalan economy. In the years between 1946 and 1965, censuses report a decline in female workers in the manufacturing sector from 22 to 18 per cent, the largest declines being in the tobacco, rubber, textile, chemical and foods industries. Employment for male workers, on the other hand, is rapidly increasing in the areas of chemicals, paper and rubber, as well as in electrical products, transportation and furniture, which are relatively new industries, first appearing in the 1965 industrial census. It is clear that new industries are creating a demand for male labour, while at the same time men are replacing women in some of the older industries. Prior to 1946, women were employed in independent artisanal industries, but Chinchilla argues that industrialization has destroyed many of these industries without a compensatory increase in the demand for female factory labour, and as a result women's overall participation in the manufacturing sector has declined (Chinchilla, 1977: 39, 48–50).[15] Thus women's participation in non-agricultural employment can vary with changes in the overall structure of the economy.

However, changes in occupational structure, and in the overall organization of an individual country's economy, do not take place in a vacuum, but are directly determined by the part the country's economy plays in the international arena. For example, in the last twenty years, global capitalist development has led to the emergence of what are known as world-market factories in many parts of the Third World, most particularly in Asia and Latin America (Elson and Pearson, 1981; Froebel et al., 1980; Van Putten and Lucas, 1985). These world-market factories produce goods exclusively for export to the rich countries of the world. The companies that run these factories may be owned by local capitalists or they may be subsidiaries of large multinationals. In either case, their choice of location is determined by cheap and compliant labour, the advantages of tax concessions and by conveniently inadequate regulations governing health and safety provisions. World-market factories produce textiles, soft toys, sports equipment and ready-to-wear clothes, but they also produce electrical goods and components for the electronics industry. In many instances, whether the company that runs the factory is formally independent or not, the very limited role which these factories play in the manufacture of the product means that they are little more than a stage in a production process controlled by multinationals.

> Some world market factories producing final consumer goods do no more than assemble together parts supplied by their customers. . . . For instance, trousers are cut out in Germany, then flown in air-containers to Tunisia, where they are sewn together, packed and flown back for sale in Germany. In such cases, the world market factory is fully integrated into the production process of the customer firm, even though in formal terms it may be independent. (Elson and Pearson, 1981: 88)

The most interesting point about these world-market factories is that the vast majority (over 80 per cent) of the workers who are employed in them are young women between the ages of 13 and 25 years. These women, of course, are the assembly-line operatives; the administrative and technical posts, which are far fewer in number, are occupied by men (Mitter, 1986: 14). A number of studies report that, when companies are asked why they employ women, they respond with reference to women's apparently innate capacities for the work – 'nimble fingers' – their docility, their disinclination to unionize, and the fact that women are cheap because, while men need an income to support a family, women do not. Susan Joekes highlights this last point in her study of women workers in the Moroccan clothing industry, where male workers and factory managers explain the fact that men earn more than women for doing the same job by saying that 'women work for lipstick'. In other words, they work to earn money to buy personal luxuries, while men work to support a family (Joekes, 1985: 183). Research also shows that employers believe that women are suited to boring, repetitive and unskilled tasks, and that they respond better to the discipline of long hours on the factory floor. A number of writers have pointed out that there is very little basis for these stereotypes in empirical fact. In their article on women's waged work in Britain, Anne Phillips and Barbara Taylor make it clear that the definition of women's jobs as unskilled often bears little relation to the actual amount of training or ability required to do them. Women's work is often deemed inferior because it is women who do it, and women workers carry their subordinate status into the workplace with them, where this status comes to define the value of the work they do (Phillips and Taylor, 1980: 79). John Humphrey discusses women workers in an electrical plant in Brazil, where, although some women did 'simple but exacting jobs', others were employed in a special sterile area in the factory manufacturing the silicone wafers from which silicone chips are made. The wafer department was the basis of the plant's productive enterprise, and all the non-supervisory workers in the department were women. These women were expected to be able to use 'sophisticated machinery in all the stages of production – photo-engraving, etching, and depositing of particles'. The machinery was highly automated and set up by technicians, but the women had to work with extreme care, take responsibility and be prepared to carry out any of the tasks in the sterile area. Women working in this area required 4–6 months' training and represented a considerable asset to the company in terms of knowledge and experience. But, in spite of this, all the women in the section were classified as unskilled 'production assistants' (Humphrey, 1985: 220–1).

Susan Joekes points out in her study of the Moroccan clothing industry that women and men machinists sit side by side, performing the same operations at the same speed, and the only difference between them is that women earn 70 per cent of what the men earn

(Joekes, 1985: 183). This undermines the argument that women are less skilled than men, and it questions the view that women are allocated to unskilled jobs because they are better suited to boring, tedious and repetitive tasks. Joekes also emphasizes that women were paid less than men for doing the same job even though they were regarded by management as producing a better quality of work, and were acknowledged as having higher educational levels. Joekes discusses the argument that technological advances in industry have tended to result in the creation of more and more repetitive, assembly-line jobs on the one hand, and a decreasing number of managerial and supervisory jobs on the other. The relative increase in the number of unskilled, low-paid jobs is advantageous to employers because it reduces the cost of the wage bill, and it eliminates the skilled worker whose knowledge of all stages of the production process could threaten managerial control. Technological advances thus lead to increases in the number of women employed, as employers take on large numbers of female workers to fill the growing numbers of unskilled jobs created by new technology. One of the problems with this argument, as Joekes points out, is that it provides only a partial explanation. Technological changes have taken place throughout industry, and the increased demand for unskilled labour must therefore be very widespread, but the demand for female labour has come from only a few industries (Joekes, 1985: 188–9). Joekes's argument is strongly supported by comparative data which show that industries which are thought appropriate for women, and industries which never, or rarely, employ women, are found in all economies; thus the entry of women into the manufacturing labour force is extremely selective and cannot be directly correlated with the increasing numbers of unskilled jobs in general.

A comparison between Guatemala, where women's employment in manufacturing has declined in relative terms, and where newly emerging electronics industries have drawn on male labour, and those countries with world-market factories, like Hong Kong and Brazil, where large numbers of young women have been drawn into the electronics industry, demonstrates that women's entry into the labour market is selective, and that the 'feminization' of industries varies from one economy to another. The stereotypes concerning appropriate work for women should not deceive us into imagining that there are particular areas of work which are always going to be designated as 'feminine'/appropriate for women. A good example of this last point is provided by examining some of the data on women's employment from the Arab region. According to Azzam et al., figures from countries with significant urban sectors, like Bahrain, Egypt, Lebanon and Kuwait, show that women tend to be employed mainly in community or in social and personal services. The authors' data show 97 per cent of the total active females in Bahrain engaged in these areas, 96 per cent in the United Arab Emirates (UAE), 99 per cent in Kuwait and 56 per cent in Lebanon (Azzam et al., 1985: 22). This stereotyping of women's employment would appear to be quite familiar, but a closer examination of the data produces some interesting points. With regard to the Gulf States (Bahrain, Kuwait, Qatar and UAE), it appears that the figures for women engaged in service occupations are not made up of large numbers of women employed as domestic servants, waitresses, cleaners and building caretakers, as we might expect from looking at women's employment in other parts of the world. In the Gulf, these jobs are socially stigmatized as being inappropriate for women because they involve too much contact with strangers, particularly men (Azzam and Moujabber, 1985: 65). In the same way, clerical and secretarial jobs are not considered stereotypically feminine, and few women are employed in such capacities because they involve non-segregated working conditions (Nath, 1978: 182). The conclusion to be drawn from the foregoing discussion is that, although the level of industrialization/economic development and the structure of the economy have some influence on women's entry into the labour market, neither of these factors can adequately explain women's participation rates in non-agricultural employment.

Women's opportunities: education and status

Having looked at women's participation rates in non-agricultural employment in terms of the level of economic development, and in terms of the changing structure of demand in the labour market, it is necessary to turn to a consideration of those factors which might be said to control the supply of women available to the labour market. One of the most important of these factors is education. Education is thought to have a positive effect on women's participation in the labour force because it improves employment opportunities for women, it encourages greater female mobility in search of employment, it is assumed to increase the aspirations and expectations of women workers, and it is supposed to weaken the barriers of cultural tradition which prevent women from entering the labour market. The effect of education on employment cannot, of course, be considered in isolation from other factors which affect the supply of women to the labour market, and which are directly and indirectly linked to education itself. Some of the most significant factors in this regard are the legal position of women, cultural values concerning the appropriate behaviour of women, the demographic structure of the population and age at marriage. Education is thus clearly linked to women's socio-economic status and to their role and position in society.

Mujahid's study of female labour-force participation rates in Jordan uses data from the Household and Fertility Surveys of 1976 to demonstrate that labour-force participation rates are positively correlated with level of education, and that participation rates rise significantly for women who have completed secondary school, but are highest for women who have received vocational and technical education (Mujahid, 1985: 117). Similar findings are available from other developing countries, but the positive relationship between jobs and education is not as straightforward as it might at first seem. One problem is that, in many cases, women's overall participation rates actually decline with an increase in primary education, and only rise again with an increase in secondary school numbers. The general argument put forward to explain why women with less than secondary education should have lower participation rates than those with no schooling at all is that those with basic primary education are not prepared to do unskilled jobs, while at the same time they are not sufficiently qualified for better-paid jobs (Mujahid, 1985: 117). There seems to be a certain amount of validity in this argument, in so far as it implies that basic educational provision may not be directly related to job acquisition.

It is clear from a number of studies that, in the initial stages of economic development, basic education confers advantages on those who acquire it, but at a later stage the supply of individuals with such education exceeds the jobs available. The result is a kind of inflation in the level of educational skills thought to be appropriate for certain jobs. In this context, women are often particularly disadvantaged because, although their education provision has increased in many developing countries in the last twenty years, it still lags far behind that of men. This point is reinforced by a comparison of female and male literacy rates, and of school enrolment figures for females and males. In Ghana, 18.4 per cent of women are literate compared to 43.1 per cent of men; in Zambia 40.2 per cent of women are literate compared to 63.1 per cent of men, and the comparable figures for Sudan are 17.9 per cent for women and 44.7 per cent for men. The school enrolment figures show less striking differences, with Ghana having 38 per cent of females between the ages of 6 and 24 years enrolled in schools, compared to 52.3 per cent of males; Zambia has 31.4 per cent of females enrolled compared to 44 per cent of males, while Sudan has 22 per cent of females and 39.9 per cent of males (Stichter, 1984: 194). Africa has some of the highest illiteracy rates in the world, but data from other regions show much the same sort of disparity between females and males. Youssef studied the literacy and school enrolment figures for a selection of Latin American and Middle Eastern countries. She found that on average, in the Latin American sample, 71 per cent of women and 78 per cent of men were literate, but in the Middle Eastern sample only 17 per cent of women were literate compared to 44 per cent of men (Youssef, 1976: 43).

The differences in the educational achievements of women and men increase as one moves up the educational system, because women do not have equal access to the higher levels of education. Whyte demonstrates that this is so even in developed countries like Switzerland, where females make up 49 per cent of primary school children, but only 23 per cent of university/tertiary school students, and in West Germany, where the percentage of females in primary school is 49 per cent but only 27 per cent at the university/tertiary level (Whyte, 1984: 200). Women's lack of access to secondary and tertiary education is even more marked in developing countries, where men's access to vocational and technical training also exceeds that of women (Martin, 1983; Robinson, 1986). The result of this differential access is that, in a situation where many individuals are chasing scarce jobs, more men than women have access to a better education and therefore to better jobs. This leaves women, whether their access to basic education has improved or not, in a disadvantaged position in the labour market. Economic development may have increased educational provision and improved women's position in an absolute sense, but it has made very little impact on relative sexual inequalities between men and women.

The relationship between education and women's participation in non-agricultural employment is further affected by the uneven distribution of women within the different sectors of the economy, and by class.[16] It is quite clear that the more highly educated women are concentrated within particular sections of the labour force, and that within those sections they have much higher rates of work participation than do women in the economy at large. This point can be demonstrated by looking at the unusual case of Kuwait. In 1961, Kuwait had a crude female participation rate of 0.4 per cent, which was strongly correlated with female seclusion and early marriage. By 1970, the participation rate of women had risen to 5.2 per cent, and behind this change was a massive increase in the education of women. The most striking result of this massive programme of modernization and education for women was the entry of women into government service, as civil servants, welfare workers and teachers (Nath, 1978: 175). The first women to move into these areas of employment were the daughters of rich merchant families in Kuwait. These families had considerable social status and political power, and the education of daughters was regarded as an index of modernization and wealth (Nath, 1978: 181). The overall participation rate for women in the labour force in Kuwait is still extremely small, but the curious selectivity of the increase in women's participation rates becomes clear on further examination of the figures. In 1970, the work participation rate for women university graduates in Kuwait was 99 per cent, with the Kuwaiti government as the sole employer. This high participation rate is remarkable by any standards, but it is particularly interesting when compared with the very low work participation rate for all Kuwaiti women in the working group 15–55 years, which was 2.3 per cent in 1965 and 5.2 per cent in 1970 (Nath, 1978: 180). The evidence from Kuwait shows that women's access to education is clearly correlated with class, and that increases in women's labour-force participation rates may mask particular concentrations of women workers in particular sectors of the economy. Education is free in Kuwait, and since 1966 it has been compulsory for the age group 6–14 years, but this has made only a small difference to the overall female participation rate in the workforce (Nath, 1978: 179). Kuwait is, of course, a very special case, but the picture which emerges is one which can be found, albeit in less striking forms, in many other countries (Al-Sanabary, 1985; Robertson, 1986).

The question of education and women's employment is further complicated by the relationship of both these factors to the demographic structure of the population and to age at marriage. The study of demography and its interrelations with marital strategies is a specialist area, which cannot be reviewed here. However, fertility levels are linked to a number of other indicators which have a direct bearing on any attempt to assess women's overall status and position in society: the female literacy rate, the sex differential in literacy rates, the female participation rate in the labour force, age at marriage and the incidence of marriage. All these factors may be used as indicators of women's status because they are directly linked to a woman's ability to choose for herself with regard to when she marries, whom she marries and how many times she marries, as well as her rights concerning access to education, economic autonomy through work, and participation in political and public life. An evaluation of these indicators and of what they actually mean for women in any particular context is a difficult task, not least because the question of women's status is itself so complex and shifting, as we saw in chapter 2. The material conditions of women's lives, the social, economic and political circumstances within which they live, interact with cultural stereotypes about the qualities, potentials and appropriate behaviour of women in ways which are not always easy to assess when we come to consider how to define women's status in any given society.

For example, one of the key values in Muslim society is that of honour, and family honour depends most critically on the modest, chaste and discreet sexual conduct of daughters, sisters and wives. Honour is a basic social principle, and a family's reputation and status in the community depend upon its vigilant maintenance. The principle of honour structures gender and kinship relationships, and it is the guiding principle behind the behavioural restrictions on Muslim women. The importance of honour as a key cultural principle explains why males within the family accept full responsibility for their kinswomen, both morally and economically. The economic and the moral, the material and the cultural, are here combined. Control of women in the kin group is vested exclusively in the hands of male members of the group, and, in exerting this control, men receive religious, judicial and social support. Women are the guardians of male honour and because of this they themselves need to be guarded. This applies to all women, but it applies most strongly to young unmarried women who are most likely to threaten the purity of family honour (Youssef, 1978: 76–8; Azzam et al., 1985: 6–7).

The concern with honour and sexual behaviour favours early marriage, and it also favours female seclusion after the age of puberty. Under these circumstances, it is not surprising that few girls continue at school after the age of 15 years, and that the numbers of young single women employed outside the home in Muslim countries are very small. Among those who are employed, a large proportion are from the most highly educated section of the population. According to Youssef, 42 per cent of all single women employed in Egypt and 35 per cent of all those employed in Syria are professionals or white-collar workers (Youssef, 1978: 78). On average, 45 per cent of all Muslim girls aged 15–19 years are already married, and in Libya and Pakistan three out of every four girls in this age group are married (Youssef, 1978: 80). The very early age of marriage is only one factor accounting for the very high fertility rates in Muslim countries.

In spite of the very low participation rates for single women in Muslim countries, the participation rates for this category are still higher than those for married women. This is because very few married women are permitted, or encouraged, to work, with the possible exception of those in the highest socio-economic groups. Youssef notes, in a sample based on Egypt, Turkey and Syria, that the work participation rate for divorced/separated women is eight times higher than that for married women, and the rate for single women is six times higher. This relationship between marital status and employment is not, of course, peculiar to Muslim countries. Youssef also records data from a sample based on Chile, Costa Rica, Ecuador and Peru, which show that on average in these countries the work participation rate for divorced/separated women is five times higher than that for married women, and the rate for single women is four times higher (Youssef, 1976: 63). Overall, these two sets of data suggest that women tend to drop out of the labour force on marriage, but if they find themselves divorced or separated they may enter it again, presumably because of economic necessity (Azzam et al., 1985: 7). The differences in participation rates between single and married women suggest that age at marriage does affect women's employment rates because early marriage reduces both the length of time women remain single and the actual number of single women in the population. This is borne out by looking at the contrary case of Latin America, where late marriage and non-marriage are correlated with relatively high female participation rates in non-agricultural employment. According to Youssef, the regional average shows 17 per cent of all adult women between the ages of 30 and 64 years as single, with an average female participation rate in non-agricultural labour of 20 per cent (Youssef, 1976: 19–20).

The relationship between women's employment and marital status is, of course, strongly affected by socio-economic class. For many poorer women there is no possibility of withdrawing from the labour force on marriage. Many married women are, in any event, the sole wage earner in their household. The birth of children can place family resources under further pressure, and, far from being an incentive for women to stay at home, it becomes an imperative which keeps them in employment. Under such circumstances, the cost of childcare can be a heavy burden, as can the task of finding suitable childcare arrangements, if there are no family members who can be relied on to help. Even when family help is forthcoming, it can still be inconsistent and unreliable, especially if the childminders are very old or very young, and this adds considerably to the strain of working full-time. The option of returning to work after the children have reached school age is not always an easy one to exercise, and it is often the most highly educated women – professional and white-collar workers – who find it easiest to do this. Of course, educational achievements of this kind are themselves linked to social class.

The determinants of women's participation rates in non-agricultural employment are extremely complex, and very varied in their effects. What is clear is that cultural stereotypes about gender, and about the appropriate behaviour of women, interact with family and kinship structures in ways which influence the ultimate effects of factors such as level of economic development, the structure of the economy and educational opportunity. The effects of gender ideologies, and of their material consequences, are very difficult to assess. One interesting point is that, whatever the ideologies about gender and work, women are in a unique position because of the way in which childbearing and sometimes motherhood too are associated with women's roles in society, and with social status and self-esteem. While marriage and parenthood are important indicators of male social worth and self-esteem in many societies, such activities are never proffered as an alternative career as they may be for women. As Ursula Sharma points out, men's work is only ever evaluated in terms of comparisons with other waged occupations; women's work, on the other hand, is evaluated and approved with reference to motherhood and domestic work (Sharma, 1986: 128–9). Earning money does not seem to be perceived as an essential part of the female role. Different societies, or different sectors of society, may approve of and encourage women's employment, they may acknowledge its necessity both economically and psychologically, but they never seem to recognize it as an intrinsic part of the feminine role, in the way that many societies do seem to see male employment as part of the masculine role. As Ursula Sharma says, talking of her work in India:

> In this respect the structure of gender ideologies in South Asia and in most western industrial societies are basically similar. Where they differ is in respect of the kind of criteria which they allow for evaluating the legitimacy of particular female occupations (compatibility with conceptions about the psychological needs of young children in the west, ideas about purdah, family honour, or pollution in South Asia). (Sharma, 1986: 129)

The effects of wage labour on women's lives

Having considered some of the determinants of women's entry into non-agricultural employment, the question which remains is what difference does this kind of employment make to women themselves? How do they perceive the advantages and disadvantages? Does working outside the home improve women's position within the home? Once again, these are questions which always have to be answered in historically and culturally specific terms: there can be no easy generalizations. Even within a single society, women's perceptions of and responses to changing work patterns are cross-cut by the experiences of race and class.

Janet Salaff's study *Working Daughters of Hong Kong* examines the family backgrounds and experiences of women working in factories, in the service sector, in white-collar jobs and in the professions. What emerges from her work is that in the low-wage economy of Hong Kong each family depends on the wages of several family members in order to survive, and daughters' wages are an increasingly crucial part of family income. As Salaff points out: 'No individual proletarian wage earner can bring home enough to fill the family rice bowls' (Salaff, 1981: 258). However, in the rapidly modernizing economy of contemporary Hong Kong, the family remains a key social institution. Economic co-operation and the pooling of the wages of family members are seen as part of an essential strategy to sustain the family, and to advance its social status and prestige. Daughters may be important wage earners, but their position and status within the family is very different from that of sons. Sons have a special place in the family because of the intense religious and cultural emphasis on the continuity of the patrilineage and the importance of ancestral tradition, and, as a result, sons rather than daughters tend to be the main recipients of family benefits. Daughters, for their part, are socialized into contributing unstintingly to their natal families before marriage, and thereafter to their husbands' families.

Salaff found that class and overall family circumstances determined the lifestyles of daughters, and the age at which they began employment. All the respondents in Salaff's sample completed primary school, but working-class women entered the labour force between the ages of 12 and 14, whereas upper-working and lower-middle-class women tended to matriculate in lower secondary school, and to start employment at about 16 years (Salaff, 1981: 259–60). Salaff emphasizes that, because the Hong Kong low-wage economy does not enable individuals to support their families unaided, most households, particularly the poorer ones, are constantly trying to increase the ratio of wage earners to dependants. The result is that during early stages in the life-cycle of the household, when there are young children and few wage earners, family resources cannot stretch to schooling for the eldest children. Women who are the eldest daughters of working-class families are sent to work as soon as they reach puberty, and all their earnings are remitted to the family fund. Often the daughter's earnings will be directly subsidizing the school fees of her younger brothers. Middle-income families, where the father earns a higher wage, have slightly larger financial resources, and this may mean that all the daughters, even the eldest, could have the chance of receiving secondary education. Household fortunes vary with the life-cycle of its members, and the most affluent period is when all the children have joined the labour force, followed by a decline in earnings when the older children marry and form families of their own. Salaff's data show clearly that position in the sibling order is a crucial determinant of educational and employment opportunities. The eldest daughters, who mature when the family resources are at a minimum, must enter waged employment immediately in many households, whereas their younger siblings may be able to remain in education longer and defer entry into the labour force, thus improving their job chances (Salaff, 1981: 261–6). Social class determines in what way and how much daughters' wages need to be used, but Salaff calculates that, on average, three-quarters of working women's incomes go to their families.

The advantages of working daughters to the family are quite clear, but the question is: what advantages do these women perceive for themselves? One possible advantage is a greater degree of self-determination. Salaff notes that most marriages are no longer arranged and that women tend to meet their potential spouses through peer-group activities. But parental control over marriage is still strong, and 15 out of the 28 women interviewed by Salaff said that they deferred marriage at their parents' request because the family was still in need of their income. Deferral of this kind did, however, appear to benefit the women themselves, who saved part of their earnings to buy household goods for their marital homes and to make contributions to their dowries (Salaff, 1981: 268).

Working daughters keep a small and regular amount for themselves from their earnings, which is agreed on by the family. Women use this money for personal effects and leisure activities, and in this sense wage labour makes leisure-time activities with peers financially possible. In recognition of the money they put into the family, working daughters are usually exempt from household tasks such as cooking, childcare and laundry (Salaff, 1981: 269). Working daughters are also given more say in family affairs, particularly as they relate to the activities of younger siblings, although their advice is usually ignored if it is in direct conflict with the parents' wishes. Salaff concludes that employment has had a favourable effect on the lives and experiences of working daughters: they have more control over marriage, over leisure activities, and over the use of their own money, and they have increased their contribution to family decision-making (Salaff, 1981: 270–1). However, Salaff also points out that, while women have experienced measurable improvements in lifestyle and opportunities, they have made little progress towards equality with men.

> In fact, the gap between men and women in education, employment, and earnings remains nearly as wide today as in the past. Hence, although the women's subjective feelings of progress are understandable, qualitative amelioration of their standing with respect to men and to their position in the family is as yet unrealized. (Salaff, 1981: 13)

The relationship between employment and increased social and economic autonomy for women is a vexed one. It is clear, however, that many women themselves feel there is a connection. Quite a number of studies from around the world show that married women often see working outside the home as a strategy to gain more economic and social independence from men. Barbara Ibrahim records the words of a Cairo factory woman: 'Work strengthens a woman's position. The woman who works doesn't have to beg her husband for every piaster she needs. She can command respect in her home and can raise her voice in any decision' (Ibrahim, 1985: 296).

Carmel Dinan has argued that in Ghana women with white-collar and professional jobs enjoy considerable freedom. They frequently choose to remain single, but they maintain an active social life, often with many men friends. These women assert an economic and social autonomy which is unusual in traditional Ghanaian society, and this is demonstrated by the fact that they are willing to restrict their relationships with kin in order to avoid the social and economic obligations which kinship entails (Dinan, 1977). This emphasizes how different these women are from many others who are dependent on marriage and kinship for access to essential resources. Christine Obbo, in her study of rural–urban migrants in Kampala, Uganda, found that men's attitudes to women's employment were contradictory. On the one hand, urban men were keen to have a partner who was a financial asset rather than a liability, and, on the other hand, they feared that women's economic autonomy would lead to a loss of male control over women (Obbo, 1980: 51).

Women and wage labour: some theoretical considerations

Urban anthropology and the study of workers in urban and industrial settings are growth areas within the discipline. Studies of this kind have always been part of anthropology, but they have grown substantially in number in the last fifteen years.[17] Feminist anthropologists have only recently begun to turn their attention to studying women's waged employment in an urban context, and to examining the relationship between productive and reproductive labour under industrial capitalism. Much of the feminist-Marxist anthropology of the last decade or so has been concerned with pre-capitalist social formations, and with the processes of transformation and articulation which characterize the relationship between rural production systems and emerging capitalism (see the opening section of this chapter). The study of women's waged employment under capitalism has been developed most systematically in sociology, and latterly in history and economics. The result of this is that feminist anthropology has had little opportunity as yet to consider how the discipline might or might not be able to contribute to the various debates about the relationship between the sexual division of labour and capitalist relations of production. Social anthropology cannot claim to have any startling new insights to offer with regard to these issues, and the theoretical sophistication of the feminist critiques already advanced make it unlikely that anthropology would be able to proffer any new theoretical models. However, this does not mean that anthropology does not have a distinctive contribution to make.

Much of feminist-Marxist analysis in the social sciences has focused on the necessity for capitalism of women's domestic labour, and on women's role as a 'reserve army' of workers who get sucked into the labour force during periods of expansion or crisis, and spewed out again when circumstances change. These two points are necessarily linked because the division of labour in the home is connected to the division of labour at work and to the conditions under which women enter the labour market. Household organization and gender ideologies play an important role in limiting women's participation in wage labour. The result is a process of mutual determination, in which education, legal provision for women and economic circumstances are also crucial factors. The idea that women workers form part of a reserve army of labour is linked to the fact that women are paid lower wages than men. The argument is that married women are dependent on their husbands, and that, should it be necessary to lay these women off in times of unemployment, employers can comfortably assume that they will be supported by their husbands' wages. This allows capitalist employers to exploit the assumption that the waged work of their married female employees is secondary to their work as wives and mothers; with the result that women can be paid wages so low that they do not even cover the costs of reproducing them as workers (Beechey, 1978: 185–91).

The 'women as a reserve army of labour' theory has been extensively criticized from a number of points of view (Milkman, 1976; Barrett, 1980: 158–72). However, the anthropological contribution to this question merely emphasizes, as many have already done, that, in so far as this view of women's labour-force participation is correct, it is only correct for particular historical moments, under specific social and economic circumstances. The comparative picture which emerges from studies of women's waged employment around the world is one of variation and complexity; there is no single explanation which can be said to characterize the relationship between women's work in the labour force and the sexual division of labour in the home. The case of the working daughters of Hong Kong is an example where capitalism draws on the labour of young, single women who usually find that their substantial contribution to household income releases them from many of the domestic responsibilities in the home. The situation of these young women cannot be explained merely with reference to the advantages of a cheap labour force, dependent on the wages of men for support during periods of unemployment. The majority of these young women, especially those in the industrial and service sectors, are not supported by a man's wage. Indeed, most of them are key wage earners within the household, with other members of the household dependent upon their wages. Feminists have already confronted this point, and they have stressed that the fact of women being key wage earners, or indeed the sole wage earner, within a household is not the issue, because it is the ideology of women as dependants which helps to keep their wages lower than those of men (Beechey, 1978: 186).

This argument has a considerable amount of force, but it does suggest that, since women are all perceived as dependants, all women will be cheap. In this regard, then, one woman is as good as another, so how do we explain why it is young, single women who make up the workforce, rather than some other group of women? There are certainly many factors related to demand in the workforce which could be discussed: employer preference, physical disabilities caused by the job which increase with age – such as deteriorating eyesight – the greater mobility of young women, their lack of childcare responsibilities, and so on. However, there are also determining factors on the supply side of the equation, and the most important of these are related to the structure and ideology of the family. Feminist scholars are undoubtedly correct when they say, as Beechey and others do, that household organization and gender ideologies play a crucial role in determining women's entry into the labour market. They are also correct when they insist that, in order to understand the relationship between the sexual division of labour and the capitalist relations of production, it is necessary to examine the ways in which pre-capitalist gender relations have been incorporated into and consolidated by the structure of productive relations under capitalism. Anthropology's contribution to this debate is to be able to provide comparative material which demonstrates, in particular historical circumstances, what the links are between gendered relations in the household and those in the workplace. Janet Salaff's study of the working daughters of Hong Kong shows that without the particular nature of the Hong Kong family, with its emphasis on continuity and corporateness, its demographic size, the privileging of sons over daughters, the strong respect for parents, and the relative freedom permitted to young, unmarried women, the industrial workforce would not be what it is and the structure of women's employment might well be of a very different kind. This is not to suggest that there are not strong economic pressures acting on these families, as there are in many other areas of South-East Asia, where daughters go out to work in order to contribute to family income. But such pressures do not explain why it should be daughters who go rather than sons, nor do they explain why more young women do not seek to move out of the 'family' earlier in order to be able to keep more of their wages for themselves or in order to be able to contribute wages to their own conjugal household while they are still young enough to work. To answer these questions it is necessary to know something about the nature of kinship and gender relations, and about the nature of gender ideologies. Anthropology is particularly well suited to analysing kinship and gender relations in comparative perspective, and there is an increasing body of available data which demonstrates the specific links between the sexual division of labour and capitalist relations of production in a wide variety of different circumstances.

A review of all the material which has been presented in this chapter on women's work, including women's agricultural and informal-sector employment, demonstrates the importance of analysing productive relations with reference to the specific nature of kinship and gender relations. For example, Maria Mies's study of the lacemakers of Narsapur shows how a particular set of gendered relations within a specific household structure have become incorporated into the capitalist relations of production. Not only is this a perfect example of an instance where the separation of the home and the workplace are not coterminous with capitalism, but it once again emphasizes that the nature of women's entry into the workforce can only be understood with reference to the specific nature of gender relations and the structure of the household – a broad understanding of the 'needs of capital', or of the macro-economic processes at work, is not enough. From the data available it seems probable that many of the observable variations in the structure and nature of women's employment in developing countries in the contemporary world are not particularly different from the variations which are known to have existed historically. In other words, women in sweatshops, women working from home, multi-wage-earning households and young women working are all features of employment which are known to have existed in the early stages of industrial capitalism in developed countries (Tilly, 1981; Tilly and Scott, 1978). However, the fact that all these different forms of employment exist simultaneously in the contemporary world – as the concrete manifestation of the uneven processes of capitalist transformation as they impinge on specific kinship and gender systems – produces an unparalleled opportunity for feminist scholars from a variety of disciplines to study the mutually determining nature of productive and reproductive relations. It also provides an opportunity for feminist scholars to release themselves from the teleology of the historical trajectory which capitalism and its intersection with kinship/gender relations have followed in western Europe.

The intense theoretical focus of much feminist and Marxist writing on the 'needs of capital', on the question whether a specific 'family' formation is the result of or is necessary for capitalism, on the argument about whether the sexual division of labour is determined by the capitalist division of labour itself, has been somewhat misleading. A number of writers have criticized the functionalism of this approach, and have pointed out that it is reductionist continually to pose questions about the changing sexual division of labour and changing household forms merely in terms of the function of these changes for capital (Bozzoli, 1983). While it is undoubtedly true that capitalism has transformed the processes of production, reproduction and consumption in societies, it has not done so simply in accordance with the needs of capital. These processes of transformation have been equally determined by the existing forms of production, reproduction and consumption; in other words, by the existing forms of kinship and gender relations. To see all change as being dictated by the nature of the capitalist relations of production is incorrect. The significance of this point will become clearer in the following section, which deals with the changing nature of 'family' forms.

The changing nature of the family

The study of the changing nature of kinship and family relations is one of the key areas of 'traditional' social anthropology. The complexities of this field of enquiry, and the brilliance of much of the scholarship associated with it, means that making even the most cautious statement is full of pitfalls. In the light of the previous discussion about modernization, industrialization and capitalist relations of production, one of the most pressing questions concerns the changes which are taking place in 'family' and household forms around the world, and whether the 'nuclear' family, with a joint congual fund and neolocal residence, is emerging as the dominant form or not.

The rise of the 'nuclear' family

Anthropological studies from around the world document changes in the structure and nature of the family. One of the common themes identified in such studies is the declining importance of the corporate lineage and the increasing significance of the elementary or 'nuclear' family. Recent studies on West Africa, for example, document change of this kind, and refer to increasing personal choice in spouse selection, a growing tendency for couples to reside in their own homes rather than with parents or kin, and an increasing emphasis on love and companionship between spouses as a basic criterion for marriage (Oppong, 1981; Harrell-Bond, 1975; Little and Price, 1973; Oppong, 1983). Soraya Altorki's study of elite marriage in Saudi Arabia also documents changes in marriage practices, recording an increase in physically separate entrances and exits in the household or separate residences altogether for married children, growing demands to see prospective spouses prior to marriage, and a reduction in contacts with kin (Altorki, 1986). She notes that increasing neolocal residence – where married couples live in their own homes – corresponds with a decline in the segregation of women, so that husbands and wives spend more time together and engage in more joint decisions (Altorki, 1986: 34–5). West Africa and Saudi Arabia are not unique, for studies from many areas of the world have produced similar conclusions. Other notable changes in marriage practices, which have received considerable attention in anthropology and which appear to be linked to processes of 'modernization', are a decrease in polygyny and an increase in divorce rates. It should be borne in mind, however, that data concerning these last two points have rarely been adequately collected over long periods of time, and many studies record such increases and decreases as they appear at particular moments in time, and as they are perceived by particular groups of individuals. The position is further complicated by the fact that the interrelation between divorce and number of marriage partners is extremely complex, with high rates of divorce and remarriage producing a phenomenon known as serial monogamy (marrying one person after another), which obviously affects any straightforward statement about polygyny giving way to monogamous marriage. None the less, there is certainly a considerable amount of evidence which supports the argument that family forms are changing, but the question remains as to how we make sense of the changes we observe. A brief look at the history of the family in Europe is useful in this regard, provided we do not assume that contemporary developments in very different areas of the world will necessarily follow the same pattern. The most illuminating points which arise from a consideration of the European material concern the critical role of class in any analysis of changing 'family' forms, and the absolute necessity of maintaining a clear distinction between the 'ideology' of the family and the structure and organization of the household.

The historical study of the changing 'family' in Europe and America has produced lively debate. Peter Laslett has argued that industrialization did not produce the 'nuclear' family structure, and he supports this with evidence which demonstrates that the 'nuclear' family existed among the rural working population long before the advent of industrialization and the rise of an urban proletariat (Laslett, 1972). What is equally important is that historical studies have produced evidence which illustrates the enormous variability in 'family'/household structure and form according to class situation (Poster, 1978), and various authors have argued that property relations and inheritance patterns play an important part in influencing the differing 'family'/household structures characteristic of different classes (Goody, 1972; Creighton, 1980). It is clear from a variety of studies that in Europe and America the idea of the 'nuclear' family supported by a male wage earner arose as part of nineteenth-century middle-class ideology (Hall, 1979; Poster, 1978). During the eighteenth and nineteenth centuries, there was a rapid development of capitalism coupled with a growth in urbanism. These factors, taken together with the spread of wage labour, resulted in the development of a rural and urban proletariat and an urban bourgeoisie. In the latter half of the nineteenth century, workers' unions gave a great deal of emphasis to the establishment of a 'family wage' – whereby a single man was paid enough to support himself and his wife and children through his work alone. The demand for a 'family wage' became one of the ideals of the organized trade-union movement, and it happened to meet with the 'approval' of the new middle classes who were extolling the virtues of a 'family' where women and children were the dependants of the father/husband. This middle-class view of 'family' life was supported by the economic and political power of the middle class, whose beliefs and values were strongly reflected in legislation of the period. Many writers have pointed out that this middle-class 'familial' ideology had much deeper historical origins, but it was the convergence of social, economic and political power which enabled the middle class to impose their values and beliefs upon the rest of society. It is important not to imagine this 'imposition' as a totally one-sided process, because the organized working class were able to use this emerging familial ideology to their own ends in their struggle to secure a 'family wage'. The end result of this process, however, was that a particular idea of the 'family' became established as both desirable and 'natural'.

Whatever the power of middle-class beliefs and values, the situation for the majority of the population was very different. The poor, the divorced, the widowed and the unmarried could not support their households on the wage of a single individual, while the women and children remained at home as dependants. For these families it was still necessary for as many household members to work as possible. Reflecting on the circumstances of the majority – the middle class and the organized working class were numerically small – it is clear why it is necessary to maintain a distinction between 'family' ideology and the actual structure and economic circumstances of the household. The middle class succeeded in establishing a definition of 'natural' family life as based on a male breadwinner with dependent wife and children, and they succeeded in defining the family as a place of private, personal relations distinct from the public arena of commercial life. But, while this ideology was powerful and desirable, there was – and still is – an enormous gap between the pervasiveness and power of the ideology, and the actual household structure and economic circum-stances of the majority of the population.[18] The questions of class difference, and of the relationship between family ideologies and the social and economic realities of household organization, are crucial in any attempt to analyse changes in 'family'/household structures.

Marriage, ideology and socio-economic change in colonial Nigeria

One of the few historical studies of non-Western society to illustrate the intersections of class, ideology and socio-economic circumstances in the context of changing marriage practices and 'family' forms is Kristin Mann's study of an educated African elite in colonial Lagos, Nigeria. Her book describes the changes in marriage, in 'family' ideology and in 'family'/household structures as a result of the development of the colonial state, the incorporation of West Africa into the world economy, and the spread of Christianity and Western education. She makes it clear that these developments altered economic opportunities, and transformed processes of capital accumulation, as well as structures of economic and political power (Mann, 1985: 9). In nineteenth-century Lagos, Europeans, and especially European missionaries, introduced middle-class Victorian values and ideas concerning what they thought were proper marital and kinship relations. Polygyny offended these white Victorians, and they therefore laid considerable emphasis on the fact that monogamy was 'the most fundamental characteristic of Christian marriage' (Mann, 1985: 44). The 1884 Marriage Ordinance prohibited polygyny among Christians, and gave Christian wives a legal right to monogamy. Europeans taught that Christian marriage should be based on love and companionship, and should not be premised on the joining of two lineages. In addition, they were responsible for transmitting middle-class Victorian values about the proper roles of men and women within marriage. Husbands were portrayed as breadwinners and providers, while women were seen as mothers whose proper place was in the 'home'. The education available to the children of elite African families naturally reinforced these stereotypes (Mann, 1985: 44–5).

Victorian 'familial' ideology had very concrete material consequences for the educated elite in Lagos. First, Christian wives usually moved to a new conjugal home after the wedding, rather than going to live with the husband's kin. Secondly, Christian marriage radically altered traditional Yoruba inheritance practices. It gave spouses rights to each other's estates, it made Christian wives and their children sole heirs to a man's property, and through the Marriage Ordinance it disinherited a man's siblings and any children by customary wives or concubines (Mann, 1985: 51). Thirdly, Christian marriage served as a way of defining the emerging educated elite, and it helped to set them off from the rest of the population. It concentrated economic resources within the elite group, and it created a network of kinship and affinal ties (those based on marriage) which worked to defend and promote the economic and political interests of the group (Mann, 1985: 53). For men, Christian marriage had advantages in the economic circumstances of the period. While polygynous marriage was advantageous in an agrarian context, where the labour of wives and children could be used to create wealth and prestige, the urban situation was rather different. Among the Lagos elite, wealth was bound up in private land, houses and luxury goods. Income was derived from trade, rents and employment in the professions and the colonial service. Educated wives and children did not contribute to the family income, but rather were a drain on it. Under these circumstances, limiting the number of wives and children – through monogamous Christian marriage – was a 'sound economic strategy' (Mann, 1985: 58).

In spite of the benefits of Christian marriage, there were also disadvantages for men. First, a man had to support his wife and children, and wives who did not retain some measure of financial autonomy could not contribute to household expenses. Secondly, the Christian laws of succession gave a wife rights to her husband's property. Quite apart from the disadvantages of Christian marriage, Yoruba marriage had some attractions for elite males. Some chose Yoruba marriage because they preferred the customary conjugal relationship and roles, but, more importantly, the status of customary unions was often ambiguous, and it was possible to manipulate and redefine conjugal relationships and roles, as well as the legal rights and duties within such unions, in a way which was not possible within Christian marriage (Mann, 1985: 60–1). As a result of the different advantages and disadvantages of Yoruba and Christian marriage, many men chose both: 'dual marriage'. Dual unions served as a means of 'maximizing resources and opportunities', and, as long as men left the status of their customary unions ill defined, it was possible to pursue a dual strategy without contravening the letter of the Marriage Ordinance (Mann, 1985: 62). Mann makes it clear that men married in different ways to meet different needs, and in order to pursue different strategies.

After the 1890s, conditions in Lagos altered and the appeal of Yoruba marriage increased for educated elite males. A severe trade depression, coupled with increasing racial discrimination in employment, threatened the position of the educated elite. Falling profits and the insecurities of professional employment led some men to postpone Christian marriage and to enter customary unions. These difficulties increased men's awareness of the financial disadvantages of Christian marriage compared to the advantages of Yoruba marriage (Mann, 1985: 70–1). There were also other changes at the time which had profound effects on marriage. In the mid-1890s, there grew up among the elite a cultural nationalist movement, which was very critical of Western marriage and which argued strongly that Yoruba marriage was not in the least inferior to Christian marriage. Indeed, Yoruba marriage was seen as being 'well suited' to the cultural environment of West Africa. During the years 1888 and 1891, the first African churches were founded. These churches provided a religious defence of Yoruba marriage, and for the first time elite males could openly practise Yoruba marriage and remain in good standing with the Christian church (Mann, 1985: 71–4).

The varying responses of elite males to Christian marriage are particularly interesting when compared to the responses of elite women. Mann argues that elite women responded to Christian marriage less ambiguously than elite men, and, where they could, such women insisted on Christian marriage. Elite women, like elite men, were socialized through education, family and church life into Western religious and cultural values, but the relationships of women and of men to these value systems were not the same. Women were seen as 'guardians of moral virtue', and their conformity to Christian values and Victorian ideals was intricately bound up with their responsibility for developing and maintaining the cultural identity and superiority of the elite. Men might 'backslide' into Yoruba marriage, but, when an elite woman failed to live up to Christian practice and ideals, it not only undermined her reputation but threatened the status of the elite as a whole (Mann, 1985: 77–9).

The marriage choices of elite women, like those of elite men, were linked to economic circumstances. Elite men could maximize their social and economic resources and opportunities by engaging in 'dual' marriage, but elite women were denied such a strategy, by both Yoruba and Christian custom. Single women were permitted to make only a single match, so it is hardly surprising that they wanted this to be of a kind which would give them the greatest prestige and legal security. When elite women withdrew from the workplace, they relinquished their economic autonomy, and became dependent upon their husbands. Education for elite women did not train them for the professions, trade was regarded as unsuitable, and they were debarred from all the posts in the colonial service except those specifically designated for women (Mann, 1985: 81). Teaching and sewing, which were regarded as suitable occupations, were very badly paid. Elite women had none of the opportunities, either social or economic, which elite men used to gain wealth and influence. For an elite woman to maintain her status and a level of economic security, it was necessary to marry an elite man who would support her and her children adequately. As Mann says, 'Once educated women's social and economic status depended upon their husbands, they had little alternative but to practise Christian marriage' (Mann, 1985: 82). Many elite women and their parents thought that the legal rights enshrined in Christian marriage would help improve the status of wives. However, many found that Christian marriage did not live up to expectations and provided few benefits. African commentators noted this disillusionment, and from the 1890s elite men and women became increasingly concerned about the position of Christian wives. Their chief anxieties were the economic vulnerability of such women, and the 'disappointment and bitterness' many women clearly experienced when the realities of Christian marriage failed to live up to their expectations. From around 1900, some contemporaries began to advocate greater economic independence for elite women, and some proposed industrial and technical training for women. According to Mann, the economic activities of elite women in the early twentieth century demonstrate changing attitudes towards marriage and women's work. Several elite women were engaged in retailing, farming, service industries and the professions. During the same period a few elite women actually began publically to defend Yoruba marriage (Mann, 1985: 82–90).

One of the conclusions of this study is that elite women and men in colonial Lagos responded differently to Christian marriage because their social and economic circumstances were different. These differing responses and expectations frequently led to conflict between spouses, and to attempts on both sides to redefine conjugal roles and responsibilities. Mann's account of marriage and social change in colonial Nigeria provides us with a very clear and dramatic example of the kinds of ideological, political, social and economic pressures which need to be taken into account in any analysis of changing marital strategies and 'family' structures. Many of the processes she describes can be observed in the contemporary African context, as well as in other parts of the world. Her study demonstrates that we cannot see marital change as part of a unidirectional progression, where corporate lineages give way to 'nuclear' families, and polygyny is replaced by monogamy. When political and economic circumstances changed for the Lagos elite from the 1890s onwards, the values and benefits of Christian marriage were reconsidered. Yoruba marriage was reassessed by contemporary commentators, conjugal roles and responsibilities were again redefined, and polygynous marriage was once again used as mechanism for gaining a broader access to dwindling resources and opportunities. It is a mistake, however, to see changes in 'family' forms as arising solely from changes in economic and political circumstances. The early colonial period provided new opportunities for women and men to redefine and renegotiate aspects of their domestic lives, but this was not true for all sections of the community.

Christian marriage was part of a socio-economic and political strategy for the elite middle class, but those outside this class pursued very different strategies. There were also differences within the elite itself. Some individuals held strongly to Yoruba marriage throughout the period, and found it morally binding and socially compelling, while others continued to adhere to Christian values and Victorian ideology even under changing political and economic circumstances. The lack of any necessary linear progression, the critical role of class, and the importance of understanding people's varying responses to and support for particular ideological structures are all key points in any attempt to analyse changes in contemporary 'family' forms.

The variety of household structures and 'family' forms

Empirical studies from Africa, South America and South Asia support the argument that there is no necessary link between urbanization, modernization and the rise of a 'nuclear' family. The very large increase in female-headed households in Africa and South America, the impact of migration and economic recession, and the reported rise in the number of women choosing not to marry at all, are all factors which undermine any straightforward theory about the increasing 'nuclearization' of family forms.

In her discussion of women in the Caribbean, Pat Ellis makes it clear that family forms in the region are very diverse. 'Nuclear' families, matrifocal families, extended families, single-parent families and female-headed households all exist (Ellis, 1986b: 7). The variety Ellis describes is not, however, the prelude to an era when 'nuclear' families will predominate. She notes that young middle-class women are questioning the institution of marriage, and experimenting with alternative sorts of relationships with men. Many women, as in other parts of the world, are rejecting marriage (Ellis, 1986b: 7; and see this chapter above). This plurality of family forms is not just characteristic of less-developed countries, but is also a notable feature of the urban societies of Europe and North America.

Joanna Liddle and Rama Joshi review the literature on the family and social change in India, and they note that the 'nuclear' family form is one among a variety of family structures. However, they dispute the idea that professional women tend to form 'nuclear' families because they are imitating a Western model, and they suggest instead that the 'nuclear' family form is attractive to such women because it allows them to escape from the demands of kin, and most particularly from the authority of their mothers-in-law. Traditionally, young wives moved into their husband's home and came immediately under the control of the mother-in-law, who ran the household. At the present time, many younger women are only too glad to escape the constraints and conflicts of this relationship (Liddle and Joshi, 1986: 142–5). A desire to escape from the constraints of kinship is a theme which arises in many studies of changing family forms around the world. Obligations to kin are often a source of serious conflict between spouses. However, Liddle and Joshi also note that, in spite of these tensions, the extended or joint family is not necessarily disappearing in urban areas, but is instead adapting to changing circumstances (Vatuk, 1972: 57). The main reasons for this appear to be economic. An increase in the employment of middle-class women has led to problems concerning household management and childcare. These problems are solved by living in a joint household, where parents or in-laws can help with domestic tasks, but where the traditional authority of the mother-in-law has been broken down. In some cases, young married couples invite their in-laws or parents to come and live with them, rather than the young wife going to reside in her parents-in-law's home – an arrangement which looks like the traditional joint family on the surface, but which is actually slightly different (Liddle and Joshi, 1986: 145–6; Ross, 1961: 172).

It would appear that in an urban context changing economic circumstances can either encourage the 'nuclearization' of family forms in order to protect 'family' resources from the depredation of kin, or promote a very different 'family' structure which depends for its survival on utilizing kinship links as a resource in their own right. These apparently contradictory tendencies should not surprise us, because they are completely comprehensible if we stop trying to categorize family forms into particular types, and instead begin to analyse varying marital/family structures as different types of strategy, where individuals and households struggle to survive and to maximize their resources and opportunities under the circumstances in which they find themselves. These circumstances are not 'purely' economic in any straightforward sense of the term, because they are also social, political, religious and ideological. All of these factors act as relevant parameters which guide, constrain and enable decision-making, but decisions based on them do not necessarily have to be 'maximizing' ones. Individuals often have to act in the interests of others rather than themselves, and in the case of households it is often a matter of having to pursue strategies which first ensure the continuity of the unit upon which all depend for survival before the interests of specific individuals can be advanced. It is also important to remember that the distribution of resources within households is rarely egalitarian, and that some members have much more control than others over decisions concerning the allocation of resources. It should be clear from the arguments made in this chapter that such hierarchies are usually premised on gender and age. If we accept that 'nuclearization' is one strategy among several, then we must also acknowledge that it is not a strategy open to all. The poor, the single, the widowed and others cannot afford to abandon the 'web of kinship' which provides their safety-net. It is for this reason that the 'nuclear' family form is associated with emerging class interests, as well as with economic growth. The converse of this, as Mann makes clear in her study of colonial Lagos, is that in times of economic recession the advantages of 'nuclearization' become less apparent, and it may be abandoned or partially abandoned in favour of other strategies.

However, economic growth and the penetration of capitalism do not always give rise to 'nuclear' family forms. In many parts of rural sub-Saharan Africa successful entry into cash-cropping has been achieved by those individuals who have used kinship links to retain their rights over the labour of others. Among the cocoa farmers of West Africa, where men have had trouble for some time in getting their sons to work for them, access to labour and to other resources through the utilization of kinship links is still absolutely crucial to successful commercial enterprise (Berry, 1984). Data from around the world are very uneven, but what there are suggest that there is very little evidence, as in Africa, that the penetration of capitalism into rural areas is necessarily giving rise to the 'nuclear' family. This is not just because the processes of capitalization are uneven and incomplete, but because, given the nature of the pre-existing forms of production, reproduction and consumption, there is no necessary link between these processes and the rise of the 'nuclear' family.

'Nuclear' family forms certainly exist in many rural areas of the world, but it is important when analysing such households to be aware of the relationship between the ideology of family life and the actualities of household economics and organization. Martine Segalen's study of rural households in Brittany, France, discusses what appear to be independent, farming and non-farming units based on the 'nuclear' family. However, she argues that at the present time these 'nuclear' households are extremely dependent on kin for the organization of their tasks, probably more dependent than they were in the time of extended households (Segalen, 1984: 169). Fathers and sons, who apparently run separate farms, may 'share' expensive agricultural machinery, and co-operate over work tasks in a variety of ways. Even when the children are not farmers, they may continue to help their parents on the farm during peak periods of labour demand, and women who are married to non-farmers may continue to help their own parents with farming tasks. Under such circumstances, grandmothers become heavily involved in the care and socialization of young children (Segalen, 1984: 173–8). As Segalen makes clear in discussing the relationships between these apparently independent 'nuclear' households: 'A constant reciprocal flow of services, contacts, and psychological help takes place, resulting in deeply intertwined household organizations, despite their formal and material separation' (Segalen, 1984: 178). The most difficult thing to explain is not the co-operation between households, which clearly has economic, social and psychological benefits, but the fact that, despite these advantages, people continue to behave as though they wanted to live in separate 'nuclear' families, they build expensive new houses when they marry, and they keep up an ideology of separateness while in fact maintaining intense contact and co-operation. Segalen's study demonstrates quite clearly that the term 'nuclear' family may obscure more than it reveals; understanding what is happening to changing family forms and household structures cannot be achieved through reference to static typologies (Wilk, 1984). Even if we can identify 'nuclear' family forms around the world, it is worth remembering that this label is likely to obscure more about their differences than it reveals about their similarities.

The importance of recognizing the distinction between the 'ideal' or 'believed' way of organizing kinship/household relations and the actualities of the way in which those relationships are organized in practice has long been a central feature of anthropological analysis. Anthropological writings of the 1940s, 1950s and 1960s emphasized changes in 'family'/household structures as a result of the colonial state, the rise of urbanism and the spread of Christianity and Western education. However, more recent work on the analysis of changing 'family'/household forms has broadened in approach to study the effects of contemporary processes of socio-economic differentiation, new ideologies and forms of state authority on the organization of domestic life and the nature of gender relations. In this chapter, I have concentrated on women's position within kinship/household structures and on the various feminist and anthropological debates concerning the sexual division of labour and the organization of gender relations within the family and the household. Feminists from a variety of disciplines have consistently and forcefully argued that the 'family' is the 'central site of women's oppression' in society. The sexual division of labour in the 'home' is related in complex and multifarious ways to the sexual division of labour in the workplace and in society at large. Women's subordinate position is the product both of their economic dependence on men within the 'family'/household and of their confinement to a domestic sphere by ideologies of mothering, caring and nurturing. The feminist anthropological position on these issues is not clear-cut, partly because the available data are of such extraordinary richness and complexity that they defy even the most serious attempt at synthesis, let alone generalization. However, it is clear that any straightforward explanation of women's subordination which does not take into account the enormous variation in women's circumstances and in gender and 'familial' ideologies would be not only reductionist but extremely ethnocentric. In the following chapter, I re-examine some of the issues raised here by looking at the role of the state in regulating 'family' life and gender relations, as well as by examining some of the ways in which women have responded to the imposition of state authority.

5

WOMEN AND THE STATE

The state is an important area of concern for both feminists and social anthropologists. Demands for the state provision of childcare, equal pay for equal work, equality of opportunity in education and employment, and free access to contraceptives and abortion are examples of the importance feminists attach to the state in the regulation of women's lives. All states have complex institutional structures, with specific economic and political histories. It would be quite misleading to make universal generalizations about the nature of states, just as it would be equally incorrect to see the state as a single, monolithic entity, capable of acting as an organic unit.

In spite of the variations in state forms, it is quite clear that state policies affect the social position of women, and that through economic, political and legal practices they determine how much control women have over their own lives. State policies also regulate sexuality and fertility, through such mechanisms as marriage laws, legal provisions governing rape, abortion, indecency and homosexuality, and programmes for population control. Western feminists have long argued that the state tends to promote a particular form of 'family'/household structure: the male wage earner, with dependent wife and children (Wilson, 1977; McIntosh, 1978; 1979). Writers have pointed to the ways in which state regulations governing wages, taxation and social security benefits combine to reproduce the segregated occupational structure of the labour force and the sexual division of labour within the family. These policies are not necessarily designed with the intention of oppressing or discriminating against women, but they are designed according to prevailing assumptions and ideologies about the role of women, the nature of the family and the proper relations between men and women. The end result is that state policies may be extremely contradictory. Regulations which are enforced with the aim of protecting mothers and children can end up discriminating against them if their lives do not conform to the assumed set of social practices and beliefs upon which state policies are based. The state then has a role not just in regulating people's lives but in defining gender ideologies, conceptions of 'femininity' and 'masculinity', determining ideas about what sorts of persons women and men should be. The assumptions about women and men which inform state policies are further reinforced by the choices forced upon individuals under the constraints imposed by the same policies. For example, those women who live with a husband or male sexual partner are assumed by the state to be dependent upon them; this means not only that many women will be dependent on male partners but that many will be forced into an independence (economic and social) which the state does not support or provide for (McIntosh, 1978: 281). However, it is also important to be clear that state institutions and policies and their relations to women cannot be analysed as if all women were affected by the state in the same way. Race, ethnicity, class, religion and sexual orientation all affect the ways in which women enter into relations with the state. But these different factors cannot be analysed as if they were merely 'additive'; their intersections will always be complex and historically specific, and will therefore require empirical analysis.

The feminist analysis of the state has developed through a variety of approaches. One early emphasis was on the welfare aspects of the state, and on the ways in which it provides for and controls women. A second approach was concerned with 'ideological state apparatuses', such as the media, schools, political parties, the church and the family, which work together to reinforce and reproduce dominant ideologies. This approach was inspired to a large extent by the work of Althusser (1971: 123–73), who suggests that under modern capitalism the dominant ideological state apparatus is the education system, which literally 'schools' children in the ruling ideology. A third approach, which has only recently developed, is concerned with state responses to women organizing – with the ways in which the state manages to disorganize, control and institutionalize women's activities, particularly women's popular organizations. It looks at the means through which women's interests are represented in state bureaucracies, often through nominated 'femocrats' whose job it is to speak officially on behalf of women. A fourth approach focuses on the unequal influence of women and men on state actions, and on their unequal access to state resources. It is the last two approaches which are of particular interest in this chapter because of the way in which they match recent developments in social anthropology. However, before we can proceed to a discussion of these developments, it is first necessary to examine some of the ways in which anthropology has traditionally approached the analysis of the state.

Anthropology and the state

For our purposes, the analysis of the state in anthropology can be broadly divided into four types of approach. The first of these is exemplified by British structural functionalism, and its attempts to categorize African political systems (Fortes and Evans-Pritchard, 1940; Middleton and Tait, 1958). The main purpose of this work was to establish how societies without state institutions maintained social order, and it laid considerable emphasis on the role of kinship. A second approach, developed in evolutionary anthropology, concerned itself with the origins of the indigenous or 'pristine' state. Early work concentrated on the identification of 'prime movers' to explain the origins of the state, such as population pressure, control of irrigation systems, warfare and technological advancements. These unilinear 'prime-mover' explanations were later rejected as over-simplistic and were replaced by models based on systems theory (Flannery, 1972; Sabloff and Lamberg-Karlovsky, 1975). The 'new archaeology' or 'processual archaeology' which produced these systemic models to explain the origins of early states in Mexico, Iran, Greece and other regions of the world produced many stimulating ideas about the role of kinship and trade in the processes of stratification which underlie state formation (e.g. Frankenstein and Rowlands, 1978). An emphasis on the role of these factors highlights the many theoretical continuities between this approach and what we may think of as the third approach to the origins of the state in social anthropology.

This third approach is associated with French structural Marxism and it developed initially out of attempts to delineate an 'African mode of production'. The two themes which emerge time and time again in this approach are (1) the role of long-distance trade in the emergence of African states and (2) the mechanisms for the control and allocation of labour which allow particular groups to control agricultural production and the resultant surpluses. According to a number of writers, kinship relations, the manipulation of marriage payments and the timing of marriage are the key variables with regard to the control of labour. Brain has argued that rights to bridewealth were a critical variable in the Zulu and Bamileke chiefdoms, where the bridewealth system resulted in chiefs having rights in approximately one-third of the female population (Brain, 1972: 173). Control of marriage and marriage payments through kinship systems are definitely one way in which particular groups and individuals can exercise domination over others. Since kinship systems are about controlling access to resources, they obviously contain the seeds of social differentation. It is not possible here to go into the very complex debates about the emergence of states in Africa, but it is important to note that various scholars have argued that relationships between women and men are of critical importance (Meillassoux, 1981: Goody, 1976).[1]

The fourth approach to the study of the state focuses on processes of incorporation (Cohen and Middleton, 1970). The study of incorporation grew out of a concern with the colonial state and the processes through which local or indigenous social formations were incorporated into emerging nation states. Early texts emphasized ethnicity, and the maintenance of ethnic boundaries in urban contexts. Later studies developed the theme of the way in which state structures penetrate local power and authority structures, and thus become involved in the manipulation of kinship and marriage rules, among other things. The state not only intervenes in marriage and inheritance laws, but also changes the geopolitical context in which local and kin-based power structures operate. New legislation concerning land tenure, taxation and debt, for example, redefines people's relations with one another and attempts to codify their relationships with and responsibilities to the state. In addition, new political structures grow up; many people under colonial rule found themselves coping with imposed adminis-trative structures; which were often nominally modelled on existing political and jural structures; and many people at the present time are constantly seeking to comprehend and exert control over the bureau-cratic structures of local government and party organization.

This brief and very schematic overview of anthropological ap-proaches to the study of the state provides the necessary background to understanding feminist approaches to the study of women and the state in social anthropology and related disciplines. As a discipline, anthropology has often been criticized for failing to consider the wider social, political and economic contexts of the local communities it has traditionally studied. A number of critics have argued that anthro-pology has neglected the analysis of the modern state and the insti-tutional structures of state power, as well as the 'world system' which provides the international context within which states operate. There is certainly some justification for an argument of this kind, but in recent years anthropology has turned to a consideration of how local systems interact with regional, national and international processes (see chapter 4). This development in social anthropology has been inspired to a considerable extent by the growth of 'peasant studies', which have undergone a particularly extensive revitalization in recent years. However, when we look at the different approaches to the study of the state in social anthropology, it is quite clear that whatever the 'type' of state under discussion, and whatever the intellectual origins of the approach used, the single unifying theme is the importance of kinship. Kinship is, of course, a 'catch-all' term, which means nothing outside its historical, political, cultural and economic specification. Feminist anthropologists have demonstrated that even in the realm of kinship, where one might expect to find an emphasis on gender relations, women have often remained quite 'invisible'. Kinship relations, particularly where they are examined in terms of their role in political and jural structures, can turn out to be the study of kin-based links between men, and women are considered merely one of the mechanisms for establishing those links. This has frequently been the case in structural-functionalist and Marxist anthropology, and the feminist critiques of Meillassoux discussed in chapter 3 are particularly relevant here.

The centrality of kinship is a theme which has been taken up by feminist anthropologists and historians when discussing the origins of class and state societies. In anthropology, much of this work has been inspired implicitly or explicitly by Engels, but it also owes a great deal to evolutionary and Marxist anthropology (Reiter, 1977; Sacks, 1974, 1979; Sanday, 1981; Silverblatt, 1978; Coontz and Henderson, 1986; Rohrlich-Leavitt, 1980; Nash, 1980; Rapp, 1977). The feminist problematic remains the question of the origins of women's subordination, and of male dominance in the political sphere of social life. The treatment of this issue with regard to the origins of class and state societies has benefited greatly from attempts to provide empirical demonstrations of how women's position changed from one of equality of power in pre-state societies to one of relative subordination under emerging state structures.[2] In many instances, this has necessitated a heavy reliance on archaeological and historical data which bring particular kinds of methodological problems, notably the question of deciding what kind of evidence should be judged as sufficient to demonstrate women's status and power in society. For example, evidence of early goddess cults has sometimes been interpreted as indicative of women's power. But a variety of feminist scholars have pointed out that representations of women in material culture and myth do not necessarily tell us anything about women's values, needs and experiences in past societies (Bamberger, 1974; Pomeroy 1975). Ann Barstow has argued, on the other hand, that we are prevented from analysing the archaeological data which are available to us because we are forced to study them in terms of our own understanding of concepts like 'dominance' and 'power', which may be wholly inappropriate for analysing/reconstructing gender relations in the archaeological and historical past (Barstow, 1978: 8–10). Such difficulties are of a familiar kind, and bring us back once again to the question of how we judge sociological evidence as indicative of greater or lesser amounts of female power, status, and so on (see chapter 3).

The same issue is raised, albeit in slightly different form, by historical ethnographic evidence. Perhaps the most notable example of this is the question of the high status of women in West African societies. Both historical and anthropological data make it clear that in certain parts of Africa in pre-colonial times women were the holders of public offices and wielded considerable political power.[3] Some societies had 'dual-sex' systems, where a woman was responsible for women's affairs and a man for the men's affairs. Kamene Okonjo describes the Omu or 'mother' of the Ibo of Nigeria, who had a group of women councillors and was responsible for women's affairs in the community, and in particular for the regulation of markets and trade (Okonjo, 1976). Bolanle Awe describes a similar situation for the Yoruba, where the Iyalode was responsible for all women and represented women's interests on the king's council (Awe, 1977). In other West African societies, there were women office-holders whose political power was not restricted to 'women's affairs'. The Queen Mother of the Asante was responsible for the continued fertility and success of the matrilineage as a whole, and Carol Hoffer records that Mende and Sherbro women could hold chiefships on the same basis as men (Lebeuf, 1971; Hoffer, 1972, 1974; Sweetman, 1984). The case of the Mende and Sherbro women chiefs is particularly interesting because they are among a minority of women office-holders who have managed to retain their political rights throughout the colonial and post-colonial periods (Hoffer, 1972: 154–9). There is no doubt that the women in these societies were powerful, and powerful in their own right, as opposed to being the wives of powerful men. However, the fact that a few senior or 'aristocratic' women could under certain circumstances hold political office and exercise political power does not necessarily tell us anything about the status and position of women in the society as a whole, nor much about the sorts of 'political' rights or power of ordinary women as social adults.

Analysing women's status and political power is further complicated by the fact that earlier ethnographies tended to look at women as the political dependants of men. Western observers found it all too easy to rediscover their own assumptions about the 'male' nature of political power in non-Western societies. This tendency is yet another example of male bias in ethnography, but the distressing fact is that it may be a particularly difficult distortion to set right, and will possibly not be displaced merely by producing evidence of powerful women who held recognizable political offices. The main reason for this, as a number of feminist writers have pointed out, is the problem of understanding the term 'power'. 'Power' as a general term incorporates a number of concepts such as force, legitimacy and authority. One of the most salient features of women's position in society is that they often have political power, but they frequently lack force, legitimacy and authority.[4] In many of the political systems in the contemporary world, women have political power – they have the vote, for example – but they lack any real authority in the exercise of that power. This makes analysing women's position in society extremely difficult. However, this does not mean that analysis is impossible. A first step might be to stop speaking generally of women's 'power' or 'role' in society, and to spell out instead the intersections between the social, economic, political and ideological spheres of social life in such a way as to build up a picture of women as particular kinds of social individuals within particular social formations. A second and related step might be to acknowledge the fact that women are social actors who are involved in social strategies, with both short- and long-term aims. Some of these strategies will be conscious attempts at organizing, but others may well be unconscious or relatively *ad hoc*.

Feminist scholars and social anthropologists have recently begun to re-examine issues concerning the analysis of the state, state institutions and the structures of state power. In both cases, this resurgence of interest can be linked to a general trend in the social and political sciences concerned with rethinking state theories, and reincorporating the state into social and political theory (Evans et al., 1985). Scholars use the term 'state' in a variety of different ways. Liberal scholars employ the term to refer to 'government', to a means of ensuring social order and economic prosperity. This approach can be contrasted with the Marxist understanding which identifies the state with the 'ruling class', and stresses the oppressive nature of the state as a mechanism for controlling other classes. Neo-Marxists, on the other hand, take an approach which emphasizes the state's relative autonomy from the dominant economic class. This view of the state sees the political elite as sharing some goals with the dominant classes, but as nevertheless separate from them. According to Poulantzas, the dominant classes are continually broken up into 'class fractions' because of competition and differences of immediate interest. As a result, the role of the state is to maintain a centralized political authority which protects the long-term interests of the dominant classes, and which simultaneously undermines the possibility of any political threat from the working classes, as well as any such threat from other 'classes' or political groups who, because of their political and economic marginality, could act against the state (Poulantzas, 1973, 287–8). Under such conditions, the state can maintain its function as a centralized political authority only if it is 'relatively autonomous' from the particular interests of dominant class fractions. However, the degree of autonomy which the state achieves can vary through time, and depends on the relations between classes and class fractions, and on the degree of social and political struggle (Poulantzas, 1973, 1975). This emphasis on the state as relatively autonomous from the dominant economic class, and on the state's role as a mediator between intra- and inter-class interests, has recently been taken up by historians and feminists (Eisenstein, 1980, 1984; Lonsdale, 1981). The chief attractions of such an approach are that it opens the way to analysing the state as constitutive of relations of power rather than solely of relations of production; it permits an investigation of the divisions of interest within the dominant class; it creates a space for asking questions about the political successes of marginal groups, and it offers the possibility of examining why certain state actions, such as those concerning gender, run counter to economic 'good sense'. The neo-Marxist approach is a potentially liberating one for those who wish to study the relationship to the state of social divisions other than those based on economic class. Race, ethnicity, religion and sexual orientation are critical social divisions, in addition to gender. All these identities, including class, define access to the state, to state resources, and to political representation and the institutions of state power.

However, in addition to the formal apparatuses of state power, there are also the legal and ideological systems which make up the state. While definitions of the state might appeal to ideas about the state as 'government' or the state as 'ruling class' or the state as 'mediator', most definitions also include some reference to the state as a bureaucratic/legal/coercive order. The inclusion of such elements in definitions owes much to Weber, who emphasized the modern state's administrative apparatus, its territoriality and its monopoly of the use of legitimate force (Weber, 1972, 1978). Administrative, legal and coercive systems are the main means through which the state structures relationships between society and the state, and they are also involved in the structuring and restructuring of many crucial social relationships within society as well – for example, family relationships. As a result, any attempt to analyse women and the state in social anthropology (and related disciplines) will have to examine not only women's access to the formal apparatus of the state and state resources, but also the impact of legal and ideological systems on women, as well as the strategies and mechanisms women have employed to defend, protect and advance their position. One area where such an analysis has already begun is in the study of women in socialist societies.

Women in socialist societies[5]

> The emancipation of women becomes possible only when women are
> enabled to take part in production on a large, social scale, and when
> domestic duties require their attention only to a minor degree. And this
> has become possible only as a result of modern large-scale industry
> which not only permits of the participation of women in production in
> large numbers, but actually calls for it and, moreover, strives to convert
> private domestic work also into a public industry. (Engels, 1972: 152)

The hopes of women's emancipation have long rested on the incorporation of women into the waged labour force. Contemporary feminists
find much to disagree with in Engels's writing, but the vast majority
continue to see the 'family' as the site of women's oppression, and to
view women's position in society as the product of complex interconnections between the productive and reproductive spheres of life.
Many socialist and communist countries have used the writings of
Marx, Engels and Lenin to construct and justify programmes of
economic and social reform, which place the emancipation of women
and their incorporation into productive activities at the centre of their
political agendas. It is not possible to make generalizations about the
nature of socialist and communist states in spite of similarities in their
ideological positions, because they all have specific social formations,
which have evolved through particular historical circumstances. However, some similarities do exist between the revolutionary states of the
Third World, the USSR, China and eastern Europe. This is largely
because these states do share a general set of assumptions about how
to promote economic development and bring about social change. In
all cases, the state plays the leading role in economic life, industrialization is strongly supported, while the agrarian sector is brought
under state control by creating co-operatives and state farms. The
result is a planned economy with a strong state sector, and a
considerable degree of state intervention concerning production,
distribution, prices and wages. At the same time, these countries are
committed to social transformations including the dismantling of 'pre-
revolutionary' social, ideological, legal, political and religious systems,
as well as the creation of welfare provisions in education, health and
housing (Molyneux, 1981: 1–2). Policies with regard to women are
based on the assumption that the oppression of women results from
class relations, and that the liberation of women will come about with
the demise of the class society, a view which is clearly derived from
Engels. In keeping with Engels's view of the 'woman question',
socialist states see the entry of women into waged work and the
socialization of domestic tasks as central to the emancipation of
women. Socialist states have, therefore, sought to introduce policies to

improve the position of women as part of a general process of social transformation. In order to assess how successful socialist states have been in their efforts to deal with the 'woman question', it is necessary to look at the outcome of state activity with regard to legal provision, family policy, education, health, employment and political representation. It is not possible to discuss all these policy areas in detail here, but a few general points will allow us to assess the successes of socialist states in their attempts to emancipate women.

Legal provision

The constitutions of socialist states declare women's equality with men in all spheres of life. They grant women the right to education and the right to work. Legal reforms have also been passed with regard to property, inheritance, marriage and religion. Such reforms, combined with rights to maternity leave, extra-domestic facilities, contraception and education, have given many women greater freedom from the control of husbands and fathers within the family, and have provided a degree of institutional support for women's participation in society outside the family. Legal reforms of this kind may not seem particularly revolutionary, especially if they merely provide for formal rather than practical equality, and if in reality laws can be ignored or evaded. After all, one only has to look at the very partial success of the equal pay legislation in the United Kingdom to see that formal equality before the law is not everything.[6] However, formal equality is not inconsequential by any means. Under many of the 'pre-revolutionary' social systems to be found in what are now socialist states, women's lack of rights in law was a crucial factor in maintaining them as subordinate to men, and a sanctioned method of limiting their access to resources, especially land. Legal reform at least ensures that men cannot claim to have legal sanctions over all areas of women's lives, just by virtue of being husbands, fathers or brothers.

Legal reform is very directly involved in the area of family policy. All the socialist states have passed legislation which seeks to redefine family relations, both between women and men, and between parents and children (Molyneux, 1985a). Laws in many socialist states have banned polygyny, child marriage and marriage payments, and have rescinded men's rights to unilateral divorce and the automatic custody of children. Marriage laws have also been amended to give women equal rights to property and inheritance. In societies where lineage or households were landholding units, the reform of marriage laws has had to go hand in hand with land reform. Many socialist states have recognized that changing relations between women and men necessarily involves changing property laws, and this has been seen as a desirable outcome. However, changes in marriage laws have not always gone smoothly. When the Chinese Communist Party introduced new marriage and land laws in 1950, the party gave direct support to a campaign to implement the Marriage Law, which set out self-consciously to destroy the 'feudal family'. The party's emphasis on destroying 'feudal' marriage was interpreted as allowing women to leave unsatisfactory marriages, and between 1950 and 1953 courts granted an average of 800,000 divorces per year. The majority of divorce plaintiffs were women. However, many of the women who tried to take advantage of the law encountered ferocious resistance from husbands, in-laws and party cadres. It seems that husbands regarded the law as a way of losing both their land and their wives. Resistance was often violent, and an enormous number of women were reported to have been murdered or driven to suicide. A government report for 1953 estimated that in the three years when the law had been in force 70,000–80,000 women had died in his way (Stacey, 1983: 176–8).

Under different circumstances, of course, state campaigns can have quite the opposite effect, especially when the ideology underpinning state policies has become sufficiently strong. A woman interviewed in South Yemen expressed her position: 'If I can say that in not allowing me to go to work or marry whom I choose they are acting as counter-revolutionaries, and defying the law of the land, then it is more difficult for them to stop me' (Molyneux, 1981: 13). The state does at least give women some legal protection in the face of opposition from husbands and kin. This protection is, however, contradictory, and is frequently frustrated by the social, cultural and economic constraints which prevent women from having recourse to law, even while it exists. Some feminists have argued that state laws maintain the 'family' as a private world in which the state hesitates to intervene. In the writings of British feminists, the reluctance of the police to intervene or take action in cases of domestic violence has always been cited as an example of the way in which the state leaves the inner workings of the family relatively untouched (Barrett, 1980: 235). One of the prevailing theories on this issue is that men acquiesce in the face of state power partly because the state grants them complete control within the domain of the family (Ortner, 1978: 28–30). Baldly stated, this view seems unduly instrumental, but it is nevertheless true that certain kinds of intervention in 'family' life are strongly resisted by women and men in both socialist and capitalist states around the world. In fact, critics of socialism often cite state 'interference' in 'private'/'family' life as one of the unacceptable features of socialist systems.

Employment

Socialist states have all pursued policies designed to draw women into wage labour, in line with the necessity of pursuing programmes of economic expansion. In Cuba, for example, prior to 1959, only 17 per cent of all wage labour was performed by women. Women were concentrated in domestic service, in the professions, and in the textile, food and tobacco industries. Fewer than 2 per cent of women were employed in agriculture, and this undoubtedly reflected their exclusion from the predominant sugar-cane industry (Croll, 1981c: 386; Murray, 1979a: 60–2). After the revolution, agricultural reforms transferred private lands to the state, and state farms were set up, but about 20 per cent of the land remained in the hands of smallholders. By the early 1960s, most of the available male labour in the rural areas had been mobilized, and, because of economic expansion, Cuba was being rapidly transformed from a country with a serious unemployment and underemployment problem to one with a growing shortage of labour. As a result, women were encouraged to enter waged agricultural production (Croll, 1981c: 387; Murray, 1979a: 63–4). However, the number of women who did enter such work was small, and the distribution of agricultural work continued to be operated on the basis of a 'natural' division of labour apparently grounded in differences of physical strength. The sexual division of labour was defined in law by Ministry of Labour resolutions 47 and 48 in 1968, which reserved some categories of work for women and restricted them from entering others. These resolutions were rescinded in 1973, but the 1976 constitution still refers to the state ensuring that women 'are given jobs in keeping with their physical make-up' (Murray, 1979a: 70; 1979b: 103; Latin American and Caribbean Women's Collective, 1980: 102–3; Croll, 1981c: 388). Both Croll and Murray point out that the need for maximum economic productivity, allied to firmly held beliefs about women's capabilities, has led to the confinement of women workers to particular sectors of the economy, and to particular types of work within these sectors (Murray, 1979b: 105; Croll, 1981c: 388–9).

Cuba is particularly interesting in this regard because of the strenuous efforts made to change women's relationship to reproductive labour as well as to productive labour. According to Murray, in the 1970s Cuba chose to spend a larger percentage of the gross national product on daycare provision for the children of working mothers than almost any other country in the world. The number of nurseries had increased from 109 in 1962 to 658 by 1975, capable of catering for 55,000 children. Nurseries take children from six weeks to six years; they provide medical care, meals and clean clothes. Most are open from

6 a.m. to 6 p.m., and some will take children as weekly boarders. However, given Cuba's economic position, even a massive commitment of this kind is not enough to provide sufficient places to meet the demand. Priority is given to working mothers, and, as Croll points out, it is often a question of which comes first, the job or the childcare (Murray, 1979a: 64–5; Croll, 1981c: 390–1).

In addition to the provision of childcare, Cuba made other attempts at socializing domestic labour, such as the provision of communal eating facilities at the place of work and laundry services. But, because of the cost of providing these services, provision has been slow and biased towards urban working women. In 1974, women's organizations called for expansion and improvement in the availability of clothes and prepared foods, and for reductions in hours worked in order to allow opportunities for training and time for domestic responsibilities. The government responded by campaigning to encourage a more equitable sharing of domestic tasks within the home between women and men. The Family Code of 1974 was widely debated in women's organizations, in workplace debates and elsewhere before it was passed. Women complained about men's lack of co-operation in domestic and family matters, and they emphasized that they were being asked to become workers without any recognition of the fact that they still had to do all the domestic labour (Latin American and Caribbean Women's Collective, 1980: 101). The outcome was that the Family Code, in addition to redefining marriage and divorce procedures, explicitly states that, where both partners are employed, both must share equally in household tasks and childcare, whatever their social responsibilities and whatever the nature of their jobs (Croll, 1981c: 391). The appropriate sections of this highly advanced legislation are read at all marriage services to 'remind men of their duty', but there is little evidence at the present time that any widespread sharing has occurred, or that women are finding it any easier to reconcile the conflicting demands of productive and reproductive activities (Murray, 1979b: 101–3). Rural women have not entered the waged labour force to any great extent – with the exception of voluntary, seasonal and temporary work – largely because the labour of many women is still needed in the smallholder sector, where it is unremunerated. Whether they are involved in waged or unwaged agricultural labour, rural women are still responsible for servicing and maintaining their households. They have responded to the dual demands of production and reproduction by informally co-operating among themselves, through setting up rotating childcare arrangements, and/or by refusing to enter waged employment. According to Croll, during an intensive campaign to encourage women to enter employment, as many as three out of four women refused to take on waged labour because of 'domestic' demands on their time, the lack of servicing facilities and the conservative attitudes of their husbands (Croll, 1981c: 391–2). Murray notes that, although more women entered the labour force in the years 1968–9 than in the previous decade, of all the women who entered the labour force in 1969, 76 per cent dropped out of it within a year, and this pattern continued in subsequent years. The Federación de Mujeres Cubanas (FMC), the Federation of Cuban Women, commissioned a special survey to investigate women's reasons for leaving the paid labour force. The 'double shift' and the lack of effective services to lighten the domestic load were again cited as major reasons, alongside the scarcity of consumer goods (which decreased the economic incentive to work), poor work conditions, and workplace administrators' lack of understanding of the 'specific' problems of women (Murray, 1979b: 99–100).

The difficulties and frustrations experienced by Cuba are not unique. This point can best be made by comparing Cuba with the Soviet Union because, on the face of it, the situation of women in the two countries is very different. One of the most noticeable features of the Soviet economy is the number of women employed in wage labour. Women comprise 51 per cent of the total labour force, 49 per cent of the industrial workers, 51 per cent of those working on collective farms and 45 per cent of state farm workers. By the end of the 1960s, 80 per cent of working-age women were employed outside the home (Buckley, 1981: 80). This is in marked contrast to Cuba, where women constitute only about 25 per cent of the waged labour force (Croll, 1981c: 387). The main impetus for the incorporation of women into wage labour in the USSR was the demographic imbalance of the sexes produced by the Revolution and by the two World Wars in the face of the necessity of maintaining high productivity and economic growth. By 1946, the sex balance of the Soviet population was highly skewed. 'Women of working age heavily outnumbered their male counterparts by a staggering twenty million' (Buckley, 1981: 80–1). Demographic factors were not the only reason for the high rate of increase in women's employment; economic factors were also crucial. The government's goal of rapid industrialization, and the need to produce food for an increasingly urbanized and industrialized population, meant an increase in labour input in both the industrial and the agricultural sectors. Thus Buckley argues that, in spite of an ideological commitment to equality for women, adherence to this commitment on guidelines set out by Marx and Engels has been less influential in promoting the highest world percentage of women in the workforce than the combined effects of demographic pressure, labour shortage and the necessity for rapid economic growth (Buckley, 1981: 84).

As in Cuba, an emphasis on economic growth and high productivity has had contradictory effects on the position of women. Women may have been drawn into the labour force in large numbers in the USSR, but several commentators have pointed out that female labour in both industry and agriculture is heavily concentrated in unskilled, manual jobs, where pay is low. Occupational segregation by sex persists in spite of an ideological commitment to equality. The position of rural women is particularly interesting. Women form the highest proportion of collective farm workers, but women work fewer days per year than men – approximately 50–100 days less. But, in addition to their work on the collectives, women contribute to the private subsidiary sector, growing vegetables and fruit, and raising livestock for household consumption. Estimates of the value of this work suggest that private plots provide 80 per cent of meat and 75 per cent of vegetables of the rural family's consumption (Croll, 1981c: 376). Most of the women agricultural workers are in the heavier, less-skilled, least-mechanized types of work (Buckley, 1981: 85). The disparity in skill levels is reflected in a disparity in formal education between men and women, although basic literacy rates for rural women are reportedly very high, at about 98.5 per cent (Croll, 1981c: 77). There are obviously many ways in which rural women do not have equality with men, and, what is more, their incorporation into waged labour has resulted in a 'tripleload', where women work on the collective farm, they continue to grow vegetables and raise livestock on the household plots, and they perform domestic tasks.[7] In both Cuba and the Soviet Union, changes in the relations of production have left the sexual division of labour largely untouched.

Childcare and domestic tasks

Like Cuba, the Soviet Union has sought to socialize childcare and domestic tasks in order to lessen women's workload. But, according to Croll, finding childcare arrangements is still the main difficulty for women in rural and urban areas. In rural areas only 7 per cent of pre-school children can be looked after in nurseries, compared to 37 per cent in urban areas. Seasonal nurseries are provided during peak periods of labour demand, but these have no equipment and are located in the fields where the women work or in local playgrounds. Only 40 per cent of collective farms have nurseries or kindergartens, and half of these are seasonal (Croll, 1981c: 378–9). A few communal dining-rooms have also been established, but these are mainly in the cities (Buckley, 1981: 90–3).

Both Cuba and the Soviet Union have failed to alleviate women's 'double burden' of productive and reproductive tasks. This is largely because, even in planned state economies with a high degree of collectivization, every household continues to be a unit of production and consumption to a certain degree, and continues, in many cases, to provide its own childcare. This is particularly the case for rural households. In urban as well as rural areas, servicing the household is very time-consuming because the supply of consumer goods and retail facilities is inadequate. The absence, in many areas, of modern plumbing, electricity supplies and modern appliances like refrigerators adds enormously to the number of hours necessary to maintain basic services within the household (Jancar, 1978: ch. 3; Buckley, 1981: 90). Time-budget surveys show that women perform most of the unremunerated domestic tasks, such as shopping, washing, cleaning, cooking and childcare, and thus sleep shorter hours and enjoy less leisure than men (Croll, 1981c: 379). The governments of both Cuba and the Soviet Union have been committed to socializing domestic tasks, but their success in this area has been very uneven, and has been considerably constrained by the cost of making such provisions.

The problems of Cuba and the Soviet Union are by no means unique; if anything they are probably typical of contemporary socialist states (Jancar, 1978; Scott, 1974). The entry of women into the labour force has served merely to intensify women's labour. The limited development of the service sector, the enormous cost of socializing childcare and domestic tasks, and the overriding emphasis on economic growth and expansion have all contributed to a situation where ideological commitment to the 'emancipation' of women has proved very difficult to realize in material terms. This general explanation for the socialist states' failure to deal with the 'woman question' – the 'lack of resources' argument – has a certain amount of force. A second argument, which is often put forward by governments and organizations within the socialist states, is that the difficulty is of an ideological or 'cultural' nature. The main problem is thought to be the beliefs and customs which underlie the sexual division of labour, particularly in the home. Cuba and China, for example, have both introduced campaigns to try to change people's attitudes to domestic work, and to alter what they see as 'reactionary' views about relations between women and men. Cuba's legislation to equalize household labour is part of such a programme. Reform at this level is clearly necessary, and it is obviously going to be a long and tortuous process. However, Elizabeth Croll points out that, although reform is necessary, to define the problem primarily in ideological terms may just be one way of avoiding more radical solutions to the problem. Emphasizing ideology 'may obscure the need to change certain material practices that sustain discriminatory beliefs against women' (Croll, 1981b: 371).

The reformation of the family

In addition to the 'lack of resources' and the 'cultural ideology' explanations for failure to change gender relations in the ways hoped for, critics have also suggested that failure could be attributed to the fact that the eradication of sexual inequality has not really been regarded as a key issue, in spite of statements to the contrary, while others have suggested that sexual divisions have survived because they are in some way necessary or functional to the social system. Maxine Molyneux makes a most convincing argument when she suggests that the answer would appear to lie somewhere in between (Molyneux, 1985a). This becomes clear when we look at what has been happening to the 'family' within socialist states.

One of the commonest fallacies about socialist states is that they pursue policies designed to 'destroy' the family. The implicit assumption which is being made is that communal living and working arrangements will necessarily involve the destruction of the family as the basic unit of society. A number of feminists have been at pains to point out that this assumption is quite erroneous. Legislation on the family, far from seeking to destroy it, is actually intended to create a specific family form which will ensure social and productive stability, and which will act as the basic unit of society, particularly with regard to the important task of socializing the young into socialist and nationalist goals. The partial maintenance of the 'family' as a unit of production and consumption in the rural areas of many socialist states is not the result of a lack of resources or of an imperfect implementation of 'socialist policies', but a direct consequence of the role the family is required to play under socialism.

Maxine Molyneux points out that it is necessary to see 'family policy' as taking place in two phases. The first is aimed at transforming what is seen as the traditional patriarchal family – a transformation which is part of an overall strategy to change the social relations of society and, in particular, the productive base on which they rest. In this phase, there is considerable emphasis on the connections between socialist development and women's emancipation, and many of the reforms which are made in an attempt to change gender and property relations, and to erode the power of 'traditional' social and religious systems, are often extremely radical (Molyneux, 1985a: 54–7). It is important, as many feminist writers have argued, to acknowledge the genuinely emancipatory effect of many of these reforms on women and on the poor. If the first phase is one of deconstruction, the second is one of reconstruction. The transformed family is reconstructed as the basic cell of society responsible for the physical and social reproduction of the next generation of workers. These responsibilities devolve most heavily on women in their roles both as waged workers and as mothers, and state policies for the future come to depend on women fulfilling both their 'new' role as workers and their 'traditional' social and domestic roles within the family. The new socialist woman, as Molyneux points out, is 'the working mother' (Molyneux, 1985a: 57). This dual role causes conflict, frustration and hard work for the women who have to live it, but it also produces conflict within state policies. After an initial period designed to 'modernize' the family and release women for wage labour, which is part of a process of restructuring and increasing the productive capacity of the economy, the second period is actually concerned with stabilizing the new social order, and bringing the family and women more in line with the state's social and economic goals. There is absolutely no question of 'getting rid' of the family (Davin, 1987a: 154–7). This point is reinforced by the extremely positive view socialist states take of heterosexual relations and monogamous marriage, in contrast to their exceptionally negative response to premarital liaisons and divorce (although both are permitted), homosexuality, illegitimacy and any alternative form of sexual and reproductive relations.[8]

The emphasis on the family as promoting social stability and economic growth through the social and physical reproduction of the next generation of workers is the key to understanding certain socialist states, notably the USSR, China and countries in eastern Europe. Maxine Molyneux points out that in the USSR sociologists have now begun to argue that too much emphasis on women's work and too little on their family roles is a major contributory factor to high rates of divorce, alcoholism and youth problems (Molyneux, 1985a: 60). The concern with the low birth-rate, which is clearly related to anxieties about the demands of the economy for labour, devolves directly on to women, who are encouraged to take social responsibility for reproduction and to expand or limit the size of their families in accordance with the wider social and economic goals of the state. In China, women are required to limit the number of children to one or at most two,[9] while in South Yemen, the eastern European countries and the USSR state policy has been designed to increase the birth-rate (Molyneux, 1981: 18).[10] In the USSR, the low birth-rate, tellingly referred to as the 'mothers' strike', is likely to result in future policy offering women more incentives to stay at home while their children are young, thus increasing the divisions between women and men both in the home and in the workplace (Molyneux, 1985a: 60).

When discussing the limitations of family reform in socialist states, it is also important to note that state policies have encountered resistance, even within what might appear to be fairly restricted terms of reference.[11] Kinship and marriage practices have proved highly resistant to change in many contexts, not just because of 'traditionalism' or 'cultural lag', but because they continue to be a necessary means of pursuing household survival strategies even under the transformed conditions of the 'new' socialist economy.[12] However, it would be a mistake to see family policy in socialist states as being the result of the imperfect implementation of socialist policies, whether because of the 'cynical' needs of the state, or because of the entrenched 'traditionalism' or cultural systems of the people concerned. The relations between the state, the family and revolutionary change are more complex than such explanations would suggest.

Judith Stacey charts the development of the Chinese revolution and the various changes in family policy which have taken place in twentieth-century China. In her analysis she makes it plain that the relationship between family transformation and macro-social change is a complex dialectic. The Chinese family did not merely resist or adapt to state policies, but family structures, both social and ideological, helped to shape the nature of state-inspired social transformations. Family change was neither a 'dependent' nor an 'independent' variable, but was instead 'inseparable from the general causes, processes, and outcomes of socialist revolution' (Stacey, 1983: 259–60). Stacey argues that the successes and the limitations of the Chinese revolution are the outcome of the interdependence of patriarchy (hierarchical male control within the Chinese family) and socialism. However, this 'marriage' of patriarchy and socialism is not built on the survival of an anachronistic, 'traditional' family form which has merely accommodated itself to socialist policies, or which has been preserved because of its utility to the socialist state. On the contrary, the family in China has undergone a revolution, in the course of which patriarchy itself served as a revolutionary force.

Stacey argues very convincingly that land reform and agricultural collectivization, far from undermining the material base of the patriarchal family, actually served to democratize access to key resources, notably land, and thereby to strengthen and secure the future of the family under the leadership of its male head. She also argues that patriarchal socialism received its most fundamental support from existing lineages in the rural areas. Producers' co-operatives were formed around existing villages or neighbourhoods, where, because of existing social systems based on lineages and patrilocal marriage, most households were already linked through male kin. With landlords and rich peasants eliminated, village lands and other resources were handed over to the egalitarian remains of former patrilineages. Collectivization actually strengthened networks among co-operating male kinsmen, who also assumed leadership roles that went along with their newly acquired economic power. The state and the rural producers collaborated in a process which 'strengthened patriarchal family security and promoted socialist development' (Stacey, 1983: 203–11).

The situation in the urban areas, where the geographic concentration of kin ties which formed the basis for patriarchal control in the rural areas does not exist, is somewhat different. Urban family life is notably less patriarchal than in pre-revolutionary urban or contemporary rural China (Stacey, 1983: 235–7). However, Stacey argues that men dominate positions in the highly favoured state sector of employment, while women retain primary responsibility for domestic labour, and that these divisions are replicated in education and political power. The net result is a gender-stratified social and economic system. These factors point to a diminution rather than an elimination of patriarchal control in the urban context. Stacey makes the very important point that, whatever the decline in 'private patriarchy' has been, it has to a considerable extent been replaced by a 'public patriarchy' (Stacey, 1983: 235–40). This 'public patriarchy' is manifest in the number of direct interventions which the state is able to make in family life, and in China, as well as in other states, it is given ideological weight by reference to the political leader as 'father of the people' (Molyneux, 1985a: 58).

Women's emancipation and women's organizations

The achievements of socialist states are not insignificant. In most instances, socialism has immensely improved the social and family life of its citizens: it has provided basic economic and social security, it has made major advances with regard to education and health provision, and it has expanded the life opportunities of many individuals. The benefits of such vast improvements have been experienced, albeit unequally, by women, and by the poor and the disadvantaged. The negative side of the equation is that women's emancipation is seen as firmly rooted in a wider process of social transformation, in such a way that policies concerning women are intimately bound up with state policy and goals. Women's emancipation may be a goal to be worked towards, but its subjugation to an overall process of social and economic transformation limits its possibilities and its progress. As the wider socio-economic goals shift and alter, so too does the commitment to women's emancipation. In the last few years, many feminists have come to realize that the issue is a political one. If the state will not alter its policies, then it must be led to do so by other representative bodies, that is by women's organizations.

Women, as might be expected from the foregoing discussion, are poorly represented in the institutional and political structures of socialist states; they have not entered into formal positions in collective decision-making in proportion to their representation in production or in the population at large (Jancar, 1978: 88–105; Croll, 1981b: 371). The situation, as in capitalist states, is a disappointing and frustrating one, and is not very convincingly explained by commentators who see it as a stage en route to a brighter future which has yet to come. As Maxine Molyneux so wittily writes: 'After all, it could reasonably be argued that if a country could send a woman to outer space it could manage to get an equal number of women and men on its politburo' (Molyneux, 1985a: 51). The lack of formal representation of women in political structures has been variously attributed to the male-dominated nature of the ruling communist parties, to the 'fraternal' ethos which guides political activity, and to the fact that many lower-level positions in the political hierarchy involve unpaid positions, which require attendance at meetings outside work hours when the demands on women's domestic labour are greatest. All these factors are pertinent. However, the broader reason for failure is perhaps one linked to the question of political representation, to the kinds of citizens women are meant to be within the modern state.

The history of women's organizations within the socialist states and the development of the relationship between socialism and feminism is a fascinating one. In both China and the USSR, early feminist movements were outspoken and active, but subsequent fears of separatism and of women's independence from the overall aims of class struggle led to women's organization being broken up, only to be reinstituted in the 1960s and 1970s as part of state-led campaigns to improved the position of women in society (Croll, 1978; Jancar, 1978: 105–21). In all socialist states, women's organizations have played a key role in explaining, implementing and arguing for government policies designed to work for the benefit of women. However, women's organizations, like trade unions and other mass organizations, only exist at the discretion of the ruling party. In spite of the campaigns in the 1960s and 1970s to raise people's consciousness about the 'dual burden' of women's work, their lower rates of pay, and their lack of equality in social and political life, many ruling parties still seem to subscribe to the view that separate women's organizations are a necessary revolutionary force in the initial stages of development, but that eventually they should become unnecessary in a socialist society, where policies on women are an integral, not a separate, part of overall socio-economic development. As a result, women's organizations are encouraged to operate as a mechanism of the ruling party by extending state policies into a female constituency, rather than as a separate pressure group which organizes women independently and which encourages them to take an active role in asserting and defining their own needs and demands. The relationship between feminism and socialism has been further complicated by the anxiety of leading party members about 'separatism', and women's groups and their leaders have often found themselves in the ambiguous position of having to defend women's rights and position, while at the same time steering clear of anything which could be construed as 'bourgeois feminism' (Croll, 1978: 310). The notable 're-establishment' of women's organizations in many socialist states in the 1960s and 1970s has not resolved this problem to any significant extent. Class struggle and class consciousness still take precedence over gender struggles and feminist consciousness. The emancipation of women is seen as a revolution within a revolution, and as a result women's organizations have been more successful in soliciting women's support for official policies than in getting official policies changed to meet women's needs (Croll, 1981b: 373).

Women in socialist societies recognize and constantly assert that socialist policies are not in themselves sufficient to bring about changes in gender relations. Many feminist scholars and activists seem now to be agreed that changes in gender relations will come about only through women organizing, through agitation on behalf of women, through the coming into being of an independent feminist movement in the various countries concerned. This argument is a forceful one, but the question it leaves unexplored is a fundamental one about the actual nature of the relationship between women and the state.

Women's access to political, decision-making and bureaucratic institutions

In socialist countries, it is quite clear that, in spite of legal equality, relative economic autonomy, and the socialist states' commitment to women's full participation in economic, social and political life, women and men do not stand in the same relation to the state. Women have equal rights as citizens of the state, but they do not seem able to exercise those equal rights. Compared to men, women make relatively little impact on state policies. Their position under socialist regimes is not the same as that of 'minority' groups – racial, ethnic and religious – who may be discriminated against and often persecuted. Women as a group are actually supposed to enjoy state support, and yet still do not reap the benefits, or at least some of the benefits, of that support. Women and men may be theoretically united in their revolutionary struggle, but in the final analysis they turn out to be different sorts of political subjects with regard to the state. In both socialist and capitalist societies, the modern state works in part through a process of politicizing women's and men's roles; it politicizes or constructs the kinds of citizens women and men are supposed to be under the state's jurisdiction. The interesting point seems to be that none of the known forms of the state, whether ancient, pristine or modern, politicizes women's roles in such a way as to give them *de facto* rather than *de jure* equality with men. The comparative data suggest that, even in states where women's emancipation and political participation receive state advancement and support, the institutions of state power, as well as formal political roles, remain male-dominated. This is an idea which has been explored in the feminist literature. Some authors have argued that the state is not neutral, because state structures and institutions are male-dominated, and as a result they serve to institutionalize male privilege. However, feminist writing has only just begun to analyse the more interesting problem of how the state inscribes gender difference into the political process in such a way that women are debarred – at least under present state forms – from becoming full political persons, whatever their rights in law. The concept of women's interests is central to feminism and feminist analysis, but it is not central to the operation of state power, in spite of the social policies followed by socialist and non-socialist states alike. The interests of women are subsumed under the general interests of all citizens, without any recognition of the fact that women are not the same sort of citizens as men. It is important to be clear that the position of women and their ability to pursue their interests are cross-cut by race and class, ethnic origin and religion, but the fact that some women may be able to exercise their rights as citizens more fully than others does not alter the relative inequalities which exist between women and men.

The test of the argument I have just made will rest to a certain extent on a thoroughgoing analysis of exactly what is meant and entailed by such terms as 'citizen', 'rights', 'law', and so on. Such analysis is clearly under way in social and political theory, and is part of the general process of 'rethinking the state' (Pateman, 1985; Held, 1987; Yeatman, 1984). However, for the purposes of the argument in this chapter, which is intended to be exploratory rather than conclusive, I should like to base my assertion that women and men have a different relationship to the state, and are therefore different sorts of political subjects under the state, on two observable features of gender–state relations: first, that state structures and policies have a differential impact on women and men, and, second, that women and men have an unequal influence on state actions. A consideration of these two features of gender–state relations opens up some very interesting lines of enquiry for feminist anthropology and for social anthropology in general.

One of these lines of enquiry concerns the anthropological study of the modern state. Earlier work in anthropology was concerned with the formation of political elites, but more recent work is beginning to focus on the anthropology of political structures in the modern state, and on issues concerning processes of bureaucratization, decision-making, power-broking and policy formation. This interest is paralled by an expanding field of enquiry concerned with elites in big business, with corporate management, decision-making processes and employee allegiance. This new work is exciting, but the anthropological study of the state still has a long way to go. There has been almost no work on democracy, on the relationship between political and cultural ideologies (except with regard to questions of nationalism), on the concept of the citizen, on the concept of political action, on forms of political representation or on civil rights. All these are issues which anthropology must tackle as a modern social science in the coming decades. Anthropology has also made little attempt to analyse those large-scale interest groups within state formations which have particular social and political philosophies: examples from western Europe would include CND (the Campaign for Nuclear Disarmament), the gay rights movement and the Green Party. In this regard, however, recent initiatives to get issues concerning anthropology and violence and anthropology and nuclear war on to the discipline's agenda are very welcome. It seems clear that any future feminist anthropology will have a very distinctive contribution to make to all these issues, but in terms of the modern state, and in the light of an increasing dissolution of discipline boundaries in the social sciences, work on the concept of political action, the concept of the citizen, civil rights and forms of political representation will be particularly crucial. Feminist anthropology has already begun to develop the theoretical and methodological tools necessary to tackle these issues through its work on personhood and the concept of the person (see chapters 2 and 3).

A further line of enquiry concerns forms of political activity – in the general sense of the term – which are outside state control, or are intended to challenge or subvert the state, or perhaps to reform it . This would include an analysis both of forms of organizing and of forms of protest. It would also have to incorporate an analysis of what we might think of as 'negative' political activity, non-participation, withdrawal. There are a certain number of precedents for work of this kind in anthropology, which will be discussed later in this chapter, but it is an area where a more sustained feminist analysis is necessary.

A third area of interdisciplinary research, which is currently of particular interest to feminist anthropologists, is the field of 'women and development'.[13] This is an area of research and practice which links questions of gender with the analysis of the state. It focuses on concerns about the nature of the management of state institutions, economic planning, policy formation, decision-making and the exercise of state power. It examines questions about male dominance and male privilege in relation to access to state resources, as well as to political power, and it also raises issues concerning gender ideologies, and how those ideologies inform planning and policy. Once again, the issue of the success or failure of state policies designed to benefit women has to be discussed in terms of what kind of economic and socio-political changes must be envisaged and implemented in order to bring about development. This broad field of enquiry overlaps with the analysis of women's organizations, of women's responses to development initiatives, and of women's reactions to and perceptions of the state and its agents. Development anthropology in general is a growth area within the discipline, and it is also the main focus of applied anthropology. It is one of the most complex and difficult areas to work in because it meshes theory and practice in ways which drastically affect people's lives, and which inevitably raise political questions, none of which has an easy answer. This is the major area in anthropology which shares with feminism a commitment to theory and practice, and as such it is not surprising that many feminist anthropologists see it as being central to the practice of a modern anthropology in the future.

In chapter 4, I described many of the changes women experience in their lives as a result of development and the penetration of capitalism into rural production systems. The deleterious effects of many development projects on women with regard to their access to and control over land, property, technology, training and decision-making – particularly in the light of the changes in productive and reproductive relations, and in relations between the sexes under colonial rule – are now well documented.[14] The effects of agricultural change on women have been very diverse, and there is a danger, as I have argued, in making easy generalizations. However, one of the notable trends which commentators have identified is the weakening of women's authority and decision-making powers because of changing productive roles under the increasing commercialization of agriculture coupled with the exclusion of women from technology, training and credit schemes. Early writers on women and development were able to demonstrate that many of the negative effects of development programmes on women were due to a neglect and/or misunderstanding of women's key role in production. Subsequent attempts to rectify past mistakes have resulted in a variety of policies and programmes aimed specifically at women. 'Women's projects' have been moderately successful in a large variety of contexts, but one area where project success has been very minimal is in improving women's participation in decision-making and bureaucratic institutions, and in improving women's political representation. This lack of success in the realm of political participation and decision-making is particularly marked, and cannot merely be explained with reference either to a lack of political will on the part of policy-makers and planners – which is not always the case – or to a neglect of or misunderstanding about women's role in production.[15] One of the main purposes of an applied feminist anthropology would seem to me to be to try to come to grips with women's particular relation to the modern state, and, instead of always framing enquiry in terms of 'the impact of development on women', to spend more time looking at women's perception of and responses to development initiatives, including their apparent lack of response.[16]

There is no easy or adequate means of characterizing the many ways in which women have been excluded from decision-making in emerging managerial and political structures, and/or have had their authority, autonomy and power in existing socio-economic systems undermined by planned social change. The neglect of women farmers and their exclusion from training, extension and credit schemes is a very clear example of a way in which the state has worked to construct gender activities and ideologies (Staudt, 1978a, 1978b, 1982). The job of government agricultural extension officers is to visit farmers and provide training, as well as information about crop varieties, agricultural services and credit schemes. There is some evidence to show that male agricultural extension officers prefer to interact with men rather than women, even in situations where women are farmers and/or heads of households, and where such interaction is not proscribed by cultural codes of behaviour. Female agricultural extension officers are the obvious solution to this sort of problem, but they are non-existent in some countries, and in others they form only a tiny proportion of agricultural extension staff (Bryson, 1981). This is largely because women have not been admitted to agricultural training in large numbers. In 1975, only 25 per cent of graduates from agricultural training institutes in Tanzania were women, and 25 per cent of these graduates were studying nutrition, not agriculture (Fortmann, 1981: 210). Thus women's exclusion from training is a double exclusion: they do not receive training either as farmers or as agricultural extension officers.

Women experience a similar sort of exclusion from the managerial, bureaucratic and decision-making posts associated with co-operatives, settlement schemes, and other forms of large-scale development projects. The managerial and decision-making structures which are characteristic of these types of development initiatives are frequently very hierarchical, and, even where schemes or co-operatives have been set up with the aim of benefiting women, the decision-maker at the top of the hierarchy is likely to be male, as is the treasurer (Jain, 1980: 30). In many cases, the existence of a male head at the top of the management structure may be balanced to a large degree by a group of able and powerful women who provide the dynamic link between the head and the other female members of the co-operative or scheme. However, in such cases it is quite common to find that this group of women are an 'elite' within the community, and that one or more of its members may be attached to the male head through kinship links – sometimes the relationship between them is one of husband and wife. Sonia Harris describes such a situation in an income-generating project for women in Jamaica, where the male head of the project was assisted by a management team of women who were co-ordinated by his wife, and all these women were of long-standing prestige and status within the community (Harris, 1986: 135–6). The emergence of individual women or groups of women as leaders or 'brokers', who mediate between the community and the individual or organization which has access to outside resources and power, is a well-recognized feature of many development initiatives which are aimed at women, or which are effectively implemented through women. However, this mediating role hardly ever involves a formal recognition of women's decision-making and organizational abilities, and in any event it only effectively empowers elite individuals and groups within the community rather than working to improve women's overall political representation and decision-making power.

One obvious way in which women might be able to improve their access to state resources, training, managerial positions and political power is through developing women's organizations. This fact has been clearly recognized, in part because of the impact of the UN 'Decade for Women' (1976–85), and one of the consequences has been the emergence of development initiatives directed towards women's groups, and in particular towards women's self-help groups. It would be quite impossible to summarize the available literature on women's groups and related development projects from around the world. Everywhere women are involved in defending their own interests, working against social, cultural, racial, economic and political discrimination. These groups of women vary widely in terms of their background, objectives and effectiveness, particularly with regard to political activities. In the last ten years, many women's groups have formed, and they are involved in an enormous variety of activities, including co-operative organizations, health provision, family planning, literacy programmes, credit schemes and protection against sexual violence (Jain, 1980; Mehta, 1982). In the following section, I introduce data on women's self-help groups in Kenya as a means of investigating some of the issues concerning the relationship between women's groups and the state.

Women's self-help groups in Kenya

It has been estimated that by 1984 there were 15,000 women's groups in Kenya, incorporating an estimated 10 per cent of the female adult population of the country (McCormack et al., 1986).[17] There is a considerable degree of disagreement about how far these contemporary groups are based on or can be considered extensions of 'traditional' women's groups or collective activities. Certainly it is known that women's seasonal labour groups, mutual-aid networks, rotating credit associations, women's age-set groups, and women's councils existed in the pre-colonial and colonial periods in Kenya. However, while the significance of these groups should not be underestimated, and while contemporary women's groups definitely incorporate some of the activities of their predecessors and, in some cases, clearly build on the history and experience of previous forms of collective action, it would be a mistake to imagine that present-day women's self-help groups are based primarily on 'traditional' forms of mutual association and co-operation. Contemporary women's groups in Kenya owe far more to the workings of the modern nation state.

One of the most outstanding features of the Kenyan state has been its mobilization of local populations, who have been encouraged to participate in self-help development initiatives. Such initiatives usually involve raising funds and doing construction work related to the provision of education, health and water services, as well as a variety of other social services and public works. This successful mobilization of local communities is known in Kenya as *harambee* ('let's unite' or 'let's pull together'), and in the last ten years a considerable amount of research has been done on the origins and functioning of *harambee* groups (Holmquist, 1979; 1984; Mbithi and Rasmusson, 1977). The origins of *harambee* lie in the period of Kenya's struggle for independence, when it was absolutely essential to find a way of forging a workable political consensus to strengthen the newly independent Kenyan state. However, its political origins do not alter the fact that most of the present-day activities of *harambee* groups are basically economic in character. Women's self-help groups clearly reflect the ethos and aims of *harambee*, and are thus strongly supported by the state. Evidence for this comes from the fact that the Kenyan government began a 'Women's Group Programme' as early as 1971, and established a Women's Bureau in 1975 just before the start of the UN 'Decade for Women'. Women's self-help initiatives vary enormously, and they include projects initiated and supported by local communities, as well as many with considerable outsider and state involvement. Holmquist makes the point, when discussing self-help in general in Kenya, that such initiatives are usually hybrid phenomena; while local initiative, local leadership and local decision-making exist, so too do external leadership and ideas, outside guidance and finance, and occasional outside control (Holmquist, 1984: 73). In this sense, self-help represents a coalition of forces or interests, rather than an absolute form of self-reliance for the community or group concerned.

The state plays a major role in the formation of women's self-help groups in a variety of ways. First, there is the political legitimacy and support which the state provides for self-help initiatives in general, one of the direct consequences of which is that non-governmental and voluntary aid organizations and private individuals and foundations can maintain their own credibility by supporting or investing in such projects. Secondly, there is the fact that, in order to be eligible for grants, women's groups must register with the Department of Social Development, which is part of the Ministry of Culture and Social Services. Groups are required to elect officers and an executive or management committee in order to register with the state, and in this way the state regularizes the management structure and forms of political representation on which women's groups are built. The Department of Social Development also employs social development assistants who channel Women's Bureau and social development grants to groups, and link groups with government technical services, such as agricultural extension officers. Thirdly, much of the work done by women's self-help groups is concerned with construction – the building of schools, digging of trenches for water pipes, and so on. While initiatives of this kind come from the local community, who also bear about 90 per cent of the costs, the state is responsible for the very high recurrent costs which are incurred once the service is installed and running. It is clear from these three points that, while the label 'self-help' is a fairly accurate reflection of the local initiative and enterprise which go into the inception of projects and groups, it should not be taken to mean a lack of state involvement. There has been an enormous amount of research on women's groups in Kenya which I cannot attempt to synthesize here, but a number of points are illustrative of some of the issues concerning the relationship between women's groups and the state (McCormack et al., 1986; Maas, 1986; Feldman, 1983; Mwaniki, 1986; Wachtel, 1975; Monsted, 1978).

Maria Maas describes a women's self-help or *harambee* group in Kulima, Kiambu district, about 45 kilometres north-west of Nairobi, the capital of Kenya. Since 1966, about a hundred women have joined the group. It began with the aim of trying to buying corrugated-iron roofs for the houses of each participant, and in order to raise the money the women worked on large farms and plantations in the district until they had earned enough to pay for a roof for each member. In 1973, the group took on a more formalized structure and organized itself into three working parties, each with its own activities and self-chosen board. One of these working groups, for example, grows maize and other crops on a field lent to them by the district council. The women are able to purchase this produce at a reduced rate, and the surplus is sold to middlewomen. The same group also has a rotating credit and savings scheme, whereby every two weeks members deposit a fixed amount of money into a fund (approximately $3 in 1980), and the entire fund is placed at the disposal of each woman on a rotating basis. The main group activity, however, is farm labour. Each woman is required to participate in the workdays or send a daughter or neighbour in her place. If she fails to do so she must pay a fine equivalent to the sum she would have earned for the group that day (Maas, 1986: 17–19).

The earnings which the three groups get from their farm labour are deposited in a joint bank account under the name of the 'Kulima Harambee Group'. A board, comprising the chairwomen of the three working groups, a treasurer and a secretary, has the task of finding safe investments for this capital. In the period since 1973, they have bought two parcels of land, and they also own two shops. The board does the preliminary work, but the final decisions concerning investment and purchase are taken at general meetings of all women members. The women's aim is to earn as much money as possible and invest it, preferably in land: 'It is better to have land than money' (Maas, 1986: 20).

The goals of the different women's self-help groups in Kenya clearly vary enormously, but some of the features of the Kulima group, such as generating income through farm labour, running a rotating credit and savings scheme, and investing in property and land, are commonly found in many such groups. Mwaniki reports that the majority of women's groups in Mbeere, on the lowland plains east of Mount Kenya, raise money by doing farm work such as clearing bush, sowing, weeding and harvesting, and that farm work is definitely the most popular means of raising money for projects (Mwaniki, 1986: 215).

The Midodoni women's group, in a location 48 kilometres north of Mombasa in Kenya, is notable because it has backing both from Faith and Development (FAD), a church-based non-governmental organization in Nairobi, and from Tototo Home Industries, a voluntary agency which seeks to help low-income women in the coastal region of Kenya. The group started in 1981 through the collaboration of the government social development adviser for the area, the chief and the group's future chairwoman. Twenty-nine women paid the equivalent of a $5 yearly membership fee, as well as a weekly subscription of two Kenyan shillings (approximately 20 cents). The group's aim was to start a water project, and in the first year they tried to raise money by selling breads and growing maize on a borrowed field, but with little success (McCormack et al., 1986: 133). The breakthrough came in 1982, when the chairwoman was able to utilize kinship links to acquire outside backing; her daughter, who was working for Faith and Development (FAD), encouraged her mother to write to the organization requesting assistance. The Midodoni women are involved in a wide range of activities, including sewing school uniforms, agricultural improvements, building houses for widows and installing piped water. The benefits of the FAD-sponsored projects have been demonstrable (McCormack et al., 1986: 134–7).

However, the group's main enterprise is the production and sale of copra (a cash crop obtained from coconuts), and the success of this enterprise owes everything to the chairwoman's successful manipulation of the assistance provided by FAD. Initially, the group had difficulty obtaining land for cultivation, and both borrowing and renting proved unsuccessful. But, in 1984, the group began acquiring land, palms and tree produce using the financial resources of the FAD project. In one case, the group bought land outright, but in other cases it merely secured access to land, palms or fruits by loaning money to local landowners who were compelled by financial difficulties to raise mortgages on their properties. By acting as a mortgagee, the group has acquired land and a variety of rights in other productive resources. This would not have been possible without the initial financial backing of FAD, who have since declined to have their funds used in this way in the future. The initiative for this scheme came from the group's chairwoman, and the enterprise has been so successful that the Midodoni women's group now has the means to continue these activities without recourse to FAD funds. It is also interesting to note that this enterprise represents a highly unusual accumulation of capital by women in what is predominantly a male sphere of activity – land ownership and copra production. According to the authors of the report, none of the local male entrepreneurs, who are mostly related to women's group members, 'can match the scale and diversity of the group's enterprises' (McCormack et al., 1986: 146).

Successful acquisition of land and investment of assets is a feature of both the Midodoni and the Kulima women's groups. The two cases are, however, slightly different, and they illustrate a number of interesting points. In the case of the Kulima Harambee Group, land acquisition represents a change in group goals. Initially, the women co-operated in order to improve the living conditions of their households, but now all of the group's income is invested in land, which is the common property of group members, and none of it is used for agrarian purposes. This means that members' households no longer benefit directly from the proceeds of the women's group activities. Maas explains this change by referring to the role that land acquisition plays in the context of changing intra-household relations. Traditionally, in this patrilineal society, a woman gains access to land through marriage, but, as her children begin to marry, major changes take place in her life. When her first son marries, she relinquishes part of her land to her new daughter-in-law, so, with each son who marries, the land she originally acquired through her own marriage diminishes in quantity. The effect of this is a gradual decline in the older woman's economic position, and ultimately she becomes dependent upon her sons and daughters-in-law for her food and other needs. However, from the beginning of this century, population growth and partial inheritance have meant increasing competition for land, and, at the present time, the amount of land each household has at its disposal is frequently insufficient to support the members of the household. Older women are increasingly aware that in this situation they are a burden to their daughters-in-law, who are struggling to produce enough food to feed their children. According to Maas, the result is that mothers-in-law and daughters-in-law often have somewhat strained relations, and, to a certain extent, the mother–son relationship conflicts with that of wife and husband (Maas, 1986: 32–8). In a situation where resources of all kinds, including financial resources, are relatively scarce, older women are very aware that they cannot necessarily rely on their sons to support them. Maas explains why these older women, who form the majority of women's group members, do not invest money in the farm or contribute to the upkeep of the younger generation, in terms of their desire to invest any resources they may gain from the women's group in improving their own circumstances. She argues that they do this so as to be able to maintain their independence *vis-à-vis* their sons and daughters-in-law (Maas, 1986: 47–8). The importance of the women's groups for these women is evidenced by their expression of lifelong commitment to the group.

Maas discusses the case of a woman who had to leave the group because of ill-health. This woman asked her daughter, who lives close by, to help work her fields, and in return she transferred her share of the assets of the women's group to her daughter, who has also become a member in her mother's place. Apparently, all the women who have to leave the group for reasons of ill-health do the same. This obviously strengthens ties between mothers and daughters, and has the added benefit of providing for the mother in her old age. The benefits for the daughter are clear, because she becomes co-owner of the women's group's land, and also gains access to a network of women through whom she can get money and work (Maas, 1986: 49–50). Maas's research indicates that members of the women's group use their investment in land, and their membership of the women's group, to help gain the support of other women, especially their daughters, and to lessen their dependence on their sons and daughters-in-law.

However, the success of the Kulima women in operating as corporate entrepreneurs, and also in using their economic success to negotiate intra-household relations, is not necessarily typical of women's self-help groups. One point that is particularly relevant to the success of the Kulima group is the age and marital status of its members. Young married women find it difficult to devote time to successful women's group activities because they have young children, and because they have less autonomy and freedom of movement than older, more senior women. Young wives are much more likely to be under the immediate control of their husbands and their kin. McCormack et al make the same point with regard to their data on the Midodoni women's group and three other groups in the coastal region of Kenya. They note that the overall age distribution of the members of all four groups shows a predominance of women over the age of 40, and, for the most part, members are women who have five or six children each (McCormack et al., 1986: 58). Like Maas, the authors explain this age distribution in terms of the greater independence and status of older women, and the fact that they are past childbearing age, and are able to delegate some of their household responsibilities to children or (in polygynous households) to younger wives. In the case of the Midodoni women's group, which has forty-five members, thirty-five women are married and the rest are widows, reflecting the high proportion of older women, as well as a low rate of remarriage. In this strongly patrilineal community, where high bridewealth is paid, divorce is infrequent and women are under the control of their husbands and fathers. A wife requires her husband's permission to join the women's group, and it is reported that the chairwoman has sometimes recruited members by approaching men and asking them to get their wives to join (McCormack et al., 1986: 149). This situation is, in part, a reflection of the very restricted opportunities for women's income generation in this area, which means that married women are forced to rely on their husbands for help in paying their subscriptions to the women's group (McCormack et al., 1986: 153).

Men's control of household income may also be relevant in other ways. In a second group studied by McCormack et al., Mapimo women's group, based north of Mombasa, in a predominantly Giriama settlement, the members of the group are involved in running a bakery. The group had its origins in an adult-literacy class, and has received financial help and technical assistance from Tototo Home Industries. Since the start of the bakery enterprise, individual members have also used the facilities to bake and sell bread for individual profit, as well as for corporate gain (McCormack et al., 1986: 190–5). It appears that the group baking enterprise makes relatively much smaller profits than the profits that members make from individual baking. This may be related in part to the inefficiency and wastage of the group enterprise, but it also seems to be linked to a certain conflict of interests between individual effort and group enterprise. In addition to the bakery, the group is involved in the cultivation of a collective field and in the running of a tea kiosk. Most agricultural labour in the area is done by women, who work on the main subsistence crop, maize, as well as on the cash crops of cotton, cashew nuts and sesame. Income from cash crop sales is often taken by the head of the household regardless of land ownership or labour input. In local Giriama practice, the husband has control over all the products of his wife's labour, but how this control is exercised and how much of her income a wife is allowed to retain is open to negotiation. It is the possibility of negotiation which is the most important factor in determining the benefit group members derive from their income-generating activities, because most of them are members of households which they do not head (McCormack et al., 1986: 209, 215). Membership of the group is again conditional upon the husband or household head. Outside of group activities, women's opportunities for earning income in the area are very limited. This means that baking activities can provide much-needed cash for the household, and household heads stand to gain as much from this as the women themselves. One woman was withdrawn from the group by her unemployed husband because she refused to give him her proceeds from baking. Male control of income can also discourage women from getting involved in individual baking. One member only bakes for the group because her husband who is a local entrepreneur takes most of the money she earns. Women's income tends to be invested in the household, either voluntarily or in accordance with the wishes of the household head. In this particular context, it seems that women's access to income does not give them greater autonomy or bargaining power within the household (McCormack et al., 1986: 217–18). Ironically, this has given rise to a rather paradoxical situation where the women's group has become increasingly dominated by women whose domestic circumstances actually allow them a degree of autonomy not permitted to the majority of women.

It is clear that members' households have benefited in tangible ways from group activities, because women now have some money to buy esentials – food and clothing – and are also able to make longer-term investments in cattle, goats, trees and school fees for children. However, the study of the Mapimo group clearly demonstrates the constraints of the household economy within which women's self-help groups and their associated income-generating activities have to operate. The overall profitability of group enterprises is affected as much by these constraints as are the economic fortunes of individual women. For example, the decision to establish an individual collective system of baking was a direct response to households' immediate need for cash, and the system serves as a substitute for wage payments to members. However, this means that the interests of the individual households compete with those of the group, and when there are problems it is the group which suffers first.

It should be clear from the preceding discussion that the success of women's self-help groups and their income-generating activities depends on the complex interaction of different sets of interests. Regardless of the success or failure of group income-generating activities, the benefits which individual women gain from the income they produce depends largely on their ability to negotiate intra-household relations. The constraints which are imposed on women by these relations, largely relations with their husbands and male kin, can be so great that they threaten the overall viability of group activities, as in the Mapimo case. Women who are old enough or senior enough to escape some or all of these constraints appear to benefit most from group enterprises. On the other hand, some of the most successful women entrepreneurs emerge because they are able to use kinship links to their advantage, as in the case of the Midodoni group chairwoman who was able to gain access to outside financial support through her daughter. This utilitization of kinship links can be compared to that in the Kulima case, where women were using their membership of the women's group to help them establish links with their daughters and with other women outside their immediate families, with a view to decreasing their dependence on intra-household links, especially those with sons and daughters-in-law. The specific nature of household and kinship relations varies from case to case, but it is clear that difficulties in negotiating such relations can arise because women's self-help groups act as a channel through which household and community members can gain access to outside resources and assistance both from the state and from non-governmental and voluntary organizations.

The fact that conflicts arise between women and men, and between different groups within communities, because women's self-help groups inevitably link household and community politics into national politics is only one part of the multifaceted relationship between women's self-help groups and the state. A second and equally important area of investigation is the way in which women's groups are actively involved in negotiating relations with the state. McCormack et al. point out that the maintenance of good relations with local politicians and government development workers requires groups to make regular contributions from their funds to events and projects which are unconnected to their own activities. Getting access to outside grants can also be costly for groups, because they have to entertain 'visitors' – that is, representatives of the grant-giving body. According to McCormack et al., entertaining visitors at the time of the UN End of Decade Conference in Nairobi cost one group 25 per cent of the profits it had made from its shop over a period of ten months (McCormack et al., 1986: 91). Women's groups are also subject to various demands on their time and labour from the state. In July 1985, the Midodoni group members worked on repairing a dirt road in the area at the request of the local sub-chief. Later in the year, they cooked bananas and took them to divisional headquarters for a meeting celebrating World Food Day. Four days after that, they again went to the divisional headquarters to sing before the guests at an assembly marking Kenyatta Day. During the year, the group spent $214 on matching dresses and headscarves to wear on such occasions. Before Kenyatta Day, the local sub-chief instructed the women members on how to present food for visitors and how to curtsey and sing for them. On the day itself, the women queued for food while the 'honoured guests' feasted, but they did not get any food, and had to return home hungry.

The members of all women's self-help groups are expected to spend a great deal of their time servicing and entertaining male representatives of the state. They are invited to many meetings and public occasions, not as representatives of their communities, but as 'handmaidens' of the real representatives of the political process. On some of these occasions, women's leaders are invited to speak, and some of them do become involved in the political process. The chairwoman of the Midodoni group, for example, is the FAD project social worker and already has a regular income of her own; she is also vice-chairwoman of the sub-location development committee, vice-chairwoman of women's groups in the division, and women's representative on the district development committee (McCormack et al., 1986: 158). This situation, however, says more about processes of differentiation within the group than it does about the empowerment of women or improvements in their political representation and decision-making abilities. Women's groups become involved in public meetings and other occasions because they are fully aware of the potential benefits for the group. The fact remains, however, that their presence – especially when they provide hospitality and entertainment – actually serves the purpose of reinforcing political links between men. The sub-chiefs and chiefs of the location encourage the women's groups to support public occasions because it is one way in which they can provide hospitality for visiting district and provincial officials, and for Members of Parliament. It is also an indication of how 'progressive' they themselves are, and of the success of development initiatives in the location. Development projects and initiatives are, of course, part of the political process itself, and are an important area of state intervention and control. Just as the chiefs gain prestige from display-ing success in this crucial area, so too do district and provincial officials, as well as Members of Parliament, especially when important outsiders are present at these public meetings and occasions.

'All the women's groups in Kiambu are mine,' said the Member of Parliament for the area. During the election campaign in 1979, Maas was able to observe the interactions between the Kulima women's group and the prospective Member of Parliament for Kiambu district. Women are in the majority in the rural areas of Kiambu, but the importance of their vote is increased by the fact that they are organized and thus tend to support prospective candidates as a group, instead of using their vote individually. The women try to reach agreement through consultation about the candidate they want to support. Appropriately enough, the women say that they are going to 'get up and dance' for a candidate when they intend to vote for them. The can-didate supported by the Kulima women's group succeeded in the election. This person is essential for the successful negotiation of the group's business transactions. He supplies information on where land is for sale and what its future value might be, and he acts as an intermediary in the purchase and sale of the group's land. He has also done much to support the water supply project in Kulima, which is very important to the women, and, at an earlier date, he introduced the growing of French beans into Kulima and guaranteed sales to buyers in Europe (Maas, 1986: 65–6). Women use their organizing ability to exert pressure on the Member of Parliament to support projects in the area, and to support the investment activities of the group. The support of these women is essential for the Member of Parliament both in national elections and in the successful manipulation of constituency politics. The Kulima women are clearly able to use their organization to obtain resources, social influence and power, and to make sure that their interests are represented at a national level. However, women's influence on resource allocation, policy formation and political deci-sions is still indirect, and although organizing has improved their ability to negotiate, as well as improving their standard of living, it has not directly contributed to an improvement in their decision-making role in local or national politics. Women's political power, such as it is, is still very indirect.

Women's organizations: formal and informal

Women's self-help groups are, of course, only one type of women's association, and only one of the many different ways in which women have been 'integrated into development'. The purpose in choosing self-help groups, as opposed to other organizational forms – such as co-operatives – or other types of 'women-oriented' development projects is to provide evidence of the kinds of autonomy and degree of political power which women do achieve.

Many types of women's association exist worldwide, and they can be used to demonstrate the very diverse nature of women's political life. It is sometimes assumed that women's groups are a form of 'domestic' gathering, where women get together to gossip, exchange news and do 'good works'. They only types of women's groups exempt from this stereotype are 'feminist groups', and the women's groups attached to the political institutions of government and to political parties. The study of women's groups in comparative perspective shows that such groups have always been political in nature, and that they should not be glossed as 'social gatherings' whose activities are devoid of relevance for the wider society. The relationship of women's groups to the state is, of course, very variable, but many groups, like the women's self-help groups in Kenya, are actually located at the interface between local kinship structures and the processes and institutions of the wider society, including the modern state. Women's groups are very frequently mechanisms for defending and reproducing class and sectional interests, and, as such, it is important not to confuse women's groups *per se* with female solidarity, or with a unitary set of women's interests common to all women.

The study of women's organizations is not new in social anthropology, and a considerable amount of research has been done – not all of it directly inspired by the 'anthropology of women' – on what are known as women's informal associations (March and Taqqu, 1986). Many scholars working on Africa, New Guinea and the Middle East have emphasized the important role of women's kinship networks in establishing and maintaining links between male-based lineage groups. Women who move from their natal home at marriage to the home of their husband have an interest in maintaining ties with both their marital and their natal lineages. As a result, women form the ties which bind the separate patrilineal groups into a wider political whole. The kinship basis of politics in these societies emphasizes the insufficiency of a 'private'/'public' distinction, and shows that the domestic and the political cannot necessarily be separated out from each other (Lamphere, 1974; Strathern, 1972; Nelson, 1974; Wolf, 1972).

Kin-based associations provide a number of different contexts in which women express solidarity and co-operate together. Okonjo describes the political importance of the *otu umuada* (the 'daughters of the lineage') among the Ibo in Nigeria. 'The *otu umuada* included all the married, unmarried, widowed, and divorced daughters of a lineage or village group. These women acted as political pressure groups in their natal villages in order to achieve desired objectives' (Okonjo, 1976: 52). The *otu umuada* was a mechanism through which women in a patrilineal society who were dispersed by marriage could maintain strong ties with their natal lineages and also co-operate together to solve disputes, perform important rituals and act as intermediaries between villages.

In addition to maintaining links between marital and natal lineages, women may also come together within their marital lineages in order to co-operate over childcare, and other forms of productive and reproductive labour. Women in many societies form co-operating groups to farm each others' fields in rotation, and in many parts of Africa the 'wives of the lineage' constitute an important political body which has considerable power over community activities and which can take action against men who mistreat their wives or insult women (Van Allen, 1972; Moore, 1986: 176–7; Ardener, 1973). Women's secret societies are often cited as an example of solidarity among women, and it is certainly true that initiation ceremonies provide a context in which women can act as a group and work together to affirm the value of women's knowledge and of links between women (Moore, 1986: 181–3). However, while these societies do cement ties between women, and while initiation forms a very important basis for shared experience and communal identity, it is also the case that, in many instances, women's secret societies are hierarchical and serve to reinforce class divisions within the community. Caroline Bledsoe's work demonstrates how the leaders of *sande*, the women's society among the Kpelle of Liberia, use their power to protect the interests of the elite lineages, to control the marriages of initiates, and to make use of the labour of initiates on their own farms. The result is that the leaders use *sande* as a way of extending their personal wealth and influence, as well as a means to protect the hierarchical relations between lineages. Consequently, the women leaders of the *sande* share a number of interests with the male leaders of the elite lineages, and the solidarity of women is cross-cut by class interests (Bledsoe, 1980; 1985). As Janet Bujra points out in her discussion of the relationship between class interests and women's interests: 'Female solidarity only over-rides class divisions in very exceptional circumstances and it may indeed contribute to the perpetuation of those class divisions' (Bujra, 1978: 30).

In addition to women's associations based on kinship and age, there are also many examples of groups which are based on occupation.

Much of the early work in anthropology on these groups concentrated on urban Africa. For example, Kenneth Little analysed the role which prostitutes' associations played in providing women who had migrated to town with the kinds of mutual support which they would formerly have had from the kinship structure in their rural homes (Little, 1966, 1972). Other well-known types of associations include women's marketing and beer-brewing associations. Nelson's study of the women beer brewers of Mathare Valley, Kenya, shows how women rely on a network of connections between women to buy and sell beer wholesale, to gain extended credit, to put up bail and help collect money for fines, and to provide help in the case of emergencies (Nelson, 1979). The women in Mathare have also used the solidarity created through their personal networks to achieve wider develop- mental and political ends. Market women in many parts of the world have very well-organized associations which are concerned with organizing markets, regulating prices, applying sanctions against individuals who break market rules and establishing credit schemes (Lewis, 1976; Little, 1973: 50–60). Rotating credit schemes are often an important feature of women's group activities within markets. The nature of such credit schemes varies enormously, but they follow a basic pattern where a group of women contribute a fixed amount to a fund on a regular basis, and the fund is then given to each contributor in rotation (Ardener, 1964; Geertz, 1962). This provides women with a method of saving, a potential source of capital for their business enterprises, and a possible source of funds to cover contingencies and emergencies. In addition to credit provision and the organization of markets and market-related activities, women's market associations have also provided the basis for organized political activity against colonial and post-colonial governments (Van Allen, 1972; Johnson, 1986; Westwood, 1984: 152–5). This demonstrates that women's groups based on economic co-operation, such as prostitutes' unions and market associations, can and do provide women with an oppor- tunity for collective political action.

Another form of women's group which has been relatively well researched consists of those groups concerned with social welfare and the church. Filomina Steady has studied the Protestant church associations of Freetown, Sierra Leone, where women come together to raise money for the church and to support charities, hospitals and other philanthropic causes. Leadership of such groups provides women with opportunities for political influence within the church, as well as status and influence within the community at large (Steady, 1976). Similar associations exist for Muslim women (Steady, 1976; Strobel, 1979). It is important in contexts of this kind not to see religion as a totally conservative force in women's lives, because such groups

do provide women with a legitimate forum for collective action, as well
as giving them status within the community as a whole. Community
status may be particularly important in cases where most, or all, of the
status positions in society are open only to men.

In addition to women's informal associations, a certain amount of
research has been done on more formal women's organizations,
although this is an area where much more anthropological work needs
to be done. Patricia Caplan has made a study of women's welfare
organizations in Madras, India. The internal structure of all the
organizations was highly bureaucratic and hierarchical, and Caplan
argues that the most effective organizations were those headed by a
leader able to command the loyalty and allegiance of the members, as
well as the respect of the community at large. The majority of the
members in the five associations studied intensively by Caplan were
upper and upper-middle class, and all but one organization were
heavily dominated by Brahmins (Caplan, 1985: 149–54). All five
associations were involved in social welfare activities, in addition to
providing recreational facilities for members. Caplan argues that social
welfare is something separate from basic social services, like health
and education, and that it is not a priority area for government
intervention, although the state makes contributions to it through the
Central Social Welfare Board (comprising voluntary and government
representatives) and through voluntary agencies. During the last thirty
years, social welfare has become identified with provision to the poor,
the disadvantaged, the handicapped, and women and children, and, at
the same time, it is women's voluntary organizations which are
primarily responsible for making social welfare provisions (Caplan,
1985: ch. 7). Social welfare and the women's organizations set up to
provide it thus become identified with a specific constellation of
'women's concerns or problems'. The state's attitudes to social welfare,
as reflected in its policies towards welfare provision, work to define
women and women's activities in a particular way. The women's
voluntary organizations, which are sometimes partly supported by the
state, are complicit in this process of definition. The position is further
complicated by the role that class plays in the reproduction of relations
between women and the state. Voluntary social welfare is actively
engaged in defining and mediating relations between classes because it
consists primarily of 'good works' carried out by the middle and upper
classes for the benefit of the working class (Caplan, 1985: 16). In
addition, voluntary social welfare is part of a process through which
the middle and upper classes reproduce themselves, and it is women
who play a vital role in this work of class reproduction (Caplan, 1985:
18).[18] As a result, women's voluntary organizations can be seen as
engaged in the production and reproduction of the state through their

involvement in the reproduction of class relations. This is not to suggest that the state is identical with the 'ruling class', but rather to emphasize that the reproduction of the state depends on a complex set of interrelations between gender and class difference (see this chapter above).

Caplan also stresses the importance of men in relation to women's group activities; a point familiar to us from the analysis of Kenyan self-help groups. Husbands often have a very ambivalent attitude towards their wives' involvement with association activities. Women from well-off households may be encouraged to participate in order to 'make a name' for the family, but in less wealthy households, where group activities may conflict with the demands of domestic duties, there may be some resistance to wives' participation (Caplan, 1985: 168–73). The interesting point is that women play a significant political role in running voluntary associations, but that their ability to do so depends, to a greater or lesser extent, on their ability to negotiate with their husbands. Caplan's study of Indian women's groups once again emphasizes that household and community politics are inevitably linked with state politics.

The role of upper-middle-class and elite women's organizations in defending the interests of the state is clearly evidenced by many of the national women's organizations which are set up under direct state patronage.[19] Audrey Wipper's analysis of Mandaleo ya Wanawake, the national women's organization of Kenya, shows that, in spite of the organization's critical position *vis-à-vis* the government in the early years of independence, it has since become a conservative force whose leadership has strong links with the ruling male elite. In the early 1970s, the president of Mandaleo ya Wanawake was the wife of a government minister, whose contacts with the business and inter-national communities helped to promote the organization and gain backing for it (Wipper, 1975: 104–5). When Mandaleo ya Wanawake was first started it concentrated on trying to improve rural living standards through self-help initiatives, and as a result the organization had an extensive rural base. In 1964, there were 42,447 members in 1,120 clubs (Wipper, 1975: 102). However, during the 1970s, the association turned much more towards philanthropy and social welfare activities, and it also started raising funds to build a 'suitable headquarters' (Wipper, 1975: 106–7). The result was considerable discontent among the ordinary members, who felt that the national executive of Mandaleo ya Wanawake and the central government were indifferent to rural needs. There is obviously considerable substance to this criticism about the shared interests between the national executive of Mandaleo and the ruling elite. The government pays lip-service to women's demands and the importance of women's interests, and in the process it consolidates its constituency. Mandaleo ya Wanawake is involved in this process because its very existence is part of a strategy of tokenism and verbal affirmation which contains what might otherwise be a radical force for change. This containment is actively promoted by Mandaleo's leaders, whose strong links with the elite mean that they have no interest in disrupting the status quo (Wipper, 1971; Wipper, 1975: 116). Research on other national women's organizations in Africa has produced very similar conclusions. [20] Janet Bujra sums up the material as follows:

> The existence of *women's* organisations in Africa is not . . . unthinkingly to be equated with the existence of any specifically *feminist* conscious-ness, or any desire to transform the class or economic structures of postcolonial society. Women's liberation is *disruptive* in its challenge to male prerogatives; organisations such as these reinforce the status quo. They serve petty bourgeois interests more than they serve women. To dismiss them out of hand because of this would be short-sighted, however. For, despite their primary significance as institutions of class control, such organisations, in bringing women into communication with each other, can provide arenas of struggle within which women who are poor and subordinated can speak out and exert pressure on those who enjoy the rewards of postcolonial society. (Bujra, 1986: 137; italics in the original)

It is clear from the discussion of women's organizations in this section – both formal and informal – that women's groups in society tend to represent particular interest groups and only rarely represent women as a whole. This fact may not be particularly surprising with regard to women's organizations in contemporary Africa and India, but it is worth reiterating that it has also been true of many kinds of women's associations in pre-capitalist contexts. The issue which this raises, however, as Bujra points out, is one about the actual and supposed relationship between women's groups and feminism, and this is something which has particular relevance when we turn to women's participation in revolutionary struggles.

State institutions and women's resistance

In recent years there has been a 'rediscovery' of early feminist move-ments and of the history of women's struggles around the world.[21] This research has gone a long way towards correcting a very biased picture of feminist struggle, which seemed to be exclusively concerned with Western feminists and their activities. Such an exclusive focus contri-buted to a feminist discourse which seemed to present the majority of the women in the world as subordinate and passive, and in need of liberation. This view of women as passive and non-political has been strongly questioned as the social sciences move away from a predominant concern with forms of women's oppression towards a consideration of the forms of women's resistance. One of the most notable forms of women's resistance has, of course, been their participation in nationalist and revolutionary struggles.

Revolutionary struggle

The very important role which women have played in many socialist revolutionary struggles has sometimes been submerged in the disappointment which many observers feel because of the inability of socialist regimes to realize their stated objectives with regard to women's emancipation. Time and time again, a pattern has emerged where women play a significant role during the armed struggle, but, once the revolutionary government is installed, women's needs and interests fade from political agendas, and the political rhetoric fails to give rise to active programmes for women's emancipation. Some of the reasons for this failure have already been discussed, but the interrelations between feminism and nationalist revolutions have a number of complex political dimensions. Maxine Molyneux discusses the Nicaraguan revolution, and she notes that during the revolution women made up approximately 30 per cent of the armed revolutionary forces, and that immediately after the revolution women were promoted into senior political positions as ministers and regional party co-ordinators. However, as the revolutionary government came under pressure from counter-revolution, military action and economic scarcity, the political pluralism, which had promoted women's political participation and a commitment to women's issues, began to show signs of disintegration. The result was that AMNLAE, the women's union, 'reduced its public identification with "feminism" and spoke increasingly of the need to promote women's interests in the context of the wider struggle' (Molyneux, 1985b: 227, 237–8). It is perhaps not surprising that the precarious existence of many revolutionary governments leaves them with few resources to devote to issues which do not seem to be directly related to survival, and in such circumstances it is not difficult to see how women's interests can be viewed as secondary to those of 'the people'.

However, the relationship between women's liberation and nationalism has a further dimension which requires discussion. Many of the revolutionary leaders, both women and men, have been, and are, committed to equality of rights and opportunities for women, as well as to the eradication of women's oppression within society. Samora Machel, the late President of Mozambique, acknowledged that 'The emancipation of women is not an act of charity. The liberation of women is a fundamental necessity for the revolution, the guarantee of its continuity and the precondition for its victory.' But, in the same speech, he also criticized Western feminism:

> There are those who see emancipation as mechanical equality between men and women. . . . If there are still no women truck drivers or tractor drivers in Frelimo, we must have some right away regardless of the objective and subjective conditions. As we can see from . . . capitalist countries, this mechanically conceived emancipation leads to complaints and attitudes which utterly distort the meaning of women's emancipation. An emancipated woman is one who drinks, smokes, wears trousers, and mini skirts, who indulges in sexual promiscuity, who refuses to have children. (quoted in Kimble and Unterhalter, 1982: 13)

Machel's image of the Western 'emancipated woman' is a very disabling one, but it does highlight the extent to which Western feminism is associated with imperialism and neo-imperialism. For the women involved in national liberation struggles, it is quite clear that in many ways Western feminism 'misses the point'. This does not mean that there are no areas of overlap: women in non-Western countries are engaged in fighting for contraception, abortion, equal opportunity for equal education, childcare facilities and an end to violence against women, in the same way as women in Western countries (Organization of Angolan Women, 1984: Mehta, 1982). But there cannot be a complete identity of interests, because the fight against imperialism and dependency alters the nature of gender politics, and undermines any simple idea of an undifferentiated community of women with shared aims. In the words of Mavis Nhlapo, representative of the ANC's women's secretariat: 'In our country white racism and apartheid coupled with economic exploitation have degraded the African woman more than any male prejudices' (quoted in Kimble and Unterhalter, 1982: 14).

The Western feminist emphasis on the primacy of gender politics and on the conern with the 'family' as the site of women's oppression makes little sense to women who are involved in a struggle for the emancipation of 'all their people' and who, in the case of South Africa, see the destruction of ordinary family life as 'one of the most grievous crimes of apartheid' (Kimble and Unterhalter, 1982: 13; Walker, 1982). This does not, of course, alter the fact that many revolutionary regimes fail to achieve and implement their stated aims with regard to women's emancipation, but it does raise the issue of how we are going to develop a feminist theory of what constitutes women's liberation. The Western feminist model of women's emancipation cannot be extended to cover the rest of the world, and it seems that the first step towards a recognition of this fact will necessitate more research which examines the position of women in concrete historical circumstances, and which makes a determined effort to break away from the idea that the trajectory of Western political development will necessarily, and beneficially, be followed elsewhere.

Religion and resistance in Iran

The inappropriateness of Western ideologies of emancipation becomes particularly clear when we turn to a consideration of the complex relations between religion, revolution and the state in the contemporary world, and to the question of women's role in revolutionary religious movements.

All states have an ideological character, because without ideological legitimation they could not survive. In many states, religion plays a key role in maintaining the structures of the state, as well as providing legitimation for state policies on the 'family', education, employment, sexuality and the media. In the case of women, the role of religious ideology in maintaining political control is most forcefully manifest in the areas of marriage, reproductive rights and the control of female sexuality. It is a truism that the great religions of the world were reform movements in their time. However, religion in the contemporary world is more often seen as a conservative force.[22] Believers of all faiths have argued that religion is not intrinsically conservative and repressive, but that the rulers – secular and ecclesiastical – who interpret its tenets and laws in the modern world have made it so. One very common feminist argument builds on this thesis and argues that, since these rulers are almost all exclusively men, it is not surprising that religion and religious change should rarely prove emancipatory for women. There is much to be said for these arguments, but one of the most striking features of the contemporary situation is that, with increasing education, urbanization, modernization and international communications, we might have expected a notable secularization of religious institutions and laws. Instead, there is some evidence for a reverse process, a religious revival evidenced by the rebirth of religious fundamentalism. The revival of fundamentalism is particularly noticeable with regard to Islam, and, while a number of countries around the world – including Pakistan, the Philippines, Algeria and Malaysia – are involved in this revival, perhaps the best example is Iran. There now exists a certain amount of literature on the Iranian revolution and its consequences for women, as well as a large body of writings by Iranian clerics on the subject of women and their role in Islamic society (Hermansen, 1983; Hussain and Radwan, 1984; Afshar, 1982). Significantly, the role of women in the Iranian revolution challenges a number of Western feminist assumptions about what constitutes emancipation and equality for women.

One apparent paradox which struck many commentators was the participation of large numbers of women in the Iranian revolution, including their massive demonstrations on the streets, and the tactics they used to prevent government soldiers from shooting at demonstrators. The large-scale participation of women was crucial to the success of the revolution and also accounted for its largely non-violent character (Tabari, 1980: 19; Nashat, 1983b: 199). Western observers were surprised to see these so-called 'secluded' women demonstrating on the streets, and they commented on the fact that the majority of women protestors were veiled. However, in spite of this, in March 1979, less than two months after the Shah had been overthrown, thousands of women used International Women's Day to demonstrate against plans to make veiling compulsory (Higgins, 1985: 477). The women who had helped to overthrow the Shah quickly protested against a more conservative Islamic definition of their role and place in society. But since those demonstrations in 1979 there appears to have been relatively little protest from women, in spite of the fact that women's rights have deteriorated significantly under Ayatollah Khomeini. This is particularly noticeable because in pre-revolutionary Iran women's rights had seen some considerable improvement. The veil was abolished in 1936, women got the vote in 1962, the unequivocal male right of divorce and men's automatic custody of children were curbed in 1973, free abortion on demand was granted in 1974, and in 1976 polygamy was banned and women won the right to maintenance after divorce (Afshar, 1987: 70–1). Within a relatively short time after Khomeini came to power, however, much of this had changed.

Many of the women who helped to overthrow the Shah did not do so because they wanted to reinstate traditional Islamic law. This is especially true of the young, educated women, many of whom had attended European and American universities and were oriented to the left, but who none the less joined forces with the opposition to bring down the Shah. These women united against the Shah because they were opposed to what they saw as cultural imperialism. The hasty Westernization programme of the Shah was accompanied by increasing social differentiation and rampant corruption. The marriage, employment and education reforms introduced by his regime did nothing to ameliorate the sense of dismay with which many people viewed the 'mimicking' of Western values and lifestyle, and the loss of national and cultural identity. Opposition to the Shah focused, in part, on the necessity of restoring Islamic values and Iranian society. 'To symbolize their rejection of the regime and to express faith in their own cultural heritage', many educated women 'began to wear a scarf or even a *chadur* (veil) to the university or workplace' (Nashat, 1983b: 199). The veil, for these young women, and the revival of religious values which its wearing signified, was not seen as something

regressive and traditional, but as something Islamic. It is this understanding of the re-adoption of the veil which explains why the same
women demonstrated so fiercely against the planned introduction by
the Ayatollah of compulsory veiling (*hijab*).[23] It is clear that these
women now feel betrayed by Khomeini's regime, and that they are
bitterly disappointed by attempts to limit their job and educational
opportunities, and to confine women to the roles of wives and
mothers. It is a terrible irony that many workers and educated women
took up the veil, not as a sign of submission and seclusion, but as an
expression of their militancy and their search for a more meaningful
female identity (Azari, 1983: 67), only to find that veiling became
compulsory under Khomeini precisely because it symbolizes the
authority and vitality of traditional Islamic ideology, with all that that
implies for women.

Women still have the vote in Iran; they are still entitled to education,
but only in single-sex institutions. They have not been barred from
employment outside the home, but layoffs, early retirement, and cuts
in maternity benefits and daycare provision aim to pressure women
into giving up their jobs (Higgins, 1985: 483). The legally permitted
age of marriage has been reduced to thirteen years. Women's ability to
get divorced has been restricted, and their right to have custody of their
young children after divorce has been removed. Polygamy is permitted, and women have been executed on charges of adultery, while men
charged with the same offence are set free after being lashed. Women
are no longer permitted to be judges, and they have been removed
from important executive posts. The success of government policies in
controlling women is symbolized by the imposition of the *hijab*.
Legislation passed in 1983 prosecutes women who fail to adhere to the
dress code with imprisonment or a fine (Nashat, 1983c: 285).[24] In the
modern Islamic state of Iran, women and men are very different sorts
of citizens. In the face of all this, the question still remains: why have
women not protested more?

The answers to this question are not particularly straightforward.
One response focuses on the lack of a broadly based women's
organization which could agitate on behalf of women. It was the urban
employed and educated, largely middle-class women who protested
for, and against, the revolution in the early stages, and their protests
were focused on nationalist and cultural issues, rather than feminist
ones. Furthermore, the number of radical middle-class women is
small, and they lack support from rural, newly urbanized and petty-
bourgeois women. The Mujahidin, the Marxist-inspired group who
form the main opposition to the Khomeini government, have spoken
out in support of women's rights, but they view women's emancipation only in the context of a wider proletarian revolution. The result is
that the Mujahidin, and other left groups, do not support immediate

action around women's issues, in spite of the large number of women active within these organizations. The lack of any organizational support for campaigns on behalf of women has meant that the present government of Iran has had little difficulty in imposing repressive measures. Without a basis from which to fight back, women have been easily 'disorganized' by a combination of patriarchal and religious forces acting through a powerful state.

The second reason for women's lack of protest against the present regime is directly connected to the existence of a rural–urban divide in Iran, and to other class-based divisions. Urban, middle-class and working women were the main beneficiaries of the reforms instituted under the Shah. For rural women and the urban poor, changes in the age at marriage, in inheritance and divorce laws, and the abolition of polygyny made little impact on their lives. This is largely because local customs continued to influence the interpretation of legal codes, and few women were aware of or directly affected by these legal reforms. However, if the Shah's reforms were of little significance, so too were Khomeini's counter-measures. Erika Friedl points out that the Muslim inheritance laws, under which women inherit half as much as men, are much more favourable than many local inheritance laws. But, just as the Family Protection Law under the Shah was never implemented in the village she studied, so the new Islamic law is currently being ignored. In the same way, the Shah's minimum age at marriage for girls of 18 years was circumvented in the past when villagers thought it necessary, and at the present time the lowering of the legal age at marriage for girls to 13 years has had no impact on actual marriage patterns in the village (Friedl, 1983: 220–1). Lack of administration and enforcement by the state, and rural women's ignorance of legal changes affecting their rights, mean that state interventions in 'family life' have had very little relevance for women at a local level, who remain under the authority of their husbands and families (Higgins, 1985: 485). There is, therefore, no impetus at a local level for protest based on the erosion of women's rights.

However, the picture is further complicated by the fact that some women from rural and smaller urban centres did protest against the Shah, but because this revolutionary activity was defined as religious activity there was no perceived conflict with their traditional roles (Hegland, 1983: 171). In fact, the revolutionary actions of these women were sanctioned by their menfolk, by religious leaders and by other women in their communities. Women's protest was therefore a religious protest, but it none the less had a very significant impact on women and on their sense of identity (Hegland, 1983: 182). Their participation in a political struggle alongside men affected the lives of rural and newly urbanized women more than the legal reforms of the Shah ever did. Women were drawn into political activity; their contribution was encouraged, sought after and publicly appreciated. The result for many women was an increased sense of power and self-confidence, an expanded political consciousness, and the perception of a greater respect for women as a consequence of their activities (Higgins, 1985: 487). All these changes can clearly be thought of as emancipatory. In some ways, it can be argued that participation in the Islamic revolution expanded the role of the Islamic woman and improved her position in society far more effectively than the legal reforms of the Shah. In this context, it is perhaps not surprising that women have not yet translated the disappointment and bitterness they currently feel at the outcome of the revolution, the increasing unemployment and inflation, and the deprivations of the Iran–Iraq war, into concerted action against the regime. Such action would, in any case, be almost impossible for the majority of poor women to contemplate taking, and most especially because the actions of the state are themselves legitimized and sanctified by Islam. Much more would be at stake in overthrowing Khomeini than merely toppling the government.

The Iranian example is a complex one, but it does show, in a most dramatic way, how religious ideology legitimizes the state and the exercise of state power. It also demonstrates how religious ideology works at both a local household level and a national or governmental level. The crucial role of Islamic ideology explains the extraordinary salience and political relevance of issues such as veiling, divorce and adultery. A woman who contravenes Islamic law does not just impugn the honour of her family, but she also questions the authority of the state. Iran provides an unsettling example of the way in which state policies encode various assumptions about the nature of women and men as citizens (Afshar, 1987: 83). Islamic thought sees women and men as having radically different natures, and it is through this difference, institutionalized in various forms and structures, that the state reproduces itself. However, religious ideology does more than legitimize patriarchal structures and state power, because it also plays a fundamental role in socialization and the creation of individual identity. Islamic ideology produces and is produced by particular notions about gendered individuals. In this world-view, men and women are equal before God, but they have different physical, emotional and mental capacities and potentials, and they have different rights and responsibilities vis-à-vis family and society as a result of these different capacities. In the words of Ayatollah Khomeini: 'Women are not equal to men, but neither are men equal to women. . . . Their roles in society are complementary. . . . Each has distinct functions according to his or her nature and constitution' (quoted in Higgins, 1985: 492). Islam structures the concept of the self, the concept of the family and the concept of the state, and, through the day-to-day actions and interactions of individuals, families and state structures, these concepts are given powerful material substance and force. Religion, as I have mentioned, is often seen as a conservative force in women's lives, and this is particularly the case where gender ideologies are fundamental to both political and religious authority. It is undeniably true that the Iranian state, constituted as it is through Islamic ideology, has brutally denied women their basic rights. However, it must also be acknowledged that the same religious ideology sanctioned women's political action, and that for many women the revolution offered a more positive sense of self, and a more positive position in an Islamic world. The apparent paradox with which we have to contend is that Islam has provided Iranian women with the opportunity for political participation, while simultaneously working as an ideology which contains and controls their participation.

'Everyday forms' of women's resistance

The Iranian example has allowed us to look at women's political protest and at the ways in which the revolutionary state has controlled, subverted and institutionalized that protest for its own ends. This raises the more general issue of how we recognize women's resistance. The lack of obvious organized political activity on the part of women in many contexts around the world and the male-dominated nature of formal politics have led some observers to suggest that women are not interested in politics, or that they are not inherently political in 'their nature', or that they content themselves with influencing the 'political world' through influencing their menfolk. All of these suppositions are incorrect, and they are easily dismissed by reference to the available data on women's political activities, as this chapter shows.

However, there is a genuine problem in recognizing women's political activity, as feminist anthropologists have long realized, because, if we look at formal political activity in any society, women are not involved in significant numbers; they often appear, in fact, to be somewhat marginal to political processes. One possible response to this problem, and one which has been adopted in social anthropology, is to say that there is something wrong with the standard definition of politics. This has led anthropologists to argue that the 'political' sphere is not something which can be separated off and simultaneously defined by its separation from a 'domestic' sphere. These two spheres interpenetrate, and thus women's activities and concerns are not individualistic and housebound, but are, in fact, political. The argument here is about the necessity of breaking down distinctions between the 'domestic' and the 'political', and about broadening the definition of politics. This argument is remarkably close, although developed in a very different context, to the feminist argument that the 'personal is political', which is itself part of an effort to extend the definition of politics to include things which are of particular concern to women – such as domestic inequality, sexuality, forms of representation, equal access to public resources for women, and so on.

The problem about needing to extend the definition of politics in order to recognize the validity of women's political activity becomes particularly acute when we turn to consider the kinds of resistance and protest which lie outside the domain of organized politics. It is one thing to suggest that we need to extend the range of issues around which organized political protest can be made; it is quite another to propose the investigation of various types of action which may not be recognizably political, and which may take forms which are hard to fit into the commonly understood typologies of organized political activity. Earlier in this chapter, I discussed women's informal and formal associations, and the political functions they perform in a variety of societies. The kinds of political action we are about to discuss can be initiated and carried out by members of such groups, but they are very often not related to group structures or to group consciousness of any kind. This makes their analysis as political acts particularly difficult because politics is usually understood as a group activity, something which groups do.

James Scott describes what he calls 'everyday forms of peasant resistance'. These forms of struggle stop short of outright collective defiance, and are characterized by the 'ordinary weapons' of relatively powerless groups: footdragging, arson, sabotage, pilfering, gossip, and so on. Such forms of resistance require little or no co-ordination or planning; they can be classed as a type of self-help; and they avoid any direct questioning of the authority or the norms of dominant/elite groups (Scott, 1985: xvi). Scott makes it clear that we should not romanticize these 'weapons of the weak', but, equally, it is important that they should not be dismissed: 'individual acts of footdragging and evasion, reinforced by a venerable popular culture of resistance and multiplied many thousand-fold, may, in the end, make an utter shambles of the policies dreamed up by . . . would-be superiors in the capital' (Scott, 1985: xvii).

Scott provides an example of an attempt by women rice transplanters to boycott landowners who had hired combine-harvesters to replace manual labour in a Malaysian village. The village was highly stratified according to landholdings, and smallholders, tenants and landless labourers were particularly dependent on the income earned from transplanting and harvesting rice. The consequences of the introduction of combine-harvesting were varied, but it was the poorer sections of the village community who were hit hardest by the removal of one very important source of wage labour: rice harvesting (Scott, 1985: 115–20). Men and women – sometimes from the same household – lost work to the combine, but the resistance to the introduction of combine-harvesters focused on women. Women were involved in transplanting and harvesting the rice fields, and, as the combines effectively removed half their seasonal earnings, they were naturally unhappy about transplanting the fields of any farmer who might use a combine at harvest-time (Scott, 1985: 248–50). The fact, however, that the farmers still required transplanters gave the women a potential bargaining point. Three out of five women's work groups decided to boycott farmers who hired combines, by refusing to transplant rice for them. This boycott did not involve any form of direct confrontation between the women and the farmers. The women let it be known through an intermediary that they were not happy about the lost harvest work and that they would be unwilling to transplant the fields of those who had hired combines the previous season. At the beginning of the 1977 season, the time came to 'make good' on this threat, but none of the three groups actually refused outright to transplant the fields of the offending farmers. Instead, they delayed and delayed, and because not all farmers had used a combine the previous season they had plenty of work to keep them occupied. The women thus kept their options open and did not provoke an open break with the combine-hiring farmers. As the nursery plants started to pass their prime, and the farmers could see the newly transplanted fields of their neighbours, they started to get nervous. After two weeks of this 'war of nerves', six farmers let it be known that they were going to engage outside labourers to do the work. At this point, the boycott collapsed because the women feared that the transplanting work would be permanently lost to outsiders (Scott, 1985: 250–1).

The attempt to stop the introduction of combines was abortive, but it was not insignificant. The women clearly recognized the weakness of their position, and they were unwilling when it came to 'the crunch' to engage in open confrontation. This compliance or lack of resistance should not be seen merely as an example of hopelessness or ineffectiveness. The women realized all along that they would probably have to give in – this was implicit in the indirectness of the boycott – but the pragmatics of survival forced them to back down and return to work. Compliance, like resistance, should be seen as a strategy, part of a process of negotiation which has no beginning and no end, while the exploitative nature of rural class relations remains. Knowing when to give in is an integral part of knowing how and when to resist, if you happen to be poor and weak.

Scott's concept of 'everyday forms of resistance' may be a useful way of approaching forms of protest and resistance which are embedded in gender relations as well as those which are an integral part of class relations. One form of women's resistance which has been well documented in social anthropology is connected to spirit possession. Ioan Lewis provides detailed accounts of instances where women are involved in spirit possession, and he interprets their prominent role in this mode of self-expression and protest as related to their exclusion from, and lack of authority in, other spheres; a sort of 'weapon of the weak' (Lewis, 1966, 1971). Lewis takes as an example the Somali pastoral nomads of north-east Africa, who are a patrilineal Muslim people. Women are regarded as weak and submissive, and it is men who dominate the practice of formal religion. Both young men and women who are unhappy or unlucky in love may be possessed by spirits, but one particular form of spirit possession afflicts married women. Somali women themselves see this latter type of possession as occurring in a context where women are struggling to survive and feed their children in a harsh environment where they are liable to neglect from a husband who is often absent following the herds, and where they are undermined by the tensions of polygynous marriage and the precariousness of women's access to resources outside marriage. 'In these circumstances, it is hardly surprising that many women's ailments, whether accompanied by definable physical symptoms or not, should so readily be interpreted by them as possession by *sar* spirits which demand luxurious clothes, perfume and exotic dainties from their menfolk' (Lewis, 1971: 75–6). Lewis recorded that several cases of spirit possession in women coincided with a husband's negotiations to marry an additional spouse. Men view this form of possession as malingering and see it as another example of women's deceitfulness, but they none the less believe in the existence of *sar* spirits (Lewis, 1971: 76). Lewis interprets spirit possession among women as a limited deterrent against the abuses of neglect and deprivation in a conjugal relationship which is biased heavily in favour of men. Women resort to spirit possession, he argues, as an oblique way of airing their grievances against their husbands and of gaining some satisfaction in the way of attention, gifts, and so on. Lewis explicitly argues that women's spirit possession is a way of making strategic interventions in a 'sex war' (Lewis, 1971: 77).[25]

Women's spirit possession leading to rites of exorcism where women make explicit demands for luxury goods and/or air their grievances against husbands and kin is well known in many societies (March and Taqqu, 1986: 76). Roger Gomm, in his work on the Digo of Kenya, supports Lewis's argument that women's spirit possession can be seen as a strategy embedded in gender relations. He notes that women who become possessed request money for travel, clothes, petrol stoves and furnishings. These are exactly the items which figure in quarrels between husbands and wives. Women are possessed by male spirits, and Gomm points out that in exorcism ceremonies the sorts of demands made by women in marriage and refused are made in the voice of a male spirit and granted (Gomm, 1975: 534). However, he cautions us against too romantic a view of this form of resistance, and he rightly argues that 'as a technique for obtaining favours from men, spirit possession has a limited time utility' (Gomm, 1975: 537). In other words, any woman who uses this strategy too often may find that her husband is unwilling to believe that she is involuntarily possessed, and will ultimately refuse to perform the necessary exorcism ceremony.

Other forms of women's resistance against their husbands include refusing to cook, refusing to have sexual intercourse, withdrawing domestic and agricultural labour, and spreading gossip about their spouses. These forms of resistance are documented for contemporary societies all over the world. However, such strategies of resistance, while undeniably effective in many instances, have a limited utility, and if used too often they will result not in a woman bettering her position, but in a total breakdown of relations, leading to divorce. The 'weapons of the weak', as Scott shows so clearly, have their limitations, and, if they are to be successful as strategies, confrontation and total breakdown must be avoided at all costs. Such forms of resistance and protest are difficult to analyse because, unlike revolutions or more formal forms of protest, they never overthrow the social, productive and reproductive relations within which they are embedded. This does not mean, however, that they are insignificant.

One of the important points about these 'everyday' forms of women's resistance is that if we confine our analysis of women's political action to the activities of women's groups – whether formal or informal – we may be neglecting an important dimension of women's political strategies. These 'everyday forms of resistance' are not, of course, peculiar to women; they are also a feature of the political activity of the oppressed, the poor and the marginal. It is, however, very difficult to develop satisfactory ways of analysing political events which are actually non-events, protests which are never openly made, demonstrations of solidarity which never seem to need an identifiable group. It is all too easy to dismiss political action of this kind as ineffective and unorganized, and/or to see it as somehow prior to real politics, a sort of pre-state or 'domestic' politics which is ultimately of little significance. James Scott makes it clear that such actions are the stuff of real politics, and that what we are witnessing is a form of withdrawal from the realm of state control. There is an increasing body of evidence which suggests that women use withdrawal as a strategy for survival. Many women try to work around the state rather than to work with it. The anthropological evidence suggests that women's politics has often been concerned with evasion and avoidance, with complex strategies of resistance and compliance. Perhaps women have tended to work outside the state because they have always been marginalized within it. This may be true, but what is interesting at the present time is the number of men – as well as women – who are now becoming involved in such strategies of resistance and withdrawal. The politics of the modern state are becoming ever more exclusive as they seek to become ever more inclusive. Social and political scientists have spent a great deal of time analysing the origins, development and functioning of the modern state; it is becoming increasingly clear that they are now being called upon to analyse what appears to be a crisis in the modern state. In the context of this crisis, alternative forms of political action will become possible, and the political activities of formerly invisible groups might take on a totally new significance.

Conclusion: the view from feminist anthropology

Is the state to some degree autonomous of the interests of men or an integral expression of them? Does the state embody and serve male interests in its form, dynamics, relation to society, and specific policies? Is the state constructed upon the subordination of women? If so, how does male power become state power? Can such a state be made to serve the interests of those upon whose powerlessness its power is erected? (MacKinnon, 1983: 643–4)

MacKinnon lays out the substantive questions about the relationship between women and the state which this chapter has tried to address. It seems clear from the data available to us that state structures and state policies do have a differential impact on women as compared to men. Women and men do not have the same relationship to the state, and, even where women's legal and democratic rights are enshrined in the state constitution, women and men remain different sorts of citizens *vis-à-vis* the state. The modern state is predicated upon gender difference, and this difference is inscribed into the political process. Even when women have equal rights under the state, they are rarely able to exercise those rights.

Feminist anthropology provides a theory of how pre-state kinship relations are transformed with the emergence of the state in such a way that women come increasingly under the control of men. This theory begins a theme in the anthropological analysis of the modern state which stresses the importance of understanding kinship relations. This theme has a number of similarities with the sociological approach to the study of the state which emphasizes how state policies promote a particular form of 'family'/household relations. The material on socialist states demonstrates this point particularly well because of the obvious difficulty such states experience in radically changing particular sets of 'family'/household relations when the production and reproduction of the state still depends upon them. However, the anthropological emphasis on kinship is slightly different from the sociological emphasis on the 'family'/household. The anthropological analysis stresses the interrelations between kinship structures and state structures in order to emphasize the mutually determining nature of kinship–state relations, rather than assuming that the process of determination is always unidirectional, i.e. from the state to the 'family'. Secondly, the anthropological approach emphasizes that women are located on a boundary between kinship relations and state structures in a way which men are not. This is particularly clear in the example of women's self-help groups in Kenya, where the success of the women's groups, and their utility for the individual women involved, depended crucially on the women's ability to negotiate both with their husbands or male kin and with the representatives and institutions of the state. Men also have to negotiate with the representatives and institutions of the state, but their ability to do so is rarely structured by their relations with their wives. This is particularly clear with regard to development policies, which tend to institutionalize men's access to the state, while marginalizing women's access, which continues to be negotiated, to a greater or lesser extend, through their husbands. This process of institutionalization is the result of state policies which are themselves formulated according to various assumptions about the nature of women and men as individuals, and about the nature of gender relations.

Women form a small minority of decision-makers, policy-makers and bureaucrats worldwide precisely because they have a different relation to the modern state, and to the formal processes of political representation, from that of men. However, in stressing this, it is important not only to present women as oppressed and discriminated against, but also to analyse their perceptions of and responses to the state. The comparative study of women's groups demonstrates the enormous variety of women's associations, and the very complex relations which exist between gender and class interests. The state converts women's interests to its own ends in part, by institutionalizing differences between women. The issues of race and class difference show quite clearly that there is no single set of women's interests which can be identified in relation to the modern state. This raises the question of how we are to understand such political aims as the 'emancipation of women' or the 'liberation of women'. The experience of colonial domination and racial discrimination fractures any simple understanding of what emancipation or liberation might entail. This in turn threatens to undermine any single interpretation of civil or human rights.

Feminist writers are fond of saying that feminism lacks a theory of the state, and feminist anthropology is no exception to this rule. However, it is clear that anthropology must develop such a theory as a matter of urgency. It is equally clear that we must move decisively away from the idea of women as necessarily passive in their response to state oppression, and begin to examine the many different ways in which they struggle, protest and stand firm in the face of state encroachment.

6

FEMINIST ANTHROPOLOGY: WHAT DIFFERENCE DOES IT MAKE?

Contemporary feminist anthropology developed out of the 'anthropology of women' of the 1970s. This modern feminist anthropology takes as its subject, not women, but gender relations. It does not purport to speak *for* women, although it certainly speaks extensively *about* women. It follows from this that feminist anthropology should not be confused with or taken to be coterminous with the study of Third World women. The idea that anthropology is concerned exclusively with studying the Third World is a common fallacy. Social anthropology certainly grew out of the geopolitics of colonial domination, and out of a Western fascination with non-Western cultures; a fascination which was, in many ways, born of a prior concern with 'self' rather than with the 'other'. Other cultures were, if you like, a way of understanding, commenting and reflecting on the peculiarity of Western culture. The question was not so much 'What are the other societies of the world like?' but rather 'Is everybody like us?' It is significant in this regard that the interpretation of 'other cultures' has often been likened in the anthropological literature to a process of translation (Crick, 1976). This is an analogy which rather aptly describes the process of rendering one culture in terms of another. Anthropology's internal response to this problem was to develop the concept of ethnocentrism – cultural bias – and to begin a process of radically interrogating the assumptions on which anthropological interpretations rest.

The 'anthropology of women' was part of this process of questioning theoretical categories, and of emphasizing the way in which theoretical suppositions underpin data collection, analysis and interpretation. The acknowledgement of 'male bias' in the discipline was a 'special' case of the recognition of the ethnocentric assumptions underlying anthropological theory. This recognition was an important step because it ultimately brought into question many of the 'taken for granted' theoretical frameworks within the 'anthropology of women' itself, such as the domestic/public and nature/culture distinctions. The material presented in chapter 2 shows how feminist anthropology was able to make significant theoretical advances – for example, breaking down the assumed identity between 'woman' and 'mother', rethinking the distinction between the 'individual' and society, and challenging the Eurocentric concept of personhood or self frequently used in anthropological writing – once it was able to stand outside the theoretical parameters laid down by the domestic/public and nature/culture divisions. The rethinking of the concept of self is currently providing an impetus for the re-evaluation of theoretical frameworks in kinship and economic anthropology, as demonstrated in the discussion of marriage and property relations in chapter 3.

Critiques based on challenges to ethnocentrism have taken anthropology a very long way, and the most significant advances in this regard have undoubtedly been made in feminist anthropology and in symbolic anthropology. The interconnections between these two approaches are many and varied, and the debt they owe each other is amply demonstrated by the discussion in chapter 2. The history of the relationship between feminist anthropology and the discipline itself is rather like the history of the feminist movement in relation to left politics. The feminist movement shares many of the political aims of the left, but to a certain extent it grew out of a dissatisfaction with the insufficiencies of left politics regarding women. In the same way, feminist anthropology shares the majority of anthropology's aims, but it has also developed in response to many of the insufficiencies and absences in disciplinary theorizing and practice. We should not be surprised, therefore, to find that feminist anthropology both mirrors and parallels the theoretical and conceptual revisions which are occurring within the discipline as well as actually providing some new theoretical initiatives (Strathern, 1987a).

Understanding difference

Probably the most outstanding contribution feminist anthropology has made to the discipline has been the development of theories relating to gender identity and the cultural construction of gender, of what it is to be a 'woman' or a 'man'. This has come to be called the 'anthropology of gender', and it is a field of research which did not exist and could not have existed before the advent of a feminist anthropology. There are now quite a number of male anthropologists working in the 'anthropology of gender', and there is a growing interest in issues relating to masculine identity and the cultural construction of masculinity. Feminist anthropology is not, however, the same thing as the 'anthropology of gender', and this is a point which obviously requires further clarification, given my earlier argument that feminist anthropology should be defined as the study of gender relations, as opposed to the study of women. The problem is really one of terminology, because it is perfectly possible to make a clear distinction between the study of gender identity and its cultural construction (the anthropology of gender) and the study of gender as a principle of human social life (feminist anthropology). This distinction is important because, although feminist anthropology cannot be simply defined as women studying women, it is even more crucial when we come to define it as the 'study of gender' that this is not taken to mean that feminist anthropology is only concerned with the cultural construction of gender and gender identity. Feminist anthropology is much more than this, as I have tried to demonstrate in previous chapters. However, it is equally important to realize that the 'anthropology of gender' as a field of enquiry is not strictly speaking a sub-discipline or a sub-section of feminist anthropology, because, while it shares many of its concerns with feminist anthropology, there are those who study the 'anthropology of gender' from a non-feminist perspective.

This suggests that, while feminist anthropology cannot be defined as women studying women, there is some sense in which it can and must be distinguished from those frameworks of enquiry which study gender or women from a non-feminist point of view. The difficulty would seem to reside, in part, in deciding what constitutes a feminist point of view. One very common answer to this question is to say that feminism is all about the difference it makes to consider things from a woman's point of view; in other words, that feminism is all about the women's perspective. On the face of it, this response would seem rather tautologous, given that we have established that feminist anthropology cannot be defined by the gender of its practitioners and their subjects. Furthermore, it says nothing about whose point of view we are referring to; are we talking about the point of view of the person who studies or that of the person studied? Perhaps we are falling into the larger trap of assuming that their points of view are identical?

In order to resolve this dilemma it is necessary to return to some of the arguments concerning the relevance of the sociological category 'woman'. The major difficulty in equating feminism with the 'woman's point of view' is that this assumes that there is a unitary woman's perspective or point of view, which can be seen to be held by an identifiable sociological category 'woman'. However, feminist anthropology strongly challenges this idea, as we have seen, because it demonstrates that there can be no universal or unitary sociological category 'woman', and therefore that there can be no analytical meaning in any universal conditions, attitudes or views ascribed to this 'woman' – for example, in the 'universal subordination of women' and the 'oppression of women'. The term 'patriarchy' is similarly deconstructed. This does not mean that women are not oppressed by patriarchal structures, but it does mean that the nature and consequences of those structures have to be specified in each instance, and not assumed.

A further problem, however, with the idea of the woman's point of view is that it presupposes some underlying 'sameness'. We have already seen that the notion of 'sameness' is brought into question by the deconstruction of the universal category 'woman', and by the empirical evidence which demonstrates that gender is everywhere experienced through the specific mediations of history, class, race, colonialism and neo-imperialism (see chapter 1). Feminist anthropology recognizes this, but at times it has often seemed as if the existence of a shared feminine identity, the commonality of gender, has somehow transcended the existence of other forms of difference. The 'anthropology of women' was excellent at considering difference based on gender: what difference did it make to be a woman, what difference did it make to see things from a woman's point of view, what difference did it make to be a woman anthropologist? The issue of gender difference was very sophisticatedly handled with regard to cultural difference. What difference did it make to be a woman in one culture as opposed to another? The concept of cultural difference has always played a key role in social anthropology because it is on the basis of such difference that anthropology has historically identified its subject: 'other cultures'.

The concept of cultural difference has been subjected to exhaustive analysis within the discipline, and it has been used to build a critique of 'culture-bound' ways of looking at the world. In other words, it has been the basis for the development of the critique of ethnocentrism. However, as I argued in chapter 1, the concept of ethnocentrism, while immensely valuable, leaves some very basic issues untouched. This is because it is formulated primarily in terms of how social anthropology can and should break out of its Western cultural assumptions, its Western way of seeing the world. The value of such a project is clear, but it none the less implies the existence of a unitary anthropological discourse which is based on Western culture. The critique of ethnocentrism is certainly designed to purify this discourse, to make it more critical and self-reflexive, but it is not necessarily intended to deconstruct it altogether. It is a remedial rather than a revolutionary programme, because, while anthropology may be rethinking its theoretical assumptions, the authority of the anthropological discourse itself is never challenged. It is still the dominant Western discourse – albeit purified – which is going to define what is anthropology and what is not anthropology, what is ethnocentric and what is not. Other agendas, other anthropologies, are not going to be heard. They are not, of course, excluded specifically, and certainly not maliciously, but they can only ever be there as present absences while we still agree that there is a unitary anthropology, a single authoritative anthropological discourse, based on the distinction between 'Western culture' and 'other cultures'.

The same sort of argument applies to the idea of 'sameness' which underlies the notion of the shared woman's perspective. Black feminists have long argued that the celebration of women *qua* women in feminist politics and academic writing, with its assumption that women have a necessary basis for unity and solidarity, privileges one particular discourse about women or 'womanhood' over others (Hooks, 1982; Davis, 1981; Carby, 1982; Hull et al., 1982; Moraga and Anzaldua, 1981). Other views of 'womanhood', other ways of looking at the 'woman question', do not get heard. They are muted (see chapter 1). Much more important, however, is that gender as difference is privileged over all other forms of difference. Other forms of difference, such as race, may be acknowledged, but if they are they tend to be treated as additive, as variations on a basic theme. To be black and be a woman becomes to be a woman and be black. Black feminists make the point that the issue of race is not additive, that the experience of race transforms the experience of gender, and that it brings into question any feminist approach which suggests that women should be treated as women first, and only after that as women differentiated by race, culture, history, and so on (Amos and Parmar, 1984; Bhavnani and Coulson, 1986; Minh-ha, 1987). The issue of the primacy or dominance of gender difference is a contentious one, because gender as a social construct has a variable reference to biological difference, which racism as a social construct does not, and certainly other forms of difference – such as those constructed around histories, colonialism, class, etc. – do not. This sometimes permits a disguised appeal to biology of the kind that 'at bottom we are all women' or 'in the final analysis we are all women together'. However, given the predominantly experiential way in which individuals and groups come to know difference or differences in the world, and given that gendered individuals experience the social construction of gender rather than its biological determinants, I am not sure that the appeal to biology can be used to justify the primacy of gender difference. But, even if it could be so used, to make such an argument misses the point somewhat. This can be demonstrated by returning briefly to the critique of 'male bias' made by the 'anthropology of women' in the 1970s.

The 'anthropology of women' made much of the woman's perspective in large part as an antidote to the overwhelming problem of male bias in the discipline. In emphasizing the importance of the woman's perspective, the 'anthropology of women' sought to uncover the similarities, as well as the differences, in women's position worldwide. They looked, therefore, for universal explanations of women's subordination. This phase did not last long because the 'anthropology of women' developed a fundamental critique of its own position, and in the process self-consciously differentiated theoretical positions emerged. However, at one stage, the 'anthropology of women' did develop a discourse about women which had pretensions to universality. Precisely because it sought to be inclusive of women in other cultures, of the variety of women's experience, activities and conditions around the world, it actually practised a notable form of exclusion. Women who did not subscribe to this discourse on women, women who did not feel that the term 'woman' applied to them as expressed in the terms of this dominant discourse, were simply not heard; they were silent. One of the main concerns of the 'anthropology of women' was to deconstruct the categories of anthropological thought, to examine its ethnocentric assumptions. But the assumptions in question – for example, those about the nature of 'woman' and 'man', and about sexually differentiated spheres of activity – were Western assumptions, and the main subject of this questioning was actually Western culture as represented in the terms and categories of anthropological discourse. In other words, the revision which the 'anthropology of women' proposed was a revision internal to Western culture, and as such it was exclusionary.

We can see, then, that the 'anthropology of women' was exclusionary in two ways. In the first place, it was actually concerned with revising Western cultural assumptions, and therefore assumed by default that all anthropologists were either Westerners or that they shared Western cultural assumptions. No consideration was given to the possibility that there might be anthropologists who had other ways of looking at the world. Secondly, it established a discourse about women which was exclusively constructed in dialogue with Western cultural assumptions. 'Other women' could not intervene in the debate except on the terms set out by those who were in charge of setting the agenda. The argument, then, is really about the political and theoretical complexities of trying to speak *about* women, while avoiding any tendency to speak *for* them. The 'anthropology of women' wanted to challenge men's right to speak for women, but in the process it found itself unintentionally speaking *for* other women. This is one reason why some critics have argued that anthropology is racist as opposed to merely ethnocentric. To acknowledge cultural bias is, of course, not the same thing as acknowledging that you may have been speaking about other women in a way which prevents them from speaking about themselves. The argument that 'we are all women together' clearly doesn't address the issue of racism, because it merely subsumes the issue of race under an argument about the primacy of gender difference. However, feminist anthropology, unlike the 'anthropology of women', has made some progress in this area, because while it acknowledges that 'women are all women together' it also emphasizes that there are fundamental differences between women – whether based on class, race, culture or history – and that that difference is something which needs to be theorized.

Perspectives on gender, race and class: the problems of sameness and difference

Feminist anthropology does not, however, need to be told that women are different. It is the one social science discipline which is actually able to demonstrate from a strongly comparative perspective that what it is to be a woman is culturally and historically variable, and that gender itself is a social construction which always requires specification within any given context. The argument is not, therefore, about whether feminist anthropology acknowledges difference between women, but about what sort of difference it acknowledges. It is true that in the past feminist anthropology was concerned with registering only two forms of difference: gender difference and cultural difference. However, the material presented in chapters 3 and 4 shows that feminist anthropology has since developed sustained theoretical positions which specify the interconnections between gender difference, cultural difference, class difference and historical difference. This is most clearly demonstrated in the debates about the penetration of capitalism, the impact of colonial domination and the changing nature of the family. The comparative perspective of feminist anthropology on all these issues, and the way in which it has made gender relations central to any critical understanding of the nature of these processes, provides a challenge to many other areas of social science enquiry. The shift towards class and historical analysis which is evident in feminist anthropology is, of course, part of a wider shift within the discipline of social anthropology itself (see chapter 4), but the distinctive contribution of feminist anthropology is the way in which it demonstrates that gender relations are central to any sustained analysis of class and historical relations. It is also worth noting that the debate in feminist anthropology about the changing nature of the family challenges many of the arguments in contemporary sociology and in contemporary feminist debates concerning the relationship between family forms and capitalist relations of production. It also challenges the idea that the teleology of Western development provides a historical model which will be necessarily and beneficially followed elsewhere.

However, it is true that feminist anthropology has only recently turned its attention to studying difference based on race, and to trying to specify how gender, class and race differences intersect in specific historical contexts. This is largely because 'radical' tendencies in social anthropology have generally failed to incorporate arguments about race into their critical revisions of the discipline. For example, during the 1960s and 1970s, a number of anthropologists, both black and white, began to develop a critique of anthropology's colonial past, and suggested that the future of the discipline would have to be one based on a critical awareness of the specific relations of colonial domination, and on an equally critical understanding of the power relations inherent in the ethnographic encounter, that is in the relationship between the anthropologist and the people studied by the anthropologist. Many black anthropologists pointed out that colonial and post-colonial anthropology had been, and continued to be, racist (Lewis, 1973; Magubane, 1971; Owusu, 1979). They based their arguments on the fact that the discipline constructed other cultures as objects of study in such a way that the significant features of the 'other' resided in its relationship to Western culture, and not in terms of its own history and development. It was further argued that anthropology had made no attempt to come to terms with the politics of black–white relations under colonialism, and was continuing to make no attempt to come to terms with these politics in the post-colonial context. The discipline responded to these criticisms in a number of ways, but in the final analysis the blow was a glancing one because anthropology heard these criticisms primarily in terms of a discourse about ethnocentrism and not in terms of a discourse about racism.

However, social anthropology took up the argument about the power relations inherent in the practice of anthropological fieldwork, as well as those concealed in the twin processes of anthropological interpretation and writing. An enormous body of literature exists on these issues, and this 'radical' strand of anthropology has continued into the present. There is currently a lively debate about the way in which anthropology provides written accounts of 'other cultures' and thus monopolizes interpretation and representation. In the process of translating the experience of another in terms of one's own experience, and then representing that experience through the structures of written language, the anthropologist effectively decides to speak *for* others. The current radicalism in anthropology experiments with forms of ethnographic writing in order to try to find some way of letting the people who are being studied speak for themselves. The aim is to produce a 'new' ethnography which would be based on the multiple authorship of anthropological texts, and which would represent both the interlocutory process of fieldwork, and the collaboration between anthropologist and informant on which the practice of social anthropology depends (Marcus and Fischer, 1986; Clifford and Marcus, 1986; Clifford, 1983).

A serious critique has yet to be written of this new approach and of its consequences and potentialities for the discipline of social anthropology (but see Strathern, 1987a, 1987b). However, it is clear that it has strong continuities with the traditional anthropological approach to cultural difference. There has always been a very fruitful tension in the way in which social anthropology handles cultural difference. The tension arises because its maintenance is essential to anthropology's larger comparative project. Anthropology has always emphasized cultural difference, if not uniqueness. It has been pointed out by some critics that an emphasis on cultural difference can be used to stigmatize, 'pathologize' and 'exoticize' those who are different (see chapter 1). Anthropology has long been aware of this problem at least in one sense, and from the beginning of this century anthropologists have recognized the necessity of setting cultural difference against the wider background of social and human similarity. This is, of course, the purpose of anthropology's comparative project, and it underlies the humanitarian ethos on which the practice of social anthropology ultimately rests. The identifiable tension in anthropology's treatment of cultural difference is that an emphasis on difference is simultaneously an emphasis on similarity or sameness.

The ambiguity surrounding sameness and difference within the overall concept of cultural difference has allowed anthropology to use the idea of ethnocentrism – cultural bias – to sidestep any suggestion that other forms of difference might exist which cannot be subsumed under the heading of cultural difference, and/or that these differences might be irresolvable. The notion that it is possible for anthropologists and for anthropology itself to be ethnocentric is based on the idea that cultures have specific ways of looking at the world, and that they are different one from another. This difference is not, however, absolute, and anthropology acknowledges this by simultaneously emphasizing the similarities and differences between cultures. It is an apparent paradox of anthropological theorizing that the purpose in recognizing ethnocentrism is not to establish absolute cultural differences, but rather to break down the barriers to cultural understanding and to investigate the basis for cultural similarities. This means that, while the critique of ethnocentrism is, in part, about recognizing cultural difference, it is also about trying to overcome or minimize such difference. The critique of ethnocentrism proceeds at a tangent to arguments about racism because the theory of ethnocentrism does not presume the differences it recognizes between cultures to be absolute. Individual anthropologists might argue that differences between cultures are radical, absolute and irreducible, but anthropology as a discourse concerned with interpreting 'other cultures' cannot afford to take such a position. Cultural differences have to be overcome, at least in part, if anthropology is to be successful in translating and interpreting the 'other culture'. The notion of rendering one culture in terms of another, which is at the heart of the anthropological endeavour, can only be achieved by negotiating the inherent tension between sameness and difference, and in so doing it does, of course, run the risk of collapsing differences which should not be collapsed.

The ethical, moral and political consequences of these kinds of arguments have been extensively discussed in anthropology. The important question here, however, is what difference does feminist anthropology make to all this, and/or what difference does all this make to feminist anthropology?

Why feminist anthropology makes a difference

There are many ways in which feminist anthropology makes a difference, and many ways in which it draws our attention to the importance of understanding difference. However, there are two main questions we need to consider: what difference does feminist anthropology make to anthropology, and what difference does it make to feminism? These two sets of relationships have not been treated equally in this book perhaps, because, while feminist anthropology has spent an enormous amount of time considering its relationship to anthropology, it has spent relatively little time considering its relationship to feminism. There are practical and historical reasons for this, but perhaps the time has come to redress the balance a little.

Anthropology and feminist anthropology

The history of the relationship between feminist anthropology and mainstream anthropology has already been described in this chapter and in chapter 1. It is quite clear from the data presented in previous chapters that feminist anthropology has made its most distinctive contribution through demonstrating why an understanding of gender relations must remain central to the analysis of key questions in anthropology and in the social sciences as a whole. The comparative perspective feminist anthropology has brought to the analysis of the cultural construction of gender, and to the debate on the sexual division of labour, including the problems raised by the development of capitalism, has enabled feminist anthropology significantly to advance the state of knowledge in these areas, both theoretically and empirically. Feminist anthropologists have only recently turned their attention to the analysis of the modern state, but it seems likely that in the next few years this area of enquiry will produce some of the most interesting and exciting work in anthropology. The centrality which anthropology gives to the study of kinship relations in the context of the modern state suggests that feminist anthropology has a distinctive contribution to make through a demonstration of the ways in which existing kinship systems structure state responses to 'family' and household forms. This very brief list is not intended to summarize the achievements of feminist anthropology, but it is intended to point to those areas where feminist anthropology has had, or will have, something useful to say. It should not be imagined that feminist anthropology is alone in saying these things, because the breaking down of discipline barriers, with the very notable move towards multi-disciplinary scholarship, has been one of the most outstanding achievements of the feminist critique in the social sciences as a whole. Feminist scholarship has sought not only to radicalize individual disciplines, but also to establish new research procedures, new standards for research and new relationships between academic theory and practice.

However, as we have seen, feminist anthropology has the clear potential to speak to fundamental theoretical issues within the discipline of social anthropology. Its emphasis on difference, and on the relationship of gender difference to other forms of difference, provides an opportunity to question the primacy which social anthropology has always accorded to cultural difference. This is not to say that cultural difference should be ignored or even displaced; this would be foolish. But it is to suggest that forms of difference in human social life – gender, class, race, culture, history, etc. – are always experienced, constructed and mediated in interrelation with each other. If we establish the a priori dominance or significance of one particular form of difference in our theoretical frameworks, then we automatically run the risk of ignoring others.

I do not think that we can necessarily establish the primacy of one form of difference over others. This is because it is quite clear, if we take the example of gender, that logically there can be no way of experiencing gender difference in some moment prior to the experience of other forms of difference. To be a black woman means to be a woman and be black, but the experience of these forms of difference is simultaneous, and not sequential or consequential. What is more important, perhaps, is that in human society these forms of difference are structurally simultaneous, in that their simultaneity does not depend on each individual's experience of them, because it is already sedimented in social institutions. It is, however, clear that in specific contexts some forms of difference may be more important than others. It follows from this that the interrelations between the various forms of difference will always require specification in given historical contexts. We cannot assume we know the significance of any particular set of intersections between class, race and gender prior to our analysis of these intersections. The task for feminist anthropologists, as for scholars in other disciplines, is to find ways of theorizing these highly variable intersections between the various forms of difference.

The consequences for social anthropology of accepting that cultural difference is only one form of difference among several is that it throws into question the primary organizing concept of social anthropology: the concept of culture. There is no generally accepted definition in social anthropology of what a culture is. In some cases a culture can be understood as referring to a society, but, in the modern world, situations where cultures and societies are isomorphic are increasingly rare. Anthropology recognizes this in so far as general definitions of 'culture' refer to systems of symbols and beliefs, the 'world-view' of a people, 'life ways', an 'ethos', and so on. The concept of culture in anthropology is in need of serious revision. However, in spite of the fluidity and uncertainty surrounding its definition, precisely because mainstream anthropology still sees the interpretation of 'other cultures' as one of its main tasks – if not *the* task – to call the primacy of cultural difference into account would certainly provoke a theoretical crisis. It remains to be seen whether feminist anthropology will do this or not.

Feminism and feminist anthropology

The contribution of feminist anthropology to feminism is rather harder to work out than its contribution to mainstream anthropology. One obvious relationship is that many feminists have used anthropological data to deconstruct essentialist arguments about women in Western culture. Feminist anthropology has also made contributions to various mainstream feminist debates about the sexual division of labour and the form of the family under capitalism. However, the question still remains as to whether feminist anthropology is able to make a theoretical or political contribution to contemporary feminism. The most important issue in this context is probably feminist anthropology's radical questioning of the sociological category 'woman' (see above and chapter 1). If feminist politics depends upon the unity of women as a 'sex-class', then what are the consequences for feminism of the work of feminist anthropologists? The answer is that an emphasis on the differences between women does not necessarily deconstruct the basis of feminist politics. Women do share similar difficulties and experiences worldwide; it is simply that these similarities must be demonstrated and specified in each case, and not assumed. The differences between women are important, and they need to be acknowledged because it cannot be part of a feminist politics for one group of women to speak for and on behalf of another. The important point is that, although women's experiences, circumstances and difficulties do overlap with those of other women, they are not isomorphic with them. In order to assert a solidarity based on commonalities between women, it is not necessary to assert that all women are, or have to be, the same.

In the final analysis, the contribution of feminist anthropology to contemporary feminism is simply to point to the value of comparison and to the importance of acknowledging difference. This may not be a very grand or a very profound contribution, but it may still be a worthwhile one. Feminist anthropology, because of the nature of the enquiry it is engaged in, has had to learn to celebrate the strength of difference. The deconstruction of the sociological category 'woman' and the dissolution of such concepts as the 'universal subordination of women' have not dissolved feminist anthropology. The justification for doing feminist anthropology has very little to do with the fact that 'women are women the world over', and everything to do with the fact that we need to be able to theorize gender relations in a way which ultimately makes a difference.

NOTES

Chapter 1 Feminism and Anthropology: The Story of a Relationship

1 I have elsewhere argued that women and men do not have separate models of the world. Women certainly have a different point of view or 'perspective' on the world, but this is the result not of a separate model but of their attempts to locate themselves within the dominant cultural model of the world, which they share with men (Moore, 1986).

2 Anthropology's pluralism is undoubtedly linked to its liberal intellectual origins. Marilyn Strathern discusses the relationship between feminism and anthropology in a recent article (Strathern, 1978a). I have developed my typology of the discipline from the one she provides in her article, but our views on the relationship of feminist anthropology to the discipline of anthropology as a whole are somewhat different.

3 This part of the argument developed out of my reading of an article by Kum-Kum Bhavnani and Margaret Coulson, where they discuss how the term 'ethnocentrism' can be used to sidestep the issue of racism. I am greatly indebted to them for this insight (Bhavnani and Coulson, 1986).

4 The effects of colonialism, the penetration of capitalist relations of production and the interventions of international development agencies on rural production system, on the sexual division of labour, and on regional politics have been extensively and very brilliantly analysed by historians of Africa and Latin America. See chapter 4 for further details.

5 Many of the criticisms of colonial anthropology have focused on how arguments about cultural uniqueness can be used to support racist and separatist ideologies and policies. In South Africa today, some Afrikaner anthropologists are still using very similar arguments to justify segregation under apartheid, just as they were in the past.

6 The argument in this section has benefited greatly from my reading of Rosalind Delmar's article 'What is feminism' (Delmar, 1986).

Chapter 2   Gender and Status: Explaining the Position of Women

1   For details of this argument, see Coward, 1983; Rosaldo, 1980: 401–9; Fee, 1974; Rogers, 1978: 125–7.

2   In 1861, Henry Maine published his *Ancient Law*, a text which discussed the historical variability of legal structures, with particular emphasis on different forms of property relations. Maine used his study of comparative law to expound a theory of the patriarchal family. His interest in property, inheritance and rights led him to a consideration of the family as the basic unit not only of ancient law but of society in general. Maine saw the family, under the control and power of the father, as the primary organizing principle of society.

   The theory of the primacy of the patriarchal family came under attack immediately from a group of scholars, who all published books at approximately the same time as Maine, proclaiming that the patriarchal family had evolved from an earlier form of social organization which had been dominated by 'mother-right' (Bachofen, 1861; McLennan, 1865; Morgan, 1877). The impetus for these proclamations came, in part, from the activities of European colonization which were producing evidence of non-patriarchal family forms (Meek, 1976). These texts were evolutionist in that they sought the origins and history of societal forms. Bachofen characterized the evolution of society as a struggle between the sexes, where 'mother-right' eventually gave way to 'father-right'. The primacy given to transitions in forms of sexual and marriage practices was also a feature of the work of McLennan and Morgan (Goody, 1976: 1–8; Schneider and Gough, 1961). The questions these nineteenth-century theorists raised – the relationship of the family to the political organization of society, changes in sexual relations and forms of marriage, the basis for types of kinship structure, and discussion concerning the related concepts of 'incest', 'power', 'private property', 'sexual antagonism' and 'descent' – established the parameters of a debate which has persisted, albeit somewhat transformed, into contemporary anthropology. The unifying theme which runs through this debate is: what are the social functions of the different forms of control of sexual relation? The theorization of sex within the phrase 'sexual relations' assumed an absolute division between the sexes, because on the one hand sexual reproduction entailed the union of two different sexes, and because on the other the existence of a sexual division of labour was attributed to the existence of men and women as different interest groups (Coward, 1983). These two points are related, since the division of labour between the sexes was seen as ultimately derived from the different roles of men and women in sexual reproduction. The social theorists of the late nineteenth and early twentieth centuries gave a prominence to the issue of women's status – women's position in society – through an emphasis on changing sexual relations and family structures in the evolution of society. The debate on the 'position of women' overspilled into concerns much closer to home with the emergence of the nineteenth-century feminist movement and the proliferation of discourse on sexuality in Western society (e.g. Foucault, 1978; Heath, 1982; Weeks, 1981, 1985).

3 For explanations and typologies of different theoretical positions, see Barrett (1980), Eisenstein (1984), Elshtain (1981) and Glennon (1979); see also chapter 1 for a discussion of the relationship between feminism and anthropology.

4 For overviews of positions in feminist anthropology, see Rapp (1979), Scheper-Hughes (1983), Rosaldo (1980), Atkinson (1982), Lamphere (1977) and Quinn (1977).

5 See Douglas (1966).

6 However, many recent analyses, especially on Austronesian communities, have challenged the association between menstruation/childbirth/ nature and pollution. Keesing argues that Kwaio women see their bodies as sites of sacred order, dangerous but not dirty or defiled (Keesing, 1985). For a parallel critique on Polynesian data, see Thomas (1987). See also Ralston (1988).

7 See Atkinson (1982: 248), Feil (1978), MacCormack (1980: 17–18) and Strathern (1981a), for a discussion of how images of women may not hold good for all sections of society or for all spheres of cultural discourse.

8 A number of scholars trace the origins of the nature/culture distinction in anthropology to Lévi-Strauss, who acknowledges a debt to Rousseau, and therefore to the particular view of culture succeeding nature which that implies. See Lévi-Strauss (1966, 1969), MacCormack (1980) and Bloch and Bloch (1980).

9 Issues of suffrage were, of course, cross-cut by distinctions of class as well as gender, because it was not only women but working-class men as well who did not have the vote.

10 See Oakley (1979: 613–6), for an analysis of the ways in which ideas about femininity and reproduction are linked in Western society.

11 Linda Pollock (1983) takes a different view from Ariès and argues that a distinctive stage or category of childhood can be traced back to a much earlier period of British history than that suggested by Ariès. This is an area where debate rages fiercely and new publication abounds, but that does not alter the general point concerning the historical and cultural variability of ideas about motherhood, childhood and family life.

12 For a development of this argument, see Greer (1984: 2–5). For a history of the family from a feminist perspective and a bibliography of the major sources, see Shanley (1979).

13 See Paige and Paige (1981: 34–41) for a summary. See also Rivière (1974: 424–7).

14 For early published examples, see Brain (1976), Boserup (1970), Bossen (1975), Remy (1975), Tinker and Bramsen (1976), Dey (1981) and Rogers (1980). See also the fuller discussion of this argument in chapter 4, which also contains criticisms of various feminist positions.

15 But see Roberts (1981) for a different and favourable view of this aspect of Sack's argument.

16 For early examples of such work, see Friedl (1975), Wolf (1972), Sanday (1974), Lamphere (1974), Nelson (1974) and Rogers (1975).

17   See Atkinson (1982: 240–9) and Ortner and Whitehead (1981b) for dis-
     cussions of recent developments in attempts to combine symbolic and
     sociological approaches to the study of gender.

18   See Ortner (1984) for an overview of theoretical developments in an-
     thropology, and Strathern (1987a) for a discussion of the parallels in
     contemporary feminist and anthropological theorization of the concept
     of 'experience'.

19   Biersack (1984) makes a comparable point for the Paiela, and she insists
     that what individual women do is, to some extent, separable from the
     cultural stereotypes of the female sex, although the conclusion of her
     analysis is rather different from Strathern's.

Chapter 3   Kinship, Labour and Household: Understanding Women's Work

1   For one of the best discussions of these issues, including summaries of
    the theoretical positions and overviews of the main area of debate, see
    the essays in Young et al. (1981).

2   Lina Fruzzetti (1985) found, in her study of women farmers in the Blue
    Nile province of Sudan, that women were thought to work in the home,
    and only in 'household related activities'. The result was that all the
    women she surveyed claimed they did not have an occupation because
    they were either wives or daughters. Out of seventeen occupations de-
    signated as male, there were none which could be publicly applied to
    women, even though they did perform a number of these occupations.

3   But see Beneria and Sen (1981), Wright (1983) and Guyer (1984) for
    critiques of Boserup.

4   In the 1950s and 1960s, anthropology appeared to lose the comparative
    methodology and the concern with social change which had so charac-
    terized earlier work. A good example of such work would be Audrey
    Richard's book *Hunger and Work in a Savage Tribe*, published in 1932;
    this was a comparative study of nutrition and economic production
    among the Bantu peoples of southern Africa. Concerns like these were
    not to re-emerge in British social anthropology until the 1970s (Goody,
    1976: 2). But, although anthropology appeared to lose interest in com-
    parative work in the 1950s and 1960s, it should be noted that Radcliffe-
    Brown claimed, in the 1950s, that the aim of his anthropology was
    ultimately a 'comparative sociology' (Radcliffe-Brown, 1958: 65). In my
    view, however, the nature of Goody's cross-cultural comparison is
    rather different from Radcliffe-Brown's search for generalizations which
    would stand up as general laws. See also Kuper (1983) for a history of
    British anthropology.

5   But see Whitehead (1977) for a critique of Goody.

6   For recent feminist critiques of Engels, see Sayers et al. (1987), Vogel
    (1983: chs 3, 5, 6), Coward (1983: chs 5, 6), Burton (1985: chs 1, 2),
    Edholm et al. (1977) and Delmar (1976). For a critique of Engels from an
    anthropological point of view, see Bloch (1983: chs 2, 3).

7 Aaby (1977: 32–3) makes this point as well. He then goes on to say why he thinks their critique does not go far enough. His work is not discussed here because it has been superseded, in my view, by more recent feminist critiques of Engels (see note 6). See also Burton (1985: chs 1, 2) for a description of Gough's, Sacks's and Leacock's positions, as well as the earlier discussion of Sacks's and Leacock's work in chapter 2.

8 'Dual systems' is a phrase which Vogel derives from Young (1980). See also Beechey (1979).

9 Social relations of reproduction are often discussed under the term 'patriarchy', which is seen to have both material and ideological components. The validity of the term 'patriarchy', the analytical separation of relations of reproduction from those of production, and the importance of this distinction for understanding women's oppression are all discussed in a series of essays in Eisenstein (1979), Sargent (1981) and Kuhn and Wolpe (1978); see also Beechey (1979) and Gittins (1985: 36).

10 Coward (1983: 146, 150–2) makes a similar argument about Engels's privileging of the family. She points out that he makes the grave error of assuming that a 'general and universal history of the family' is possible.

11 But see O'Laughlin (1977) as an example of this argument and Edholm et al. (1977) for a critique of her position.

12 Meillassoux is not the only writer to have discussed women as the 'means of reproduction' in pre-capitalist societies: see also Hindess and Hirst (1975), Taylor (1975). My discussion of Meillassoux's work is drawn directly from a series of articles written by feminist crities, the substance of whose arguments I have tried to 'reproduce' as best I can; see Edholm et al. (1977), O'Laughlin (1977), Rapp (1977), Mackintosh (1977, 1979), Harris (1981), Harris and Young (1981) and Ennew (1979).

13 See Van Baal (1975) for a discussion of Lévi-Strauss's work on this subject.

14 Meillassoux never defines his concept of the 'domestic community' with any precision. This is partly because he is trying to construct the idea of a 'unit' which would be present in all modes of production with a certain level of development (basically subsistence cereal production), and which would act as the basic unit of production and consumption. In this sense, Meillassoux's 'domestic community' bears a strong resemblance to Sahlins's 'household' as defined in his 'domestic mode of production' (Sahlins, 1974: chs 2 and 3). See Edholm et al. (1977: 108–9) and Harris (1981: 53) for elaboration of this point.

15 Meillassoux mentions women's control over crops in a single, brief passage (1981: 77), but he does not discuss how women get rights to agricultural land or what rights they have over the products of their labour. He merely assumes that women lose all rights to the cereal crops they produce (a situation which in reality would be most unlikely), and his comments exemplify the way in which he portrays women as passive 'objects', who apparently take no action and employ no social strategies of their own. In a similar way, he assumes that all women's kinship links are defined through male 'filiation', and this is also most unlikely (Meillassoux 1981: 76–8).

16   See Dwyer (1978), Bledsoe (1985) and Caplan and Bujra (1978) for discussions of the way in which social differentiation, age and other 'interest groups' can be involved in situations where women 'exploit' each
other.

17   In anthropology, this is a view taken, for example, by Bujra (1978: 20)
and Whitehead (1981). This view has also been expressed in a variety of
ways by writers analysing domestic labour in capitalist societies; see
Burton (1985: ch. 4), Molyneux (1979) and Beechey (1978) for overviews
of the 'domestic labour debate', and Gittins (1985: ch. 6), Barrett (1980)
and Delphy (1984) for analyses of the relationship between capitalism
and women's oppression.

18   It is also important to note that definitions of the home, motherhood,
childhood, etc., are not fixed, but change in response to social,
economic, legal and ideological circumstances. This point was discussed
in chapter 3, but see also Hall (1979) and Rapp et al. (1979).

19   For good overviews of the literature on households and on the difficulties of definition and cross-cultural comparison, see Netting et al.,
(1984) and Wilk and Netting (1984).

20   My argument here is based on the work of Olivia Harris (1981) and Jane
Guyer (1981), although similar arguments have been made by many
other feminist scholars.

21   See Harris (1981: 54–5, 63) for an explanation of how the distinction
between intra- and inter-household relations is linked to the distinction
between use-values and exchange-values in Marxist analyses.

22   See Guyer (1981: 98–9) for further discussion of the point, and Roberts
(1979), Whitehead (1981) and Dey (1981) for further examples.

23   A review of the literature shows that women are frequently obliged to
work both on 'household fields' and on their husbands' 'private fields',
with the result that their own enterprises are neglected or relegated to
second place (Rogers, 1980). See Berry (1984) for a discussion of Yoruba
women and their continuing obligation to provide labour for household
subsistence production and for their husbands' 'private' enterprises.
Berry shows how these obligations prevent women from allocating sufficient labour time to their own enterprises, and may also restrict the
amount of other labour they can recruit. She also points out the asymmetrical and very restricted rights women have in their husbands'
labour. The problem of women's access to resources is not of course
restricted to patrilineal societies. Christine Okali's work on the matrilineal Akan people of Ghana, who grow cocoa as a cash crop, shows that
women are more likely to be engaged in own-account cocoa farming if
they are not living with their husbands, or if they are not married (Okali,
1983: 56). See Guyer (1980) for a comparison between a 'male farming
system' and a 'female farming system', and the different ways in which
the sexual division of labour operates and in which access to labour is
secured. In the same article, Guyer points out that, with commoditiza-
tion, the use of women's labour becomes an area of negotiation and
tension between women and men.

24 An earlier idea that kinship is not important in 'industrial' society has now been rejected. This idea was the logical extension of an overemphasis on the importance of the 'nuclear' family; see Stivens (1978, 1981) for an analysis of kin ties among middle-class Australians, and the famous study by Young and Willmott (1962) of kin relations in Bethnal Green, London.

25 Debates about kinship in anthropology are complex, and frequently impossible to relate sensibly to empirical data. British anthropologists, like Evans-Pritchard and Fortes, who are the 'founding fathers' of Anglo-Saxon kinship theory as it relates to lineages and corporate descent groups, see kin relations as the organizing principle of social, economic, political and religious life. French Marxist anthropologists, on the other hand, take the opposite view and argue that it is the nature of productive and reproductive relationships which determines the nature of kinship. This is only one small part of an endlessly ramifying debate which feminist anthropologists have yet to tackle in any sustained way; but see Tsing and Yanagisako (1983) and Coontz and Henderson (1986).

26 But see Weiner (1976, 1979) for contrary arguments about matrilineal systems, which emphasize the importance of links between women.

27 Such ideas are frequently expressed in indigenous ideologies, where women are associated with the 'individualizing' interests of the household, while men are associated with the 'communal' interests of the lineage or descent group; see Moore (1986: 110–11) for further references on this point.

28 See Rogers (1980).

29 Early work in the Caribbean and among black populations in the Americas (Gonzalez, 1965; Smith, 1962; Smith, 1956, 1970, 1973; Stack, 1974) made use of the term 'matrifocal'. Matrifocality (female-centredness) is found in many different kinds of kinship systems, and is not the same thing as matrilineality (descent) or matrilocality (residence). Matrifocality, like many kinship terms, does not describe a single, empirically fixed arrangement, but refers to a wide range of possibilities (Peters, 1983: 114). Kinship classifications, like many things in anthropology, suffer from the problem of having to account for the specific situation pertaining in a particular community, while simultaneously providing a basis for cross-cultural comparison. The most obvious examples are the terms 'patrilineal' and 'matrilineal'. Systems classified as patrilineal, for example, may have little in common except an ideology of descent through men. Descent ideology is only one part of the system, and it is likely that there are various contexts – access to land, rights to titles, residence patterns – when other types of kinship links (bilateral, for example) will be stressed. This has led some anthropologists to argue that terms like 'patrilineal' and 'matrilineal' are theoretically and empirically insufficient. See Eades (1980), Kuper (1982), Leach (1961) and Karp (1978b) for critiques of kinship classification based on descent rules and corporate groups. Other anthropologists have tried to stress that what defines kinship systems is the way in which they are operationalized

and manipulated. For example, Bledsoe (1980), Verdon (1980) and Comaroff (1980b) have all approached kinship systems from a behavioural, contextual and decision-making point of view. Possibly the most useful approach is a median one, which sees kinship systems in their specific historical contexts and tries to analyse their working out in practice; see Karp (1978a), as an example.

30 Bush et al. (1986) point out the different circumstances of the variety of 'units' subsumed under the term 'female-headed household'; see also Youssef and Hefler (1983). Geisler et al. (1985) make a similar point for the Northern Province of Zambia, where female-headed households are thought to constitute more than a third of the total in some areas; see also Moore and Vaughan (1987).

31 Lévi-Strauss (1969) discusses women as exchanged through marriage. See Comaroff (1980b: 26–31) for a summary of the structuralist approach to marriage and the exchange of women in the context of a re-evaluation of the meaning of marriage payments.

32 This approach to marriage in anthropology is heavily influenced by jurisprudence, and is consequently known as the jural approach. There have now been a number of criticisms of it, particularly with regard to how it privileges event over process, structure over strategy, and object over subject. For interesting discussions of its limitations, see Comaroff (1980b) and Whitehead (1984).

33 At the time of the writing of this book, China is once again undergoing a period of rapid change, including a re-evaluation of communes and their place in the rural economy, among many other things. It therefore seems likely that as a result some of what Elizabeth Croll describes in her work, including certain legal provisions, may have changed or will change in the near future.

34 The actual relationship between betrothal gifts and dowry payments is further complicated by the fact that the Marriage Law of 1950 abolished betrothal gifts, characterizing them as 'paying for' the bride. Under the present circumstances, there is therefore a tension between the families of brides who wish to be compensated for the loss of a valuable daughter, and the families of grooms who wish their sons to marry 'in the new way' and thus get their wives for 'free'. Croll (1984: 56) cites the example of one father who wanted a betrothal gift for his own daughter, but had allowed his sons to marry 'in the new way' so that he would not have to pay anything for his daughters-in-law.

35 The literature on marriage payments in anthropology is very extensive, and there are a number of different approaches. An instructive comparison can be made, for example, between Goody and Tambiah (1973) and Comaroff (1980b). The variability in the organization, form and value of bridewealth and dowry payments in different societies is enormous, and Hirschon has even suggested that the differences within these categories are almost as great as the differences between them (Hirschon, 1984: 10).

36 Dowry in Greece takes very varied forms from one region to another; see Du Boulay (1974), Campbell (1964) and Loizos (1975), for classical ethnographic accounts of dowry systems and their variation.

37 Looking at questions of property, inheritance, labour and marriage has also allowed feminist writers to begin a re-evaluation of the concept of person, particularly as this is defined through the rights which one person may have in another; see, for example, Strathern (1984a, 1984b). See also note 31.

38 Personal jewellery seems to be the one area of a woman's property which is considered her own, although it is not always clear whether she is in a position to dispose of it without reference to others; see Sharma (1980: 50–3).

39 However, for a marvellous contrast with Ursula Sharma's work, see Joao de Pina-Cabral's discussion of female power and wealth in north-western Portugal, where women inherit land and are apparently tremendously powerful within the household (Pina-Cabral, 1984).

40 The state, of course, constructs gender and kinship relations in a particular way, and distorts aspects of those relations for its own purposes. This issue will be discussed in chapter 5.

41 Singer makes the point that bridewealth transactions have been almost exclusively treated from the male point of view in anthropology (Singer, 1973). See also Ogbu (1978), who discusses bridewealth in sixty societies from both female and male perspectives.

Chapter 4   Kinship, Labour and Household: The Changing Nature of Women's Lives

1 Anthropology has been far tardier in analysing the penetration of capitalism into rural production systems than many other disciplines, and almost all of the best work has been done by scholars outside anthropology. However, see Ortner (1984) for an overview of theoretical developments in anthropology since the 1960s, and see Guyer (1981) and Nash (1981) for discussions of this particular transition within anthropology. See also Marcus and Fischer (1986) and Clifford and Marcus (1986) for the way in which this transition is currently affecting theoretical developments in anthropology.

2 Meillassoux is by no means alone in making this kind of argument; see also Wolpe (1972) on South Africa and Laclau (1971) on Latin America. The kinds of theories espoused by Meillassoux and others are only one set of theories among many which try to account for capitalism and its effects on the changing world economy, notable among which are 'development economics', 'dependency theory', 'underdevelopment' and 'world systems theory'. For a comparison of these theories and their consequences, and a critique of them, see Cooper (1981) and Blomstrom and Hettne (1985).

3 I have already detailed some of the feminist criticisms of this work in chapter 3. Most of the other criticisms focus on the concept of 'mode of production'. For criticisms from anthropology, see Sahlins (1976), Firth (1975), Goodfriend (1979) and O'Laughlin (1977). For a thorough and up-to-date appraisal, which tries to deal directly with the value of the concept of mode of production for empirical analysis, see Binsbergen

and Geschiere (1985). For a critique of the notion of articulation, see Foster-Carter (1978).

4 See, for example, the comments of Ranger (1978), Cliffe (1978) and Bernstein (1979). Historians have produced the most outstanding work in this area, especially with regard to Africa. Within anthropology, Meillassoux and other Marxist writers have not addressed themselves directly to this issue because they have tended to see capitalism as dominant without questioning the nature of that dominance sufficiently. They have not enquired, therefore, into patterns of local resistance to capitalism, or into the ways in which local groups have exploited capitalism or, indeed, transformed its relations for their own purposes. For example, African workers in the plantations and mines started, at a very early date, to organize in order to protect their interests within the wage labour markets; see Cohen (1980) and Van Onselen (1976). For an example of how women worked with men to organize and protest with regard to employment in the mines, see Parpart (1986). Questions of women's resistance will be discussed further in chapter 5.

5 See Acker (1980) for an overview of the predominant approaches to the study of gender and class. For discussions on the difficulties of conceptualizing the intersections between gender and class in developing societies, and for criticisms of the 'sex-blind' nature of much Marxist analysis, see Eisenstein (1979), Kuhn and Wolpe (1978), Hartmann (1979), Jaggar and Rothenberg (1984) and Barrett (1980).

6 There has been much discussion in the feminist literature of the relationship between family structures under capitalism and the differentiation between male and female workers in the labour force. This discussion is usually referred to as the 'domestic labour debate'. The central subject in the debate is women's domestic labour in the home. The main issues which are discussed are (1) what are the connections between the division of labour in the home and the divisions in the workplace; (2) why are women in the capitalist workforce consistently subjected to poorer pay and working conditions than men; (3) what is the process by which domestic labour is assigned to women; and (4) what role does gender ideology play in maintaining divisions of labour in the workplace. Most approaches tend to analyse the problem by asking 'What functions does women's labour perform under capitalism?' or 'Is the separation of the home and the workplace inevitable under capitalism such that capitalism is ultimately the cause of the "privatized" family?' This debate has been very well reviewed in the literature (see Molyneux, 1979; Kaluzynska, 1980). Both Barrett (1980: ch. 5) and Burton (1985: ch. 4) provide good introductory summaries and critiques. The debate has been very influential in feminist theorizing, and it is certainly complex, but I have chosen not to structure my discussions of women's work in terms of this debate because the situation in many developing countries seems to me to be very different from the history of the development of capitalism in what is now termed the 'developed world'. And, in particular, the position of women, while having some undoubted similarities, seems to require a somewhat different sort of analysis. The complexities

of women's working lives are discussed in this and the following sections while my theoretical conclusions are presented at the end of my discussion in a way which, I hope, will make clear some of my reasons for not structuring this section in terms of the 'domestic labour debate'.

7   See also Gaitskell et al. (1983: 88).

8   This point is made very forcefully by Bujra (1986: 124–7). Much of my argument in this and the following section draws on Bujra's insightful comments on these issues.

9   For further studies of women in the informal economy, see Schuster (1982) and MacGaffey (1983).

10 For another study of successful women entrepreneurs in West Africa, see Robertson (1984).

11 Cliffe discusses the process through which the capitalist relations of production gradually transform what had been voluntary and mutual help on the farm from neighbours, relatives or beer parties into the hiring of casual labour (Cliffe, 1982: 263).

12 Izzard also emphasizes the importance of acknowledging the 'economic imperative' underlying the migration of women (Izzard, 1985: 271). This view is contrary to that of writers like Caldwell (1969), Adepoju (1983) and Majumdar and Majumdar (1978), who see women's migration as primarily related to marriage and to 'following husbands'.

13 See also Schuster (1982) on this point.

14 Youssef worked out these figures on the basis of a sample of countries classified into industrialized (22) and underdeveloped (28) according to per capita income and the activity rate of adult males in non-agricultural work. She drew figures on these indicators from data published by the International Labour Office and the United Nations, Department of Economic and Social Affairs (Youssef, 1976).

15 Many studies have noted the decline in the work participation of women in the early stages of economic development, and this is usually attributed to a progressive decrease in their work participation in traditional sectors of employment: cottage industries, agriculture and petty trade. Such decreases are only partly offset by increases in the participation of women in expanding modern sectors, like manufacturing and services. See Boserup (1970).

16 The question of determining the class of women is a difficult one. In studies of class in developed capitalist societies, the class of a woman is often assumed to be determined by the occupational status of the household head, who is usually a male. Feminist writers have questioned this approach, and have indicated situations where both husband and wife are employed but in different occupational strata (e.g. Stanworth, 1984). Other feminist approaches have included the analysis of women as domestic labourers as a distinctive class (e.g. Dalla Costa and James, 1972), and the argument that women's experience of class is determined by their position in the relations of reproduction in the home (e.g. West, 1978). In many developing countries, class formation is not yet complete, and capitalist relations of production exist alongside non-capitalist relations of production; this further adds to the complications of as-

cribing class status to women. However, what is clear is that if occupational status, level of education and relations to the capitalist mode of production are used as indicators then, in many developing countries, a significant proportion of households contain individuals from a range of different classes. In this chapter I have defined women's class by using a dual definition based on the woman's occupational status and on her relationship to the dominant mode of production.

17 Probably the most substantial body of early literature dealing with these issues in social anthropology was produced by the Rhodes Livingstone Institute, Northern Rhodesia (now Zambia). This literature dealt with urban anthropology, ethnic difference and workers in the mines of the copper belt. It also studied non-corporate groupings, voluntary associations, church groups, unions and political parties. See Brown (1975).

18 For a brilliant overview of this material, see Gittins (1985: ch. 1).

Chapter 5   Women and the State

1 However, arguments about controlling the means of production and productive surpluses through controlling the labour of women and junior men are enormously complicated by the arguments concerning the role of slave labour (see Asad, 1985; Meillassoux, 1971; Miers and Kopytoff, 1977; Robertson and Klein, 1983).

2 See, for example, Rohrlich-Leavitt (1977, 1980), McNamara and Wemple (1977), Silverblatt (1978), Sacks (1979) and Sanday (1981).

3 There are also many recorded instances of women office-holders in other parts of the world, notably Polynesia.

4 The implicit, and sometimes explicit, definition of 'power' used in much feminist anthropology is the ability to make someone do what they do not wish to do, to act effectively on persons and things, to take decisions which are not of right allocated to the actor's role or to the actor as an individual. 'Authority' is defined more simply as the right to make a particular decision or follow a particular course of action, and to command obedience. The crucial point, as feminists have pointed out, is that power and authority are, in some senses, separate, because the one may not imply the other (March and Taqqu, 1986: 1–5).

5 There is a certain amount of disagreement concerning definitions of socialism and how well the term applies to particular societies. I follow Maxine Molyneux in using the term 'socialist' to refer to countries which have an expressed commitment to constructing a socialist society on the basis of what are understood as the principles of Marxism and Leninism, which have a high level of social redistribution, and where production and distribution are organized by the state according to principles of planned economic development (Molyneux, 1981: 32).

6 This legislation made it illegal for employers to differentiate between women and men undertaking 'like work'. However, the legislation has certainly not resulted in equal pay for equal work. In 1985, women's average gross hourly earnings were 74.0 per cent of men's, and women's

average gross weekly earnings were 65.9 per cent of men's (Department of Employment, 1985: part A, tables 10 and 11).

7 This situation is similar to that noted for rural China by Elizabeth Croll; see the discussion of her work in chapter 4.

8 Hostility to premarital liaisons, divorce, illegitimacy and homosexuality is not of course restricted to socialist states. However, the suppression of what are seen as 'non-normative' sexual practices under socialist regimes has often been particularly brutal. See, for example, Arguelles and Rich (1984).

9 The control of family size is more easily achieved in urban settings than in rural ones. This is partly because state controls are harder to avoid in urban contexts, and they are also reinforced by material circumstances like shortage of housing, job scarcity and the provision of state support for the elderly, which alleviates any pressure to have children in order to provide support for one's old age. In rural areas, family sizes are slightly harder to control because of the dependence of rural households on family labour – the hiring of labour is not permitted. Couples who restrict themselves to one child receive benefits in the form of higher wages, better jobs and perhaps preferential education for the child. Those who exceed the prescribed number of children are usually punished with wage cuts, reduced maternity leave, loss of political positions, etc. In some cases women have been involuntarily sterilized, and Stacey reports one incident of a father being ordered to be sterilized after the birth of a third child (Stacey, 1983: 274–80; Davin, 1987a: 158–60; Saith, 1984). The most drastic effect of the single-child policy is the re-emergence of the infanticide of girl babies. Some claims may be exaggerated, but the party, the Youth League and the Women's Federation have issued repeated denunciations of the practice, and it is recognized at the highest levels as a serious problem (Davin, 1987b).

10 See Jancar (1978: 51–6). One of the most blatant attempts to encourage women to have children is the Soviet system of medals. Women were given the title of Mother Heroine if they gave birth to and raised ten children. Those who had seven, eight or nine children earned the Order of the Glory of Motherhood, while those with only five or six received the Motherhood Medal (Buckley, 1981: 94).

11 Judith Stacey discusses rural resistance to communalism and family reform during the period of the Great Leap Forward in China (Stacey, 1983: ch. 6). In Afghanistan in 1980, a decree banning bridewealth and a further one making education for women compulsory had to be abandoned in the face of increasing opposition from rural areas (Molyneux, 1985a: 56). See Molyneux (1981: 4) for further examples.

12 See the discussion of Elizabeth Croll's work in chapter 4 and Croll (1981b and 1981c); see also Davin (1987a).

13 In the last ten years there has been an enormous amount of literature published on women and development. For bibliographies of earlier work on women and development, see Buvinic (1976), Rihani (1978), ISIS (1983) and Nelson (1979). Feminist theories of development fall into three main categories – liberal, Marxist and socialist-feminist; see

Bandarage (1984) and Jaquette (1982) for information on this typology, and, for criticisms of their work, see Staudt (1986a).

14   See Rogers (1980), Boulding (1977), International Labour Office (1981), Tinker and Bramsen (1976), Nelson (1981), Dauber and Cain (1981) and Jahan and Papanek (1979). For arguments about the decline of women's status under colonialism, see Etienne and Leacock (1980). For examples of writers who link women's subordination to the dependency and marginalization of Third World economies under international capitalism, see Nash (1977), Beneria and Sen (1982), Saffioti (1978) and Schmink (1977).

15   Elise Boulding has calculated that women represent only 6 per cent of policy-makers worldwide (Boulding, 1978: 36).

16   These issues are beginning to receive much-needed treatment by feminist scholars writing in the field of women and development; see, for example, Staudt (1985, 1986a), Staudt and Jaquette (1983) and Charlton (1984).

17   Estimates of the number of women's groups in Kenya vary: Maas (1986) gives a figure of 6,000, involving approximately 500,000 women, based on a report in *The Daily Nation* for 3 December 1979. Feldman uses Woman's Bureau figures for 1978 and gives the number of women's groups as 8,000, incorporating approximately 300,000 women (Feldman, 1983).

18   The argument is that women are involved in class reproduction because they are engaged in what Papanek (1979) has called 'family status production work', i.e. creating the lifestyle, milieu and cultural context appropriate to their class level. In addition, see Sharma (1986), who also makes use of Papanek's concept of 'status production work' in a study of Indian women. Caplan views voluntary organizations as being involved in the ideological reproduction of the dominant class, and she suggests – after Althusser (see this chapter above) – that social welfare institutions might be important as ideological state apparatuses under capitalism in contexts where the role of education and the media are constrained by their 'non-availability' to the mass of the population (Caplan, 1985: 214).

19   In many Third World states, educated women have been placed in positions of power within the state, and, while criticisms abound concerning the tokenism of such actions and the lack of resources and support many of these 'ministries of women' receive, the fact that women have been so placed requires some serious consideration. One very common feminist view is that having more women in positions of power would not just alter the form and content of policies and programmes, but would also lead to alternative methods of making decisions, reaching consensus and running bureaucratic institutions. This argument suggests that it is possible that, if more women were to be involved in state institutions, it is not only the nature of decisions which could change, but the nature of the state itself. However, while women are being encouraged to take a more active part in decision-making in many contexts, there has as yet been little serious consideration of whether the incorporation of large

numbers of women into state structures would alter state policy and planning in such a way as to allow women to become equal participants and beneficiaries. There is an urgent need for more theoretical and empirical work. See note 16.

20 See Schuster (1979) and Geisler (1987) for a discussion on the Zambian Women's League; Bujra (1986: 136–7) on the Gambian Women's Federation; Smock (1977) on Ghana; Fluehr-Lobban (1977) on the Sudan; and Steady (1975) on Sierra Leone.

21 The literature on feminist and nationalist movements in the Third World includes both historical and contemporary studies, and is particularly rich; see, for example, Jayawardena (1986), Croll (1978), Nashat (1983a), Walker (1982), Eisen (1984), Urdang (1979, 1984), Everett (1981) and Davies (1983).

22 For overviews of the history of Hinduism, Buddhism, Christianity and Islam, and their views of and effects of women, with special reference to their influence on population and education, see Carroll (1983).

23 'The Qur'an advocates neither the veil nor segregation of the sexes; rather it insists on sexual modesty. It is also certain on historical grounds that there was no veil in the Prophet's time, nor was there segregation of the sexes in the sense Muslim societies later developed it' (Rahman, 1983: 40).

24 Afshar gives the punishments for failure to observe *hijab* as much more severe than this. The open defiance of *hijab*, and appearance in public without it, is punishable by seventy-four lashes. The officials who detain such women do not need to take them to court, since the crime is self-evident; the punishment is immediate. Women who are inadequately covered are also likely to be attacked on the streets by members of the 'Party of God', the Hezbolahis carrying guns and knives, and are lucky to survive (Afshar, 1987: 73).

25 Iris Berger suggests that to see women's spirit possession simply as a thinly disguised protest against men misses the equally important point that it also offers women a degree of status and authority in ritual situations which is normally denied them in the context of formal religious observance (Berger, 1976).

REFERENCES

Aaby, Peter 1977 'Engels and women'. *Critique of Anthropology*, 3 (9–10): 25–53.

Abbott, Susan 1976 'Full-time farmers and weekend wives'. *Journal of Marriage and the Family*, 38 (1): 165–73.

Abu Nasr, Julinda, Khoury, Nabir and Azzam, Henry (eds) 1985 *Women, Employment and Development in the Arab World*. Berlin: Mouton.

Acker, Joan 1980 'Women and stratification: a review of recent literature'. *Contemporary Sociology*, 9: 25–39.

Adepoju, Aderanti 1983 'Patterns of migration by sex'. In C. Oppong (ed.), *Female and Male in West Africa*, 54–66. London: George Allen & Unwin.

Afonja, Simi 1981 'Changing modes of production and the sexual division of labor among the Yoruba'. *Signs*, 7 (2): 299.

Afshar, Haleh 1982 'Khomeini's teachings and their implications for women'. *Feminist Review*, 12: 59–72.

Afshar, Haleh 1987 'Women, marriage and the state in Iran'. In H. Afshar (ed.), *Women, State and Ideology*, 70–86. London: Macmillan.

Ahmed, Iftikhar (ed.) 1985 *Technology and Rural Women: Conceptual and Empirical Issues*. London: Allen & Unwin.

Allison, Caroline 1985 'Women, land, labour and survival: getting some basic facts straight'. *Institute of Development Studies Bulletin*, 16 (3): 24–30.

Al-Sanabary, Nagat 1985 'Continuity and change in women's education in the Arab states'. In E. Fernea (ed.), *Women and the Family in the Middle East*, 93–110. Austin: University of Texas Press.

Althusser, Louis 1971 *Lenin and Philosophy and Other Essays*. London: New Left Books.

Altorki, Soraya 1986 *Women in Saudi Arabia*. New York: Columbia University Press.

Amos, Valerie and Parmar, Pratibha 1984 'Challenging imperial feminism'. *Feminist Review*, 17: 3–19.

Anderson, M. 1980 *Approaches to the History of the Western Family, 1500–1914*. London: Macmillan.

Ardener, Edwin 1975a 'Belief and the problem of women'. In S. Ardener (ed.), *Perceiving Women*, 1–17. London: Dent.

Ardener, Edwin 1975b 'The problem revisited'. In S. Ardener (ed.), *Perceiving Women*, 19–27. London: Dent.

Ardener, Edwin 1978 'Problems in the analysis of events'. In E. Schwimmer (ed.), *Yearbook of Symbolic Anthropology*, 103–23. London: C. Hurst & Co.

Ardener, Shirley 1964 'The comparative study of rotating credit associations'. *Journal of the Royal Anthropological Institute*, 94: 201–29.

Ardener, Shirley 1973 'Sexual insult and female militancy'. *Man*, 8: 422–40.

Arguelles, Lourdes and Rich, B. Ruby 1984 'Homosexuality, homophobia, and revolution: notes toward an understanding of the Cuban lesbian and gay male experience'. *Signs*, 9 (4): 683–99.

Arhin, Kwame 1979 *West African Traders in Ghana in the 19th and 20th Centuries*. Harlow: Longman.

Ariès, P. 1973 *Centuries of Childhood*. Harmondsworth: Penguin.

Arizpe, Lourdes 1977 'Women in the informal labor sector: the case of Mexico City'. In Wellesley Editorial Committee (eds), *Women and National Development: The Complexities of Change*, 25–37. Chicago: University of Chicago Press.

Asad, Talal (ed.) 1973 *Anthropology and the Colonial Encounter*. London: Ithaca Press.

Asad, Talal 1985 'Primitive states and the reproduction of production relations'. *Critique of Anthropology*, 5 (2): 21–33.

Atkinson, Jane Monnig 1982 'Anthropology: a review essay'. *Signs*, 8 (2): 236–58.

Awe, Bolanle 1977 'The Iyalode in the traditional Yoruba political system'. In A. Schlegel (ed.), *Sexual Stratification*, 144–95. New York: Columbia University Press.

Azari, Farah 1983 'Islam's appeal to women in Iran: illusions and reality'. In F. Azari (ed.), *Women of Iran*, London: Ithaca Press.

Azzam, Henry 1979 *The Participation of Arab Women in the Labour Force: Development Factors and Policies*. International Labour Office Working Paper, WEP 2–21/WP80.

Azzam, Henry, Abu Nasr, Julinda and Lorfing, I. 1985 'An overview of Arab women in population, employment and economic development'. In J. Abu Nasr et al. (eds), *Women, Employment and Development in the Arab World*, 5–37. Berlin: Mouton.

Azzam, Henry and Moujabber, C. 1985 'Women and development in the Gulf States'. In J. Abu Nasr et al. (eds), *Women, Employment and Development in the Arab World*, 59–72. Berlin: Mouton.

Bachofen, J. J. 1861 *Myth, Religion and Mother Right*. London: Swann Sonnenschein.

Bamberger, Joan 1974 'The myth of matriarchy: why men rule in primitive society'. In M. Rosaldo and L. Lamphere (eds), *Women, Culture and Society*, 263–80. Stanford: Stanford University Press.

Bandarage, Asoka 1984 'Women in Development: liberalism, Marxism and Marxist-feminism'. *Development and Change*, 15: 495–515.

Barnes, J. A. 1973 'Genetrix: genitor: nature: culture?'. In J. Goody (ed.), *The Character of Kinship*, 61–73. Cambridge: Cambridge University Press.

Barrett, Michèle 1980 *Women's Oppression Today*. London: Verso.

Barstow, Anne 1978 'The uses of archaeology for women's history: James Mellaart's work on the Neolithic Goddess at Cataar Huyuk'. *Feminist Studies*, 4 (3): 7–18.

Bay, Edna G. (ed.) 1982 *Women and Work in Africa*. Boulder, Colorado: Westview Press.

Beck, Lois and Keddie, Nikki (eds) 1978 *Women in the Muslim World*. Cambridge, Mass.: Harvard University Press.

Beechey, Veronica 1978 'Women and production: a critical analysis of some sociological theories of women's work'. In A. Kuhn and A. M. Wolpe (eds), *Feminism and Materialism*, 155–97. London: Routledge & Kegan Paul.

Beechey, Veronica 1979 'On patriarchy'. *Feminist Review*, 3: 66–82.

Beechey, Veronica 1983 'What's so special about women's employment?' *Feminist Review*, 15: 23–45.

Beinart, William 1982 *The Political Economy of Pondoland, 1860–1930*. Cambridge: Cambridge University Press.

Bell, Diane 1980 'Desert politics: choices in the marriage market'. In M. Etienne and E. Leacock (eds), *Women and Colonization*, 239–69. New York: Praeger.

Bell, Diane 1983 *Daughters of the Dreaming*. Melbourne: McPhee Gribble.

Beneria, Lourdes 1981 'Conceptualising the labour force: the underestimation of women's economic activities'. In N. Nelson (ed.), *African Women in the Development Process*, 10–28. London: Frank Cass.

Beneria, Lourdes 1982a *Women and Development: The Sexual Division of Labor in Rural Societies*. New York: Praeger.

Beneria, Lourdes 1982b 'Accounting for women's work'. In L. Beneria (ed.), *Women and Development*, 119–47. New York: Praeger.

Beneria, Lourdes 1982c 'Introduction'. In L. Beneria (ed.) *Women and Development*, xi–xxiii. New York: Praeger.

Beneria, Lourdes and Sen, Gita 1981 'Accumulation, reproduction and women's role in economic development: Boserup revisited'. *Signs*, 7 (2): 279–98.

Beneria, Lourdes and Sen, Gita 1982 'Class and gender inequalities and women's role in economic development: theoretical and practical implications'. *Feminist Studies*, 8 (1).

Berger, Iris 1976 'Rebels or status-seekers? Women as spirit mediums in East Africa'. In N. Hafkin and E. Bray (eds), *Women in Africa*, 157–81. Stanford: Stanford University Press.

Berkner, Lutz K. 1972 'The Stem family and the development cycle of the peasant household: an 18th century Austrian example'. *American Historical Review*, 77 (2): 398–418.

Bernstein, Henry 1979 'African peasantries: a theoretical framework'. *Journal of Peasant Studies*, 6 (4): 421–33.

Berry, Sara S. 1975 *Cocoa, Custom and Socio-Economic Change in Rural Western Nigeria*. Oxford: Clarendon Press.

Berry, Sara S. 1984 *Fathers Work for their Sons*. Berkeley: University of California Press.

Bettelheim, Bruno 1962 *Symbolic Wounds: Puberty Rites and the Envious Male*. London: Thames & Hudson.

Bhavnani, Kum-kum and Coulson, Margaret 1986 'Transforming socialist-feminism: the challenge of racism'. *Feminist Review*, 23: 81–92.

Biersack, Aletta 1984 'Paiela "women-men": the reflexive foundations of gender ideology'. *American Ethnologist*, 118–38.

Binsbergen, Wim Van and Geschiere, Peter (eds) 1985 *Old Modes of Production and Capitalist Encroachment: Anthropological Explorations in Africa*. London: KPI.

Blackwood, B. 1934 *Both Sides of Baka Passage*. Oxford: Clarendon Press.

Bledsoe, Caroline H. 1980 *Women and Marriage in Kpelle Society*. Stanford: Stanford University Press.

Bloch, Maurice 1975 'Property and the end of affinity'. In M. Bloch (ed.), *Marxist Analyses in Social Anthropology*. London: Malaby Press.

Bloch, Maurice 1983 *Marxism and Anthropology*. Oxford: Oxford University Press.

Bloch, Maurice and Bloch, Jean 1980 'Women and the dialectics of nature in eighteenth-century French thought'. In C. MacCormack and M. Strathern (eds), *Nature, Culture and Gender*, 25–41. Cambridge: Cambridge University Press.

Blomstrom, Magnus and Hettne, Bjorn 1985 *Development Theory in Transition*. London: Zed Press.

Boon, J. 1974 'Anthropology and nannies'. *Man*, 9: 137–40.

Boserup, Esther 1970 *Women's Role in Economic Development*. London: George Allen & Unwin.

Bossen, Laurel Herbenar 1975 'Women in modernizing societies'. *American Ethnologist*, 2 (4): 587–601.

Bossen, Laurel Herbenar 1984 *The Redivision of Labor: Women and Economic Choice in Four Guatemalan Communities*. Albany: State University of New York Press.

Boulding, Elise 1977 *Women in the Twentieth Century World*. New York: John Wiley.

Boulding, Elise 1978 *Handbook of International Data on Women*. Beverly Hills: Sage.

Boulding, Elise 1983 'Measures of women's work in the Third World: problems and suggestions'. In M. Buvinić et al., *Women and Poverty in the Third World*, 286–99. Baltimore: Johns Hopkins University Press.

Boxer, Marilyn 1982 'For and about women: the theory and practice of women's studies in the United States'. In N. Keohane, M. Rosaldo and B. Gelpi (eds), *Feminist Theory: A Critique of Ideology*, 237–71. Brighton: Harvester Press.

Bozzoli, Belinda 1983 'Marxism, feminism and South African studies'. *Journal of Southern African Studies*, 9 (2): 139–71.

Brain, James 1976 'Less than second-class: women in rural settlement schemes in Tanzania'. In N. Hafkin and E. Bay (eds), *Women in Africa*, 265–84. Stanford: Stanford University Press.

Brain, Robert 1972 *Bangwa Kinship and Marriage*. Cambridge: Cambridge University Press.

Brown, Judith 1970 'A note on the division of labour by sex'. *American Anthropologist*, 72 (5): 1073–8.

Brown, Penelope and Jordanova, L. J. 1982 'Oppressive dichotomies: the nature/culture debate'. In The Cambridge Women's Studies Group (ed.), *Women in Society*, 224–41. London: Virago.

Brown, Richard 1973 'Anthropology and colonial rule: Godfrey Wilson and the Rhodes–Livingstone Institute, Northern Rhodesia'. In T. Asad (ed.), *Anthropology and the Colonial Encounter*, 173–99. London: Ithaca Press.

Bryceson, Deborah 1985 'Women's proletarianisation and the family wage in Tanzania'. In H. Afshar (ed.), *Women, Work and Ideology in the Third World*, 128–52. London: Tavistock.

Bryson, Judy 1981 'Women and agriculture in sub-Sahara Africa: implications for development'. In. N. Nelson (ed.), *African Women in the Development Process*, 29–46. London: Frank Cass.

Buckley, Mary 1981 'Women in the Soviet Union'. *Feminist Review*, 8: 79–106.

Bujra, Janet 1975 'Women "entrepreneurs" of early Nairobi'. *Canadian Journal of African Studies*, 9: 213–34.

Bujra, Janet 1978 'Female solidarity and the sexual division of labour'. In P. Caplan and J. Bujra (eds), *Women United, Women Divided*, 13–45. London: Tavistock.

Bujra, Janet 1986 ' "Urging women to redouble their efforts . . . ": class, gender and capitalist transformation in Africa'. In C. Robertson and I. Berger (eds), *Women and Class in Africa*, 117–40. New York: Africana Publishing Company.

Bukh, Jette 1979 *The Village Woman in Ghana*. Uppsala: Scandinavian Institute of African Studies.

Burman, Sandra (ed.) 1979 *Fit Work for Women*. London: Croom Helm.

Burman, Sandra 1984 'Divorce and the disadvantaged: African women in urban South Africa'. In R. Hirschon (ed.), *Women and Property, Women as Property*, 117–39. London: Croom Helm.

Burton, Clare 1985 *Subordination: Feminism and Social Theory*. Sydney: George Allen & Unwin.

Bush, Ray, Cliffe, Lionel and Jansen, Valerey 1986 'The crisis in the reproduction of migrant labour in southern Africa'. In Peter Lawrence (ed.), *World Recession and the Food Crisis in Africa*, 283–99. London: James Currey.

Buvinić, Mayra 1976 *Women and World Development: Annotated Bibliography*. Washington, DC: Overseas Development Council.

Caldwell, John 1969 *African Rural Migration*. Canberra: Australian National University Press.

Campbell, J. K. 1964 *Honour, Family and Patronage*. Oxford: Clarendon Press.

Caplan, Patricia 1984 'Cognatic descent, Islamic law and women's property on the East Africa coast'. In R. Hirschon (ed.), *Women and Property, Women as Property*, 23–43. London: Croom Helm.

Caplan, Patricia 1985 *Class and Gender in India: Women and their Organisations in a South Indian City.* London: Tavistock.

Caplan, Patricia and Bujra, Janet (eds) 1978 *Women United, Women Divided.* London: Tavistock.

Carby, Hazel 1982 'White women listen! Black feminism and the boundaries of sisterhood'. In Birmingham University Centre for Contemporary Cultural Studies (eds), *The Empire Strikes Back: Race and Racism in 70s Britain.* London: Hutchinson.

Carroll, Theodora Foster 1983 *Women, Religion, and Development in the Third World.* New York: Praeger.

Chaney, Elsa and Schmink, Marianne 1976 'Women and modernization: access to tools'. In J. Nash and H. Safa (eds), *Sex and Class in Latin America*, 160–82. New York: Praeger.

Charlton, Sue Ellen M. 1984 *Women in Third World Development.* Epping: Bowker.

Chinchilla, Norma 1977 'Industrialization, monopoly capitalism, and women's work in Guatemala'. In Wellesley Editorial Committee (eds), *Women and National Development*, 38–56. Chicago: University of Chicago Press.

Chodorow, Nancy 1978 *The Reproduction of Mothering: Psychoanalysis and the Sociology of Gender.* Berkeley: University of California Press.

Cliffe, Lionel 1978 'Labour migration and peasant differentiation: Zambian experiences'. *Journal of Peasant Studies*, 5 (3): 326–46.

Cliffe, Lionel 1982 'Class formation as an "articulation" process: East African cases'. In H. Alavi and T. Shanin (eds), *Introduction to the Sociology of 'Developing Societies'*, 262–78. London: Macmillan.

Clifford, James 1983 'On ethnographic authority'. *Representations*, 1: 118–46.

Clifford, James and Marcus, George (eds) 1986 *Writing Culture.* Berkeley: University of California Press.

Cock, Jacklyn 1980 *Maids and Madams: A Study in the Politics of Exploitation.* Johannesburg: Ravan Press.

Cohen, Abner 1981 *The Politics of Elite Culture: Explorations in the Dramaturgy of Power in a Modern African Society.* Berkeley: University of California Press.

Cohen, Robin 1980 'Resistance and hidden forms of consciousness amongst African workers'. *Review of African Political Economy*, 19: 8–22.

Cohen, Ronald and Middleton, John (eds) 1970 *From Tribe to Nation in Africa: Studies in Incorporation Processes.* Scranton, Pennsylvania: Chandler Publishing Company.

Collier, Jane and Rosaldo, Michelle 1981 'Politics and gender in simple societies'. In S. Ortner and H. Whitehead (eds), *Sexual Meanings*, 275–329. Cambridge: Cambridge University Press.

Collier, J. et al. 1982 'Is there a family? New anthropological views'. In B. Thorne and M. Yalom (eds), *Rethinking the Family: Some Feminist Questions*, 25–39. New York: Longman.

Comaroff, John L. 1980a 'Bridewealth and the control of ambiguity in a Tswana chiefdom'. In J. Comaroff (ed.), *The Meaning of Marriage Payments*, 161–95. London: Academic Press.

Comaroff, John L. 1980b 'Introduction'. In J. Comaroff (ed.), *The Meaning of Marriage Payments*, 1–47. New York: Academic Press.

Comaroff, John L. and Roberts, Simon 1977 'Marriage and extramarital sexuality: the dialectics of legal change among Kgatla'. *Journal of African Law*, 21: 97–123.

Coontz, Stephanie and Henderson, Peta (eds), 1986 *Women's Work, Men's Property: The Origins of Gender and Class*. London: Verso.

Cooper, Frank 1981 'Africa and the world economy'. *African Studies Review*, 24 (2/3): 1–86.

Coward, Rosalind 1983 *Patriarchal Precedents*. London: Routledge & Kegan Paul.

Creighton, Colin 1980 'Family, property and the relations of production in western Europe'. *Economy and Society*, 9: 128–67.

Crick, Malcolm 1976 *Explorations in Language and Meaning: Towards a Semantic Anthropology*. London: Malaby Press.

Croll, Elizabeth 1978 *Feminism and Socialism in China*. London: Routledge & Kegan Paul.

Croll, Elizabeth 1981a *The Politics of Marriage in Contemporary China*. Cambridge: Cambridge University Press.

Croll, Elizabeth 1981b 'Women in rural production and reproduction in the Soviet Union, China, Cuba and Tanzania: socialist development experiences'. *Signs*, 7 (2): 360–74.

Croll, Elizabeth 1981c 'Women in rural production and reproduction in the Soviet Union, China, Cuba and Tanzania: case studies'. *Signs*, 7 (2): 375–99.

Croll, Elizabeth 1984 'The exchange of women and property: marriage in post-revolutionary China'. In R. Hirschon (ed.), *Women and Property, Women as Property*, 44–61. London: Croom Helm.

Dalla Costa, Mariarosa and James, Selma 1972 *The Power of Women and the Subversion of Community*. Bristol: Falling Wall Press.

Dauber, Roslyn and Cain, Melinda (eds) 1981 *Women and Technological Change in Developing Countries*. Boulder, Colorado: Westview Press.

Davies, Miranda (ed.) 1983 *Third World–Second Sex: Women's Struggles and National Liberation*. London: Zed Press.

Davin, Delia 1987a 'Engels and the making of Chinese family policy'. In J. Sayers et al. (eds), *Engels Revisited*, 145–63. London: Tavistock.

Davin, Delia 1987b 'Gender and population in the People's Republic of China'. In H. Afshar (ed.), *Women, State and Ideology*, 111–29. London: Macmillan.

Davis, Angela 1981 *Women, Race and Class*. London: The Women's Press.

Deere, Carmen Diana 1983 'The allocation of familial labour and the formation of peasant, household income in the Peruvian sierra', In M. Buvinic, M. Lycette and W. P. McGreevey (eds), *Women and Poverty in the Third World*, 104–29. Baltimore: Johns Hopkins University Press.

Deere, Carmen Diana and Léon de Léal, Magdalena 1981 'Peasant production, proletarianization, and the sexual division of labor in the Andes'. *Signs*, 7 (2): 338–60.

Delmar, Rosalind 1976 'Looking again at Engels' *Origin of the Family, Private Property and the State*'. In J. Mitchell and A. Oakley (eds), *The Rights and Wrongs of Women*, 271–87. Harmondsworth: Penguin.

Delmar, Rosalind 1986 'What is feminism?' In J. Mitchell and A. Oakley (eds), *What is Feminism?*, 8–33. Oxford: Basil Blackwell.

Delphy, Christine 1984 *Close to Home: A Materialist Analysis of Women's Oppression*. London: Hutchinson.

Department of Employment 1985 *New Earnings Survey*. London: HMSO.

Dey, Jennie 1981 'Gambian women: unequal partners in rice development projects?' In N. Nelson (ed.), *African Women in the Development Process*, 109–22. London: Frank Cass.

Dinan, Carmel 1977 'Pragmatists or feminists: the professional single women of Accra'. *Cahiers d'études africaines*, 19: 155–76.

Dixon, Ruth 1985 'Seeing the invisible women farmers in Africa: improving research and data collection methods'. In J. Monson and M. Kalb (eds), *Women as Food Producers in Developing Countries*, 19–35. Los Angeles: UCLA African Studies Centre.

Donzelot, J. 1980 *Policing the Family*. London: Routledge & Kegan Paul.

Douglas, Mary 1966 *Purity and Danger*. London: Routledge & Kegan Paul.

Douglas, Mary 1968 'The relevance of tribal studies'. *Journal of Psychosomatic Research*, 12: 21–8.

Douglas, Mary 1973 *Natural Symbols*. Harmondsworth: Penguin.

Drummond, L. 1978 'The transatlantic nanny: notes on a comparative semiotics of the family in English-speaking societies'. *American Ethnologist*, 5 (1): 30–43.

Du Boulay, Juliet 1974 *Portrait of a Greek Mountain Village*. Oxford: Clarendon Press.

Dwyer, Daisy 1978 'Ideologies of sexual inequality and strategies for change in male–female relations'. *American Ethnologist*, 5 (2): 227–40.

Eades, Jeremy 1980 *The Yoruba Today*. Cambridge: Cambridge University Press.

Edholm, Felicity, Harris, Olivia and Young, Kate 1977 'Conceptualising women'. *Critique of Anthropology*, 3 (9 and 10): 101–30.

Eisen, Arlene 1984 *Women and Revolution in Vietnam*. London: Zed Books.

Eisenstein, Zillah (ed.) 1979 *Capitalist Patriarchy and the Case of Socialist Feminism*. New York: Monthly Review Press.

Eisenstein, Zillah 1980 *The Radical Future of Liberal Feminism*. New York: Longman.

Eisenstein, Zillah 1984 *Feminism and Sexual Equality: Crisis in Liberal America*. New York: Monthly Review Press.

Ellis, Pat (ed.) 1986a *Women of the Caribbean*. London: Zed Press.

Ellis, Pat 1986b 'Introduction: an overview of women in Caribbean society'. In P. Ellis (ed.), *Women of the Caribbean*, 1–24. London: Zed Press.

Elshtain, Jean Bethke 1981 *Public Man, Private Woman: Women in Social and Political Thought*. Princeton: Princeton University Press.

Elson, Diane and Pearson, Ruth 1981 'Nimble fingers make cheap workers: an analysis of women's employment in Third World export manufacturing'. *Feminist Review*, 7: 87–107.

Engels, Friedrich 1972 (1884) *The Origin of the Family, Private Property, and the State*. New York: Pathfinder Press.

Ennew, Judith 1979 'The material of reproduction: anthropological views on historical materialism and kinship'. *Economy and Society*, 8 (1): 99–124.

Etienne, Mona 1980 'Women and men, cloth and colonization: the transformation of production–distribution relations among the Baule (Ivory Coast)'. In M. Etienne and E. Leacock (eds), *Women and Colonization*, 214–38. New York: Praeger.

Etienne, Mona and Leacock, Eleanor 1980 *Women and Colonization*. New York: Praeger.

Evans, Peter, Rueschemeyer, Dietrich and Skocpol, Theda (eds) 1985 *Bringing the State Back In*. Cambridge: Cambridge University Press.

Everett, Jana Matson 1981 *Women and Social Change in India*. New Delhi: Heritage.

Faithorn, Elizabeth 1976 'Women as persons: aspects of female life and male–female relationships among the Kafe'. In P. Brown and G. Buchbinder (eds), *Man and Woman in the New Guinea Highlands*. Washington, DC: American Anthropological Association, Special Publication, No. 8.

Fapohunda, Eleanor 1982 'The child-care dilemma of working mothers in African cities: the case of Lagos, Nigeria'. In E. Bay (ed.), *Women and Work in Africa*, 277–88. Boulder, Colorado: Westview Press.

Fee, Elizabeth 1974 'The sexual politics of Victorian social anthropology'. In M. Hartmann and L. Banner (eds), *Clio's Consciousness Raised*. New York: Harper.

Feil, D. K. 1978 'Women and men in the Enga Tee'. *American Ethnologist*, 5 (2): 263–79.

Feldman, Rayah 1983 'Women's groups and women's surbordination: an analysis of policies towards rural women in Kenya'. *Review of African Political Economy*, 27/28: 67–85.

Fernea, Elizabeth (ed.) 1985 *Women and the Family in the Middle East*. Austin: University of Texas Press.

Firth, Raymond 1975 'The skeptical anthropologist: social anthropology and Marxist views on society'. In M. Bloch (ed.), *Marxist Analyses in Social Anthropology*, 29–60. London: Malaby Press.

Flandrin, J.-L. 1979 *Families in Former Times*. Cambridge: Cambridge University Press.

Flannery, Kent 1972 'The cultural evolution of civilizations'. *Annual Review of Ecology and Systematics*, 3: 399–426.

Fluehr-Lobban, Carolyn 1977 'Agitation for change in the Sudan'. In A. Schlegel (ed.), *Sexual Stratification*, 127–43. New York: Columbia University Press.

Fortes, Meyer 1949 *The Web of Kinship among the Tallensi*. London: Oxford University Press.

Fortes, Meyer 1969 *Kinship and the Social Order*. Chicago: Aldine.

Fortes, Meyer and Evans-Pritchard, E. 1940 *African Political Systems*. London: Oxford University Press.

Fortmann, Louise 1981 'The plight of the invisible farmer: the effect of national agricultural policy on women in Africa'. In R. Dauber and M. Cain (eds), *Women and Technological Change in Developing Countries*, 205–14. Boulder, Colorado: Westview.

Foster-Carter, Aidan 1978 'Can we articulate "articulation"?'. In J. Clammer (ed.), *The New Economic Anthropology*, 210–49. New York: St Martin's Press.

Foucault, Michel 1978 *The History of Sexuality*, vol. 1. London: Allen Lane.

Fox, R. 1967 *Kinship and Marriage*. London: Penguin.

Frankenstein, S. and Rowlands, M. 1978 'The internal structure and regional context of Early Iron Age society in south–western Germany'. *Bulletin of the Institute of Archaeology*, 15: 73–112.

Friedl, Erika 1983 'State, ideology and village women'. In G. Nashat (ed.), *Women and Revolution in Iran*, 217–30. Boulder, Colorado: Westview Press.

Friedl, Ernestine 1967 *Vasilika*. New York: Holt, Rinehart & Winston.

Friedl, Ernestine 1975 *Women and Men: An Anthropologist's View*. New York: Holt, Rinehart & Winston.

Froebel, Folker, Heinrichs, Jürgen and Kreye, Otto 1980 *The New International Division of Labour*. Cambridge: Cambridge University Press.

Fruzzetti, Lina 1985 'Farm and hearth: rural women in a farming community'. In H. Afshar (ed.), *Women, Work and Ideology in the Third World*, 37–65. London: Tavistock.

Gaitskell, Deborah, Kimble, Judy, Maconachie, Moira and Unterhalter, Elaine 1983 'Class, race and gender: domestic workers in South Africa'. *Review of African Political Economy*, 27/28: 86–108.

Gathorne-Hardy, J. 1972 *The Rise and Fall of the British Nanny*. London: Hodder & Stoughton.

Geertz, Clifford 1962 'The rotating credit association: a "middle rung" development'. *Economic Development and Cultural Change*, 10 (3): 241–63.

Geertz, Hildred 1961 *The Javanese Family*. New York: Free Press.

Geisler, Gisela 1987 'Sisters under the skin: women and the women's league in Zambia'. *Journal of Modern African Studies*, 25 (1): 43–66.

Geisler, Gisela, Keller, Bonnie and Chuzo, Pia 1985 *The Needs of Rural Women in Northern Province: Analyses and Recommendations*. Lusaka: Government Printer.

Gilligan, Carol 1982 *In a Different Voice*. Cambridge, Mass.: Harvard University Press.

Gillison, Gillian 1980 'Images of nature in Gimi thought'. In C. MacCormack and M. Strathern (eds), *Nature, Culture and Gender*, 143–73. Cambridge: Cambridge University Press.

Gittins, Diana 1985 *The Family in Question*. London: Macmillan.

Glennon, L. M. 1979 *Women and Dualism*. London: Longman.

Gomm, Roger 1975 'Bargaining from weakness: spirit possession on the South Kenya coast'. *Man*, 10 (4): 530–43.

Gonzalez, N. 1965 'The Consanguineal household and matrifocality'. *American Anthropologist*, 67: 1541–9.

Gonzalez, N. 1970 'Toward a definition of matrifocality': In N. Whitten and J. F. Szwed (eds), *Afro-American Anthropology: Contemporary Perspectives*. New York: Free Press.

Goodale, Jane 1971 *Tiwi Wives*. Seattle: University of Washington Press.

Goodale, Jane 1980 'Gender, sexuality and marriage: a Kaulong model of nature and culture'. In C. MacCormack and M. Strathern (eds), *Nature, Culture and Gender*, 119–42. Cambridge: Cambridge University Press.

Goodenough, W. H. 1970 *Description and Comparison in Cultural Anthropology*. Chicago: Aldine.

Goodfriend, Douglas 1979 'Plus ça change, plus c'est la même chose: the dilemma of the French structural Marxist'. In S. Diamond (ed.), *Toward a Marxist Anthropology*, 93–124. The Hague: Mouton.

Goody, Jack (ed.) 1971 *The Developmental Cycle in Domestic Groups*. Cambridge: Cambridge University Press.

Goody, Jack 1972 'The evolution of the family'. In P. Laslett and R. Wall (eds), *Household and Family in Past Time*, 103–24. Cambridge: Cambridge University Press.

Goody, Jack 1976 *Production and Reproduction*. Cambridge: Cambridge University Press.

Goody, Jack 1977 *The Domestication of the Savage Mind*. Cambridge: Cambridge University Press.

Goody, Jack and Tambiah S. J., 1973 *Bridewealth and Dowry*. Cambridge: Cambridge University Press.

Gough, Kathleen 1959 'The Nayars and the definition of marriage'. *Journal of the Royal Anthropological Institute*, 89 (2): 23–34.

Gough, Kathleen 1972 'An anthropologist looks at Engels'. In N. Glazer-Malbin and H. Youngelson Waehrer (eds), *Woman in a Man-Made World*. Chicago: Rand McNally.

Gough, Kathleen 1975 'The origin of the family'. In Rayna R. Reiter (ed.), *Toward an Anthropology of Women*, 51–76. New York: Monthly Review Press.

Greer, Germaine 1984 *Sex and Destiny: The Politics of Human Fertility*. London: Secker & Warburg.

Gugler, Josef 1969 'Urbanisation in East Africa'. In R. Apthorpe and P. Rigby (eds), *Society and Social Change in East Africa*. Kampala: Nkanga Editions.

Guyer, Jane I. 1980 'Food, cocoa, and the division of labour by sex in two West African societies'. *Comparative Studies in Society and History*, 22 (3): 355–73.

Guyer, Jane I. 1981 'Household and community in African studies'. *African Studies Review*, 24 (2/3): 87–138.

Guyer, Jane I. 1984 'Naturalism in models of African production'. *Man*, 19 (3): 371–88.

Hall, C. 1979 'The early formation of Victorian domestic ideology'. In S. Burman (ed.), *Fit Work for Women*, 15–32. London: Croom Helm.

Hammel, E. A. 1961 'The family cycle in a coastal Peruvian slum and village'. *American Anthropologist*, 63: 989–1005.

Hammel, E. A. 1972 'The Zadruga as process'. In P. Laslett and R. Wall (eds), *Household and Family in Past Time*, 335–73. Cambridge: Cambridge University Press.

Hansen, Karen Tranberg 1986a 'Domestic service in Zambia'. *Journal of Southern African Studies*, 13 (1): 57–81.

Hansen, Karen Tranberg 1986b 'Sex and gender among domestic servants in Zambia'. *Anthropology Today*, 2 (3): 18–23.

Hareven, Tamara 1982 *Family Time and Industrial Time*. Cambridge: Cambridge University Press.

Harrell-Bond, Barbara E. 1975 *Modern Marriage in Sierra Leone: A Study of the Professional Group*. The Hague: Mouton.

Harris, Olivia 1981 'Households as natural units'. In K. Young et al. (eds), *Of Marriage and the Market*, 49–68. London: CSE Books.

Harris, Olivia and Young, Kate 1981 'Engendered structures: some problems in the analysis of reproduction'. In J. Kahn and J. Llobera (eds), *The Anthropology of Pre-Capitalist Societies*, 109–47. London: Macmillan.

Harris, Sonia 1986 'An income-generating project for women in rural Jamaica'. In P. Ellis (ed.), *Women of the Caribbean*, 135–46. London: Zed Press.

Hartmann, Heidi 1979 'The unhappy marriage of Marxism and feminism: towards a more progressive union'. *Capital and Class*, 8: 1–33.

Hay, Margaret Jean 1976 'Luo women and economic change during the colonial period'. In N. Hafkin and E. Bay (eds), *Women in Africa*, 87–110. Stanford: Stanford University Press.

Hay, Margaret Jean and Stichter, Sharon (eds) 1984 *African Women South of the Sahara*. London: Longman.

Hay, Margaret Jean and Wright, Marcia (eds) 1982 *African Women and the Law: Historical Perspectives*. Boston University papers on Africa, vol. 7. Boston, Mass.: Boston University.

Heath, Stephen 1982 *The Sexual Fix*. London: Macmillan.

Hegland, Mary 1983 'Aliabad women: revolution as religious activity'. In G. Nashat (ed.), *Women and Revolution in Iran*, 171–94. Boulder, Colorado: Westview Press.

Held, David 1987 *Models of Democracy*. Cambridge: Polity Press.

Hermansen, Marcia 1983 'Fatimeh as a role model in the works of Ali Shari'ati'. In G. Nashat (ed.), *Women and Revolution in Iran*, 87–96. Boulder, Colorado: Westview Press.

Higgins, Patricia 1985 'Women in the Islamic Republic of Iran: legal, social and ideological changes'. *Signs*, 10 (3): 477–94.

Hill, Polly 1963 *Migrant Cocoa-Farmers of Southern Ghana*. Cambridge: Cambridge University Press.

Hill, Polly 1969 'Hidden trade in Hausaland'. *Man*, 4 (3): 392–409.

Hindess, Barry and Hirst, Paul 1975 *Pre-Capitalist Modes of Production*. London: Routledge & Kegan Paul.

Hirschon, Renée 1984 'Introduction: property, power and gender relations'. In R. Hirschon (ed.), *Women and Property, Women as Property*, 1–22. London: Croom Helm.

Hoffer, Carol 1972 'Mende and Sherbro women in high office'. *Canadian Journal of African Studies*, 6 (2): 151–64.

Hoffer, Carol 1974 'Madam Yoko: ruler of the Kpa Mende confederacy'. In M. Rosaldo and L. Lamphere (eds), *Woman, Culture and Society*, 173–87. Stanford: Stanford University Press.

Holmquist, Frank 1979 'Class structure, peasant participation, and rural self-help'. In J. Barkan and J. Okumu (eds), *Politics and Public Policy in Kenya and Tanzania*. New York: Praeger.

Holmquist, Frank 1984 'Self-help: the state and peasant leverage in Kenya'. *Africa*, 54 (3): 72–91.

Hooks, Bell 1982 *Ain't I a Woman? Black Women and Feminism*. London: Pluto Press.

Huizer, Gerrit and Mannheim, Bruce (eds) 1979 *The Politics of Anthropology*. The Hague: Mouton.

Hull, Gloria, Scott, Patricia and Smith, Barbara (eds) 1982 *All the Women Are White, All the Blacks Are Men, But Some of Us Are Brave*. New York: The Feminist Press.

Humphrey, John 1985 'Gender, pay and skill: manual workers in Brazilian industry'. In H. Afshar (ed.), *Women, Work and Ideology in the Third World*, 214–31. London: Tavistock.

Huntingdon, Suellen 1975 'Issues in woman's role in economic development: critique and alternatives'. *Journal of Marriage and the Family*, 37: 1001–12.

Hussain, Freda and Radwan, Kamelia 1984 'The Islamic revolution and women: quest for the Quranic model'. In F. Hussain (ed.), *Muslim Women*. London: Croom Helm.

Ibrahim, Barbara Lethem 1985 'Cairo's factory women'. In E. Fernea (ed.), *Women and the Family in the Middle East*, 293–9. Austin: University of Texas Press.

International Labour Office 1981 *Women in Rural Development: Critical Issues*. Geneva: International Labour Office.

ISIS (Women's International Information and Communication Service) 1983 *Women in Development: A Resource Guide for Organisation and Action*. Geneva: ISIS.

Izzard, Wendy 1985 'Migrants and mothers: case-studies from Botswana'. *Journal of Southern African Studies*, 11 (2): 258–80.

Jaggar, Alison and Rothenberg, Paula 1984 *Feminist Frameworks: Alternative Theoretical Accounts of the Relations between Women and Men*. New York: McGraw-Hill.

Jahan, Rounaq and Papanek, Hanna (eds) 1979 *Women and Development: Perspectives from South and Southeast Asia*. Dacca: University Press.

Jain, Devaki 1980 *Women's Quest for Power*. Ghaziabad: Vikas Publishing House.

Jancar, Barbara Wolfe 1978 *Women under Communism*. Baltimore: Johns Hopkins University Press.

Jaquette, Jane 1982 'Women and modernization theory: a decade of feminist criticism'. *World Politics*, 34 (2): 267–84.

Jayawardena, Kumari 1986 *Feminism and Nationalism in the Third World*. London: Zed Press.

Jelin, Elizabeth 1977 'Migration and labour force participation of Latin American women: the domestic servants in the cities'. In Wellesley Editorial Committee (eds), *Women and National Development: The Complexities of Change*, 129–41. Chicago: University of Chicago Press.

Joekes, Susan 1985 'Working for lipstick? Male and female labour in the clothing industry in Morocco'. In H. Afshar (ed.), *Women, Work and Ideology in the Third World*, 183–213. London: Tavistock.

Johnson, Cheryl 1986 'Class and gender: a consideration of Yoruba women during the colonial period'. In C. Robertson and I. Berger (eds), *Women and Class in Africa*, 237–54. New York: Africana Publishing Company.

Jones, Christina 1982 'Women's legal access to land'. In B. Lewis (ed.), *Invisible Farmers: Women and the Crisis in Agriculture*, 196–238. Washington, DC: USAID.

Kaberry, Phyllis 1939 *Aboriginal Woman: Sacred and Profane*. London: Routledge & Kegan Paul.

Kaluzynska, Eva 1980 'Wiping the floor with theory – a survey of writings on housework'. *Feminist Review*, 6: 27–54.

Karp, Ivan 1978a *Fields of Change among the Iteso of Kenya*. London: Routledge & Kegan Paul.

Karp, Ivan 1978b 'New Guinea models in the African savannah'. *Africa*, 48 (1): 1–16.

Katzman, David 1978 *Seven Days a Week: Women and Domestic Service in Industrializing America*. New York: Oxford University Press.

Keesing, Roger 1985 'Kwaio women speak: the micropolitics of autobiography in a Solomon Island society'. *American Anthropologist*, 87: 27–39.

Keller, Bonnie 1979 'Marriage by elopement'. *African Social Research*, 27: 565–85.

Keohane, Nannerl, Rosaldo, Michelle and Gelpi, Barbara (eds), 1982 *Feminist Theory: A Critique of Ideology*. Brighton: Harvester Press.

Kimble, Judy and Unterhalter, Elaine 1982 'We opened the road for you, you must go forward: ANC women's struggles, 1912–1982'. *Feminist Review*, 12: 11–35.

Kitching, Gavin 1980 *Class and Economic Change in Kenya: The Making of an African Petite Bourgeoisie 1905–1970*. New Haven: Yale University Press.

Kuhn, Annette and Wolpe, Ann-Marie (eds) 1978 *Feminism and Materialism: Women and the Modes of Production*. London: Routledge & Kegan Paul.

Kuper, Adam 1982 'Lineage theory: a critical retrospect'. *Annual Review of Anthropology*, 11: 71–95.

Kuper, Adam 1983 *Anthropology and Anthropologists*. 2nd edition. London: Routledge & Kegan Paul.

Kurian, Rachel 1982 *Women Workers in the Sri Lanka Plantation Sector*. Geneva: International Labour Office.

Lacan, Jacques 1980 *Ecrits: A Selection*. London: Tavistock.

Laclau, Ernesto 1971 'Feudalism and capitalism in Latin America'. *New Left Review*, 67: 19–38.

Lamphere, Louise 1974 'Strategies, cooperation, and conflict among women in domestic groups'. In M. Rosaldo and L. Lamphere (eds), *Women, Culture and Society*, 97–112. Stanford: Stanford University Press.

Lamphere, Louise 1977 'Anthropology: a review essay'. *Signs*, 2 (3): 612–27.

Laslett, Peter 1972 'The history of the family'. In P. Laslett and R. Wall (eds) *Household and Family in Past Time*, 1–89. Cambridge: Cambridge University Press.

Latin American and Caribbean Women's Collective 1980 *Slaves of Slaves: The Challenge of Latin American Women*. London: Zed Press.

Leach, Edmund 1961 *Rethinking Anthropology*. London: Athlone Press.

Leacock, Eleanor 1972 Introduction to F. Engels, *The Origin of the Family, Private Property and the State*. New York: International Publishers.

Leacock, Eleanor 1978 'Women's status in egalitarian society: implications for social evolution'. *Current Anthropology*, 19 (2): 247–75.

Leacock, Eleanor 1980 'Montagnais women and the Jesuit program for colonization'. In M. Etienne and E. Leacock (eds), *Women and Colonization*, 25–42. New York: Praeger.

Lebeuf, Annie 1971 'The role of women in the political organization of African societies'. In D. Paulme (ed.), *Women of Tropical Africa*, 93–120. Berkeley: University of California Press.

Lévi-Strauss, Claude 1963 *Structural Anthropology*. New York: Basic Books.

Lévi-Strauss, Claude 1966 *The Savage Mind*. Chicago: University of Chicago Press.

Lévi-Strauss, Claude 1969 *The Elementary Structures of Kinship*. London: Tavistock.

Lévi-Strauss, Claude 1971 'The family'. In H. Shapiro (ed.), *Man, Culture and Society*, 333–57. London: Oxford University Press.

Lewis, Barbara 1976 'The limitations of group action among entrepreneurs: the market women of Abidjan, Ivory Coast'. In N. Hafkin and E. Bay (eds), *Women in Africa*, 135–56. Stanford: Stanford University Press.

Lewis, Barbara 1984 'The impact of development policies on women'. In M. Hay and S. Stichter (eds), *African Women South of the Sahara*, 170–87. London: Longman.

Lewis, Diane 1973 'Anthropology and colonialism'. *Current Anthropology*, 14 (5): 581–602.

Lewis, Ioan 1966 'Spirit possession and deprivation cults'. *Man*, 1 (3): 307–29.

Lewis, Ioan 1971 *Ecstatic Religion*. Harmondsworth: Penguin.

Liddle, Joanna and Joshi, Rama 1986 *Daughters of Independence: Gender, Caste and Class in India*. London: Zed Press.

Lipshitz, Susan 1978 *Tearing the Veil*. London: Routledge & Kegan Paul.

Little, Kenneth 1966 *West African Urbanisation: A Study of Voluntary Associations in Social Change*. Cambridge: Cambridge University Press.

Little, Kenneth 1972 'Voluntary associations and social mobility among West African women'. *Canadian Journal of African Studies*, 6 (2): 275–88.

Little, Kenneth 1973 *African Women in Towns: An Aspect of Africa's Social Revolution*. Cambridge: Cambridge University Press.

Little, Kenneth and Price, Anne 1973 'Some trends in modern marriage among West Africans'. In C. Turnbull (ed.), *Africa and Change*, 185–207. New York: Knopf.

Loizos, Peter 1975 'Change in property transfer among Greek Cypriot villagers'. *Man*, 10 (4): 503–23.

Longhurst, Richard 1982 'Resource allocation and the sexual division of labour: a case study of a Moslem Hausa village in northern Nigeria'. In L. Beneria (ed.), *Women and Development*, 95–117. New York: Praeger.

Lonsdale, John 1981 'The state and social processes in Africa'. *African Studies Review*, 24 (2/3): 139–225.

Maas, Maria 1986 *It is Always a Good Thing to Have Land*. Leiden: African Studies Centre, Research Report 26.

MacCormack, Carol 1980 'Nature, culture and gender: a critique'. In C. MacCormack and M. Strathern (eds), *Nature, Culture and Gender*, 1–24. Cambridge: Cambridge University Press.

MacCormack, Carol and Strathern, Marilyn (eds), 1980 *Nature, Culture and Gender*. Cambridge: Cambridge University Press.

McCormack, Jeanne, Walsh, Martin and Nelson, Candace 1986 *Women's Group Enterprises: A Study of the Structure of Opportunity on the Kenya Coast*. Boston, Mass.: World Education Inc.

MacGaffey, Janet 1983 'How to survive and get rich amidst devastation: the second economy in Zaïre'. *African Affairs*, 82 (328): 351–66.

MacGaffey, Janet 1986 'Women and class formation in a dependent economy: Kisangani entrepreneurs'. In C. Robertson and I. Berger (eds), *Women and Class in Africa*, 161–77. New York: Africana Publishing Company.

McIntosh, Mary 1978 'The state and the oppression of women'. In A. Kuhn and A. M. Wolpe (eds), *Feminism and Materialism*, 254–89. London: Routledge & Kegan Paul.

McIntosh, Mary 1979 'The welfare state and the needs of the dependent family'. In S. Burman (ed.), *Fit Work for Women*, 153–72. London: Croom Helm.

Mackinnon, Catharine 1983 'Feminism, Marxism, method, and the state: toward feminist jurisprudence'. *Signs*, 8 (4): 635–58.

Mackintosh, Maureen 1977 'Reproduction and patriarchy: a critique of Claude Meillassoux, *Femmes, Greniers et Capitaux*'. *Captial and Class*, 2: 119–27.

Mackintosh, Maureen 1979 'Domestic labour and the household'. In S. Burman (ed.), *Fit Work for Women*, 173–91. London: Croom Helm.

Mackintosh, Maureen 1981 'Gender and economics: the sexual division of labour and the subordination of women'. In Kate Young et al. (eds), *Of Marriage and the Market*, 1–15. London: CSE Books.

McLennan, J. F. 1865 *Primitive Marriage*. Chicago.

McNamara, John and Wemple, Suzanne 1977 'Sanctity and power: the dual pursuit of medieval women'. In R. Bridenthal and C. Koonz (eds), *Becoming Visible: Women in European History*, 90–118. Boston, Mass.: Houghton Mifflin.

Magubane, Bernard 1971 'A critical look at indices used in the study of social change in colonial Africa'. *Current Anthropology*, 12 (4–5): 419–45.

Maine, Henry 1917 (1861) *Ancient Law*. London: Dent.

Majumdar, P. and Majumdar, I. 1978 *Rural Migrants in an Urban Setting*. Delhi: Hindustan Publishing Corporation.

Malinowski, B. 1913 *The Family among the Australian Aborigines*. London: London University Press.

Malinowski, B. 1960 (1927) *Sex and Repression in Savage Society*. London: Routledge & Kegan Paul.

Mandeville, Elizabeth 1975 'The formality of marriage: a Kampala case study'. *Journal of Anthropological Research*, 31: 183–95.

Mandeville, Elizabeth 1979 'Poverty, work and the financing of single women in Kampala'. *Africa*, 49: 42–52.

Mann, Kristin 1985 *Marrying Well: Marriage, Status and Social Change among the Educated Elite in Colonial Lagos*. Cambridge: Cambridge University Press.

March, Kathryn and Taqqu, Rachelle 1986 *Women's Informal Associations in Developing Countries: Catalysts for Change?* Boulder, Colorado: Westview Press.

Marcus, George and Fischer, Michael 1986 *Anthropology as Cultural Critique*. Chicago: University of Chicago Press.

Martin, Carol 1983 'Skill-building or unskilled labour for female youth: a Bauchi case'. In C. Oppong (ed.), *Female and Male in West Africa*, 223–35. London: George Allen & Unwin.

Mathieu, Nicole-Claude 1978 'Man-culture and woman-nature?' *Women's Studies*, 1: 55–65.

Mba, Nina Emma 1982 *Nigerian Women Mobilized: Women's Political Activity in Southern Nigeria, 1900–1965*. Berkeley: Institute of International Studies.

Mbithi, Philip and Rasmusson Rasmus, 1977 *Self-Reliance in Kenya: The Case of Harambee*. Uppsala: Scandinavian Institute of African Studies.

Meek, R. 1976 *Social Sciences and the Ignoble Savage*. Cambridge: Cambridge University Press.

Mehta, Shushila 1982 *Revolution and the Status of Women in India*. New Delhi: Metropolitan Books.

Meigs, Anna 1976 'Male pregnancy and the reduction of sexual opposition in a New Guinea Highlands society'. *Ethnology*, 15: 393–407.

Meillassoux, Claude 1960 'Essai d'interprétation du phénomène économique dans les sociétés traditionelles d'autosubsistance'. *Cahiers d'études africaines*, 4: 38–67.

Meillassoux, Claude (ed.) 1971 *The Development of Indigenous Trade and Markets in West Africa*. London: Oxford University Press.

Meillassoux, Claude 1981 *Maidens, Meal and Money*. Cambridge: Cambridge University Press.

Merrick, Thomas and Schmink, Marianne 1983 'Households headed by women and urban poverty in Brazil'. In M. Buvinic et al. (eds), *Women and Poverty in the Third World*, 244–71. Baltimore: Johns Hopkins University Press.

Middleton, John and Tait, David (eds) 1958 *Tribes Without Rulers*. London: Routledge & Kegan Paul.

Miers, Suzanne and Kopytoff, Igor 1977 *Slavery in Africa*. Madison: University of Wisconsin Press.

Mies, Maria 1982 *The Lace Makers of Narsapur*. London: Zed Press.

Milkman, Ruth 1976 'Women's work and economic crisis: some lessons of the Great Depression'. *Review of Radical Political Economics*, 8 (1): 73–97.

Milton, Kay 1979 'Male bias in anthropology'. *Man*, 14: 40–54.

Minh-ha, Trinh 1987 'Difference: a special Third World women issue'. *Feminist Review*, 25: 5–22.

Mintz, Sidney 1971 'Men, women and trade'. *Comparative Studies in Society and History*, 13: 247–69.

Miranda, Glaura Vasques de 1977 'Women's labor force participation in a developing society: the case of Brazil'. In Wellesley Editorial Committee (eds), *Women and National Development: The Complexities of Change*, 261–74. Chicago: University of Chicago Press.

Mitchell, Juliet 1974 *Psychoanalysis and Feminism*. London: Allen Lane.

Mitter, Swasti 1986 *Common Fate, Common Bond: Women in the Global Economy*. London: Pluto Press.

Molyneux, Maxine 1977 'Androcentrism in Marxist anthropology'. *Critique of Anthropology*, 3 (9 and 10): 55–81.

Molyneux, Maxine 1979 'Beyond the domestic labour debate'. *New Left Review*, 116: 3–27.

Molyneux, Maxine 1981 'Socialist societies old and new: progress towards women's emancipation?' *Feminist Review*, 8: 1–34.

Molyneux, Maxine 1985a 'Family reform in socialist states: the hidden agenda'. *Feminist Review*, 21: 47–64.

Molyneux, Maxine 1985b 'Mobilisation without emancipation? Women's interests, the state, and revolution in Nicaragua'. *Feminist Studies*, 11 (2): 227–54.

Monsted, Mette 1978 *Women's Groups in Rural Kenya and their Role in Development*. Copenhagen: Centre for Development Research.

Moore, Henrietta L. 1986 *Space, Text and Gender: An Anthropological Study of the Marakwet of Kenya*. Cambridge: Cambridge University Press.

Moore, Henrietta and Vaughan, Megan 1987 'Cutting down trees: women, nutrition and agricultural change in the Northern Province of Zambia, 1920–1986'. *African Affairs*, 86 (345): 523–40.

Moraga, Cherrie and Anzaldua, Gloria (eds) 1981 *This Bridge Called My Back: Writings by Radical Women of Color*. New York: Kitchen Table, Women of Color Press.

Morgan, Lewis Henry 1877 *Ancient Society*. New York: Henry Holt.

Mueller, Martha 1977 'Women and men, power and powerlessness in Lesotho'. In Wellesley Editorial Committee (eds), *Women and National Development: The Complexities of Change*, 154–66. Chicago: University of Chicago Press.

Mujahid, G. B. S. 1985 'Female labour force participation in Jordan'. In J. Abu Nasr et al. (eds), *Women, Employment and Development in the Arab World*, 103–30. Berlin: Mouton.

Murray, Colin 1981 *Families Divided: The Impact of Migrant Labour in Lesotho*. Cambridge: Cambridge University Press.

Murray, Nicola 1979a 'Socialism and feminism: women and the Cuban revolution, part 1'. *Feminist Review*, 2: 57–73.

Murray, Nicola 1979b 'Socialism and feminism: women and the Cuban revolution, part 2'. *Feminist Review*, 3: 99–108.

Mwaniki, Nyaga 1986 'Against many odds: the dilemmas of women's self-help groups in Mbeere, Kenya'. *Africa*, 56 (2): 210–28.

Nash, June 1977 'Women in development: dependency and exploitation'. *Development and Change*, 8 (2): 161–82.

Nash, June 1980 'Aztec women: the transition from status to class in empire and colony'. In M. Etienne and E. Leacock (eds), *Women and Colonization*, 134–48. New York: Praeger.

Nash, June 1981 'Ethnographic aspects of the world capitalist system'. *Annual Review of Anthropology*, 10: 393–424.

Nash, June and Safa, Helen (eds) 1976 *Sex and Class in Latin America*. New York: Praeger.

Nashat, Guity (ed.) 1983a *Women and Revolution in Iran*. Boulder, Colorado: Westview Press.

Nashat, Guity 1983b 'Women in the ideology of the Islamic Republic'. In G. Nashat (ed.), *Women and Revolution in Iran*, 195–216. Boulder, Colorado: Westview Press.

Nashat, Guity 1983c 'Epilogue'. In G. Nashat (ed.), *Women and Revolution in Iran*, 285–9. Boulder, Colorado: Westview Press.

Nath, Kamla 1978 'Education and employment among Kuwaiti women'. In L.

Beck and N. Keddie (eds), *Women in the Muslim World*, 172–88. Cambridge, Mass.: Harvard University Press.

Nelson, Cynthia 1974 'Public and private politics: women in the Middle Eastern world'. *American Ethnologist*, 1 (3): 551–63.

Nelson, Nici 1978 'Women must help each other'. In P. Caplan and J. Bujra (eds), *Women United, Women Divided*, 77–98. London: Tavistock.

Nelson, Nici 1979 *Why Has Development Neglected Rural Women? A Review of the South Asian Literature*. New York: Pergamon Press.

Nelson, Nici (ed.) 1981 *African Women in the Development Process*. London: Frank Cass.

Nelson, Nici 1986 'Rural–urban child fostering in Kenya: migration, kinship ideology and class'. Paper presented at the ASA UK Conference, University of Kent, Canterbury.

Netting, Robert, Wilk, Richard and Arnould, Eric 1984 'Introduction'. In R. McC. Netting et al. (eds), *Households: Comparative and Historical Studies of the Domestic Group*, xiii–xxxviii. Berkeley: University of California Press.

Nzula, A. T., Potekhin, I. I. and Zusmanovich, A. Z. 1979 *Forced Labour in Colonial Africa*. London: Zed Press.

Oakley, A. 1976 'Wisewoman and medicine man: changes in the management of childbirth'. In J. Mitchell and A. Oakley (eds), *The Rights and Wrongs of Women*, 17–58. Harmondsworth: Penguin.

Oakley, A. 1979 'A case of maternity: paradigms of women as maternity cases'. *Signs* 4 (4): 607–31.

O'Barr, Jean 1975 'Making the invisible visible: African women in politics and policy'. *African Studies Review*, 18 (3): 19–27.

Obbo, Christine 1980 *African Women: Their Struggle for Economic Independence*. London: Zed Press.

O'Brien, Denise and Tiffany, Sharon (eds) 1984 *Rethinking Women's Roles: Perspectives from the Pacific*. Berkeley: University of California Press.

Ogbu, John 1978 'African bridewealth and women's status'. *American Ethnologist*, 5 (2): 241–62.

Okali, Christine 1983 *Cocoa and Kinship in Ghana*. London: KPI.

Okeyo, Achola Pala 1980 'Daughters of the lakes and rivers: colonization and the land rights of Luo women'. In M. Etienne and E. Leacock (eds), *Women and colonization*, 186–213. New York: Praeger.

Okonjo, Kamene 1976 'The dual sex political system in operation: Igbo women and community politics in midwestern Nigeria'. In N. Hafkin and E. Bay (eds), *Women in Africa*, 45–58. Stanford: Stanford University Press.

Olafson Hellerstein, E., Hume, L. Parker and Offen, K. 1981 *Victorian Women*. Brighton: Harvester Press.

O'Laughlin, Bridget 1977 'Production and reproduction: Meillassoux's *Femmes, Greniers et Capitaux*'. *Critique of Anthropology*, 2 (8): 3–32.

Oppong, Christine 1980 'From love to institution: indicators of change in Akan marriage'. *Journal of Family History*, 5: 197–209.

Oppong, Christine 1981 *Middle Class African Marriage*. London: George Allen & Unwin.

Oppong, Christine (ed.) 1983 *Female and Male in West Africa*. London: George Allen & Unwin.

Organization of Angolan Women 1984 *Angolan Women: Building the Future*. London: Zed Press.

Ortner, Sherry 1974 'Is female to male as nature is to culture?' In M. Rosaldo and L. Lamphere (eds), *Woman, Culture and Society*, 67–88. Stanford: Stanford University Press.

Ortner, Sherry 1978 'The virgin and the state'. *Feminist Studies*, 4 (3): 19–35.

Ortner, Sherry 1984 'Theory in anthropology since the sixties'. *Comparative Studies in Society and History*, 26: 126–66.

Ortner, Sherry and Whitehead, Harriet (eds) 1981a *Sexual Meanings: The Cultural Construction of Gender and Sexuality*. Cambridge: Cambridge University Press.

Ortner, Sherry and Whitehead, Harriet 1981b 'Introduction: accounting for sexual meanings'. In S. Ortner and H. Whitehead (eds), *Sexual Meanings*, 1–27. Cambridge: Cambridge University Press.

Owusu, Maxwell 1979 'Colonial and postcolonial anthropology of Africa: scholarship or sentiment?' In G. Huizer and B. Mannheim (eds), *The Politics of Anthropology*, 145–160. The Hague: Mouton.

Paige, K. E. and Paige, J. M. 1981 *The Politics of Reproductive Ritual*. Berkeley: University of California Press.

Papanek, Hannah 1979 'Family status production: the "work" and "non-work" of women'. *Signs* 4 (4): 775–81.

Parkin, David 1978 *The Cultural Definition of Political Response*. London: Academic Press.

Parkin, David 1980 'Kind bridewealth and hard cash: eventing a structure'. In J. Comaroff (ed.), *The Meaning of Marriage Payments*, 197–220. London: Academic Press.

Parpart, Jane 1986 'The household and the mine shaft: gender and class struggles on the Zambian copperbelt, 1926–64'. *Journal of Southern African Studies*, 13 (1): 36–56.

Pateman, Carole 1985 *The Problem of Political Obligation: A Critique of Liberal Theory*. Cambridge: Polity Press.

Peters, Pauline 1983 'Gender, development cycles and historical process: a critique of recent research on women in Botswana'. *Journal of Southern African Studies*, 10 (1): 83–105.

Phillips, Anne and Taylor, Barbara 1980 'Sex and skill: notes towards a feminist economics'. *Feminist Review*, 6: 79–88.

Pina-Cabral, Joao de 1984 'Female power and the inequality of wealth and motherhood in north-western Portugal'. In R. Hirschon (ed.), *Women and Property, Women as Property*, 75–91. London: Croom Helm.

Pollock, Linda 1983 *Forgotten Children: Parent-Child Relations from 1500 to 1800*. Cambridge: Cambridge University Press.

Pomeroy, Sarah 1975 *Goddesses, Whores, Wives and Slaves: Women in Classical Antiquity*. New York: Schocken Books.

Poster, Mark 1978 *Critical Theory of the Family*. London: Macmillan.

Poulantzas, Nicos 1973 *Political Power and Social Classes*. London: New Left Books.

Poulantzas, Nicos 1975 *Classes in Contemporary Capitalism*. London: New Left Books.

Quinn, Naomi 1977 'Anthropological studies of women's status'. *Annual Review of Anthropology*, 6: 181–225.

Radcliffe-Brown, A. R. 1950 'Introduction'. In A. R. Radcliffe-Brown and D. Forde (eds), *African Systems of Kinship and Marriage*, 1–85. London: Oxford University Press.

Radcliffe-Brown, A. R. 1958 *Method in Social Anthropology*. Chicago: University of Chicago Press.

Rahman, Fazlur 1983 'Status of women in the Qur'an' In G. Nashat (ed.), *Women and Revolution in Iran*, 37–54. Boulder, Colorado: Westview Press.

Ralston, Caroline 1988 'Changes in the lives of ordinary women in post-contact Hawaii'. In M. MacIntyre and M. Jolly (eds), *Family and Gender in the Pacific*. Sydney: Cambridge University Press (forthcoming).

Ranger, Terence 1978 'Growing from the roots: reflections on peasant research in Central and Southern Africa'. *Journal of Southern African Studies*, 5: 99–133.

Rapp, Rayna 1977 'Gender and class: an archaeology of knowledge concerning the origin of the state'. *Dialectical Anthropology*, 2: 309–16.

Rapp, Rayna 1979 'Anthropology: a review essay'. *Signs*, 4 (3): 497–513.

Rapp, Rayna 1982 'Family and class in contemporary America: notes toward an understanding of ideology'. In B. Thorne and M. Yalom (eds), *Rethinking the Family: Some Feminist Questions*, 168–87. New York: Longman.

Rapp, Rayna, Ross, E. and Bridenthal, R. 1979 'Examining family history'. *Feminist Studies*, 5 (1).

Register, Cheri 1980 'Literary criticism: review essay'. *Signs*, 6: 268–82.

Reiter, Rayna Rapp 1975 Introduction to R. Reiter (ed.), *Toward an Anthropology of Women*, 11–19. New York: Monthly Review Press.

Reiter, Rayna Rapp 1977 'The search for origins: unraveling the threads of gender hierarchy'. *Critique of Anthropology*, 3 (9 and 10): 5–24.

Remy, Dorothy 1975 'Underdevelopment and the experience of women'. In R. Reiter (ed.), *Toward an Anthropology of Women*, 258–71. New York: Monthly Review Press.

Richards, Audrey 1932 *Hunger and Work in a Savage Tribe: A Functional Study of Nutrition among the Southern Bantu*. London: Routledge.

Richards, Audrey 1939 *Land Labour and Diet in Northern Rhodesia: An Economic Study of the Bemba Tribe*. London: Oxford University Press.

Richards, Audrey I. 1950 'Some types of family structure amongst the Central Bantu'. In A. R. Radcliffe-Brown and Daryll Forde (eds), *African Systems of Kinship and Marriage*, 207–51. London: Oxford University Press.

Rihani, May 1978 *Development as if Women Mattered*: An *Annotated Bibliography with a Third World Focus*. Washington, DC: Overseas Development Council.

Rivière, P. G. 1974 'The couvade: a problem reborn'. *Man*, 9: 423–35.

Roberts, Pepe 1979 'The integration of women into the development process: some conceptual problems'. *Institute of Development Studies Bulletin*, 10 (3).

Roberts, Pepe 1981 'Sisters and wives: the past and future of sexual equality by Karen Sacks'. *Signs*, 7 (2): 503–5.

Robertson, Claire 1975 'Ga women and change in marketing conditions in the Accra area'. *Rural Africana*, 2.

Robertson, Claire 1976 'Ga women and socioeconomic change in Accra, Ghana'. In N. Hafkin and E. Bay (eds), *Women in Africa*, 111–33. Stanford: Stanford University Press.

Robertson, Claire 1984 *Sharing the Same Bowl: A Socioeconomic History of Women and Class in Accra, Ghana*. Bloomington: Indiana University Press.

Robertson, Claire 1986 'Women's education and class formation in Africa, 1950–1980'. In C. Robertson and I. Berger (eds), *Women and Class in Africa*, 92–113. New York: Africana Publishing Company.

Robertson, Claire and Berger, Iris (eds) 1986 *Women and Class in Africa*. New York: Africana Publishing Company.

Robertson, Claire and Klein, Martin (eds) 1983 *Women and Slavery in Africa*. Madison, Wisconsin: University of Wisconsin Press.

Rogers, Barbara 1980 *The Domestication of Women: Discrimination in Developing Societies*. London: Tavistock.

Rogers, Susan Carol 1975 'Female forms of power and the myth of male dominance: model of female/male interaction in peasant society'. *American Ethnologist*, 2: 727–57.

Rogers, Susan Carol 1978 'Women's place: a critical review of anthropological theory'. *Comparative Studies in Society and History*, 20: 123–62.

Rohrlich-Leavitt, Ruby 1977 'Women in transition: Crete and Sumer'. In R. Bridenthal and C. Koonz (eds), *Becoming Visible: Women in European History*, 36–59. Boston: Houghton Mifflin.

Rohrlich-Leavitt, Ruby 1980 'State formation in Sumer and the subjugation of women'. *Feminist Studies*, 6 (1).

Rohrlich-Leavitt, Ruby, Sykes, Barbara and Weatherford, Elizabeth 1975 'Aboriginal woman: male and female anthropological perspectives'. In R. Reiter (ed.), *Toward an Anthropology of Women*, 110–26. New York: Monthly Review Press.

Rosaldo, Michelle Z. 1974 'Woman, culture and society: a theoretical overview'. In M. Rosaldo and L. Lamphere (eds), *Women, Culture and Society*, 17–42. Stanford: Stanford University Press.

Rosaldo, Michelle Z. 1980 'The use and abuse of anthropology: reflections on feminism and cross-cultural understanding'. *Signs*, 5 (3): 389–417.

Rosaldo, Michelle Z. and Lamphere, Louise 1974 *Women, Culture and Society*. Stanford: Stanford University Press.

Ross, Aileen 1961 *The Hindu Family in its Urban Setting*. Toronto: University of Toronto Press.

Rubin, Gayle 1975 'The traffic in women: notes on the "political economy" of sex'. In R. Reiter (ed.), *Toward An Anthropology of Women*, 157–210. New York: Monthly Review Press.

Sabloff, Jeremy and Lamberg-Karlovsky, Carl (eds) 1975 *Ancient Civilization and Trade*. Albuquerque: University of New Mexico Press.

Sacks, Karen 1974 'Engels revisited: women, the organization of production, and private property'. In M. Rosaldo and L. Lamphere (eds), *Woman, Culture and Society*, 207–22. Stanford: Stanford University Press.

Sacks, Karen 1976 'State bias and women's status'. *American Anthropologist*, 78 (3): 565–9.

Sacks, Karen 1979 *Sisters and Wives: The Past and Future of Sexual Equality.* Westport, Conn.: Greenwood Press.

Saffioti, Helen 1978 *Women in Class Societies.* New York: Monthly Review Press.

Sahlins, Marshall 1974 *Stone Age Economics.* London: Tavistock.

Sahlins, Marshall 1976 *Culture and Practical Reason.* Chicago: University of Chicago Press.

Saith, Ashwani 1984 'China's new population policies: rationale and some implications'. *Development and Change*, 15 (3): 321–58.

Salaff, Janet 1981 *Working Daughters of Hong Kong.* Cambridge: Cambridge University Press.

Sanday, Peggy 1974 'Female status in the public domain'. In M. Rosaldo and L. Lamphere (eds), *Women, Culture and Society*, 189–206. Stanford: Stanford University Press.

Sanday, Peggy 1981 *Female Power and Male Dominance: On the Origins of Sexual Inequality.* Cambridge: Cambridge University Press.

Sargent, Lydia (ed.) 1981 *The Unhappy Marriage of Marxism and Feminism: A Debate on Class and Patriarchy.* London: Pluto Press.

Sayers, Janet, Evans, Mary and Redclift, Nanneke (eds) 1987 *Engels Revisited: New Feminist Essays.* London: Tavistock.

Scheper-Hughes, Nancy 1983 'Introduction: the problem of bias in androcentric and feminist anthropology'. *Women's Studies*, 10: 109–16.

Schlegel, Alice (ed.) 1977 *Sexual Stratification: A Cross-Cultural View.* New York: Columbia University Press.

Schmink, Marianne 1977 'Dependent development and the division of labor by sex: Venezuela'. *Latin American Perspectives*, 4: 153–79.

Schneider, David and Gough, Kathleen (eds) 1961 *Matrilineal Kinship.* Berkeley: University of California Press.

Schrijvers, Joke 1979 'Vivicentrism and anthropology'. In G. Huizer and B. Mannheim (eds), *The Politics of Anthropology*, 97–115. The Hague: Mouton.

Schuster, Ilsa M. 1979 *The New Women of Lusaka.* Palo Alto: Mayfield Publishing Co.

Schuster, Ilsa M. 1982 'Marginal lives: conflict and contradiction in the position of female traders in Lusaka, Zambia'. In E. Bay (ed.), *Women and Work in Africa*, 105–26. Boulder, Colorado: Westview Press.

Scott, Hilda 1974 *Does Socialism Liberate Women? Experiences from Eastern Europe.* Boston, Mass.: Beacon Press.

Scott, James 1985 *Weapons of the Weak: Everyday Forms of Peasant Resistance.* New Haven: Yale University Press.

Segalen, Martine 1984 'Nuclear is not independent: organization of the household in the Pays Bigouden Sud in the nineteenth and twentieth centuries'. In R. Netting et al. (eds), *Households: Comparative and Historical Studies of the Domestic Group*, 163–86. Berkeley: University of California Press.

Sender, John and Smith, Sheila 1986 *The Development of Capitalism in Africa.* London: Methuen.

Shanley, M. L. 1979 'The history of the family in modern England'. *Signs*, 4 (4): 740–50.

Shapiro, Judith 1981 'Anthropology and the study of gender'. In E. Langland and W. Gove (eds), *A Feminist Perspective in the Academy*, 110–29. Chicago: University of Chicago.

Sharma, Ursula 1980 *Women, Work and Property in North-West India*. London: Tavistock.

Sharma, Ursula 1984 'Dowry in India: its consequences for women'. In R. Hirschon (ed.), *Women and Property, Women as Property*, 62–74. London: Croom Helm.

Sharma, Ursula 1986 *Women's Work, Class and the Urban Household*. London: Tavistock.

Siltanen, Janet and Stanworth, Michelle (eds) 1984 *Women and the Public Sphere: A Critique of Sociology and Politics*. London: Hutchinson.

Silverblatt, Irene 1978 'Andean women in the Inca Empire'. *Feminist Studies*, 4 (3): 37–61.

Singer, A. 1973 'Marriage payments and the exchange of people'. *Man*, 8 (1): 80–92.

Siskind, Janet 1973 *To Hunt in the Morning*. London: Oxford University Press.

Siskind, Janet 1978 'Kinship and mode of production'. *American Anthropologist*, 80 (4): 860–72.

Smith, M. G. 1962 *West Indian Family Structure*. Seattle: University of Washington Press.

Smith, Raymond T. 1956 *The Negro Family in British Guiana*. London: Routledge & Kegan Paul.

Smith, Raymond T. 1970 'The nuclear family in Afro-American kinship'. *Journal of Comparative Family Studies*, 1: 55–70.

Smith, Raymond T. 1973 'The matrifocal family'. In J. Goody (ed.), *The Character of Kinship*, 121–44. Cambridge: Cambridge University Press.

Smock, Audrey 1977 'Ghana: from autonomy to subordination'. In J. Griele and A. Smock (eds), *Women's Roles and Status in Eight Countries*, 173–216. New York: Wiley.

Southall, Aidan 1961 'Introductory summary'. In A. Southall (ed.), *Social Change in Modern Africa*, 1–66. London: Oxford University Press.

Stacey, Judith 1983 *Patriarchy and Socialist Revolution in China*. Berkeley: University of California Press.

Stacey, Judith and Thorne, Barrie 1985 'The missing feminist revolution in sociology'. *Social Problems*, 32 (4): 301–16.

Stack, Carol 1974 *All Our Kin: Strategies for Survival in a Black Community*. New York: Harper & Row.

Stanworth, Michelle 1984 'Women and class analysis'. *Sociology*, 18 (2): 159–70.

Staudt, Kathleen 1978a 'Administrative resources, political patrons, and redressing sex inequities: a case from western Kenya'. *Journal of Developing Areas*, 12 (4): 399–414.

Staudt, Kathleen 1978b 'Agricultural productivity gaps: a case study of male preference in government policy implementation'. *Development and Change*, 9 (3): 439–57.

Staudt, Kathleen 1979 'Class and sex in the politics of women farmers'. *Journal of Politics*, 4 (2): 492–515.

Staudt, Kathleen 1982 'Women farmers and inequities in agricultural services'. In E. Bay (ed.), *Women and Work in Africa*, 207–24. Boulder, Colorado: Westview Press.

Staudt, Kathleen 1985 *Women, Foreign Assistance, and Advocacy Administration*. New York: Praeger.

Staudt, Kathleen 1986a 'Women, development and the state: on the theoretical impasse'. *Development and Change*, 17: 325–33.

Staudt, Kathleen 1986b 'Stratification: implications for women's politics'. In C. Robertson and I Berger (eds), *Women and Class in Africa*, 197–215. New York: Africana Publishing Company.

Staudt, Kathleen and Jaquette, Jane (eds) 1983 *Women in Developing Countries: A Policy Analysis*. New York: Haworth.

Steady, Filomina 1975 *Female Power in African Politics: The National Congress of Sierra Leone*. Pasadena: California Institute of Technology.

Steady, Filomina 1976 'Protestant women's associations in Freetown, Sierra Leone'. In N. Hafkin and E. Bay (eds), *Women in Africa*, 183–212. Stanford: Stanford University Press.

Stichter, Sharon 1984 'Some selected statistics on African women'. In M. Hay and S. Stichter (eds), *African Women South of the Sahara*, 183–94. London: Longman.

Stivens, Maila 1978 'Women and their kin: kin, class and solidarity in a middle-class suburb of Sydney, Australia'. In P. Caplan and J. Bujra (eds), *Women United, Women Divided*, 157–84. London: Tavistock.

Stivens, Maila 1981 'Women, kinship and capitalist development'. In K. Young et al. (eds), *Of Marriage and the Market*, 112–26. London: CSE Books.

Stivens, Maila 1985 'The fate of women's land rights: gender, matriliny, and capitalism in Rembau, Negeri Sembilan, Malaysia'. In H. Afshar (eds.), *Women, Work and Ideology in the Third World*, 3–36. London: Tavistock.

Stoler, Ann 1977 'Class structure and female autonomy in rural Java'. In Wellesley Editorial Committee (eds), *Women and National Development: The Complexities of Change*, 74–89. Chicago: University of Chicago Press.

Strathern, Marilyn 1972 *Women in Between: Female Roles in a Male World: Mount Hagen, New Guinea*. London: Seminar Press.

Strathern, Marilyn 1980 'No nature, no culture: the Hagen case'. In C. MacCormack and M. Strathern (eds), *Nature, Culture and Gender*, 174–222. Cambridge: Cambridge University Press.

Strathern, Marilyn 1981a 'Culture in a netbag: the manufacture of a subdiscipline in anthropology'. *Man* 16 (4): 665–88.

Strathern, Marilyn 1981b 'Self-interest and the social good: some implications of Hagen gender imagery'. In S. Ortner and H. Whitehead (eds), *Sexual Meanings*, 166–91. Cambridge: Cambridge University Press.

Strathern, Marilyn 1984a 'Domesticity and the denigration of women'. In D. O'Brien and S. Tiffany (eds), *Rethinking Women's Roles: Perspectives from the Pacific*, 13–31. Berkeley: University of California Press.

Strathern, Marilyn 1984b 'Subject or object? Women and the circulation of valuables in Highlands New Guinea'. In R. Hirschon (ed.), *Women and Property, Women as Property*, 158–75. London: Croom Helm.

Strathern, Marilyn 1987a 'An awkward relationship: the case of feminism and anthropology'. *Signs*, 12 (2): 276–92.

Strathern, Marilyn 1987b 'Out of context: the persuasive fictions of anthropology'. *Current Anthropology*, 28 (3): 1–77.

Strobel, Margaret 1979 *Muslim Women in Mombasa*. New Haven: Yale University Press.

Strobel, Margaret 1982 'Africa women'. *Signs*, 8 (1): 109–31.

Sweetman, David 1984 *Women Leaders in African History*. London: Heinemann.

Tabari, Azar 1980 'The enigma of veiled Iranian women'. *Feminist Review*, 5: 19–31.

Tanner, Nancy 1974 'Matrifocality in Indonesia and Africa and among black Americans'. In M. Rosaldo and L. Lamphere (eds), *Women, Culture and Society*, 129–56. Stanford: Stanford University Press.

Taussig, Michael 1979 *The Devil and Commodity Fetishism in South America*. Chicago: University of Chicago Press.

Taylor, John 1975 'Pre-capitalist modes of production'. *Critique of Anthropology*, 4/5: 127–155.

Thomas, Nicholas 1987 'Unstable categories: tapu and gender in the Marquesas'. *Journal of Pacific History*, 22 (3–4): 123–38.

Thorne, B. 1982 'Feminist rethinking of the family: an overview'. In B. Thorne and M. Yalom (eds), *Rethinking the Family: Some Feminist Questions*, 1–24. New York: Longman.

Tilly, Louise 1981 'Paths of proletarianization: organization of production, sexual division of labor, and women's collective action'. *Signs*, 7 (2): 400–17.

Tilly, Louise and Scott, Joan 1978 *Women, Work and Family*. New York: Holt, Rinehart & Winston.

Tinker, Irene 1981 'New technologies for food-related activities: an equity strategy'. In R. Dauber and M. Cain (eds), *Women and Technological Change in Developing Countries*, 51–88. Boulder, Colorado: Westview Press.

Tinker, Irene and Bramsen, Michele (eds) 1976 *Women and World Development*. Washington, DC: Overseas Development Council.

Tsing, Anna L. and Yanagisako, Sylvia J. 1983 'Feminism and kinship theory'. *Current Anthropology*, 24 (4): 511–16.

Urdang, Stephanie 1979 *Fighting Two Colonialisms: Women in Guinea-Bissau*. New York: Monthly Review Press.

Urdang, Stephanie 1984 'Women in national liberation movements'. In M. Hay and S. Stichter (eds), *African Women*, 156–69. London: Longman.

Vallenga, D. D. 1977 'Differentiation among women farmers in two rural areas of Ghana'. *Labour and Society*, 2 (2).

Van Allen, Judith 1972 'Sitting on a man: colonialism and the lost political institutions of Igbo women'. *Canadian Journal of African Studies*, 6 (2): 165–81.

Van Baal, J. 1975 *Reciprocity and the Position of Women: Anthropological Papers*. Amsterdam: Van Gorcum Assen.

Van Onselen, Charles 1976 *Chibaro*. London: Pluto Press.

Van Putten, Maartje and Lucas, Nicole 1985 *Made in Heaven: Women in the International Division of Labour*. Amsterdam: Evert Vermeer Stichting.

Vatuk, S. 1972 *Kinship and Urbanization: White Collar Migrants in North India.* Berkeley: University of California Press.

Vaughan, Megan 1983 'Which family?: problems in the reconstruction of the history of the family as an economic and cultural unit'. *Journal of African History*, 24: 275–83.

Vaughan, Megan 1987 *The Story of an African Famine.* Cambridge: Cambridge University Press.

Verdon, Michel 1980 'Descent: an operational view'. *Man*, 15 (1): 129–50.

Vogel, Lise 1983 *Marxism and the Oppression of Women.* London: Pluto Press.

Wachtel, Eleanor 1975 'A farm of one's own: the orientation of women's group enterprise in Nakuru, Kenya'. *Rural Africana*, 29: 69–80.

Walker, Cherryl 1982 *Women and Resistance in South Africa.* London: Onyx Press.

Wallman, Sandra 1979 Introduction to S. Wallman (ed.), *The Social Anthropology of Work*, 1–24. London: Academic Press.

Walvin, J. 1982 *A Child's World: A Social History of English Childhood 1800–1914.* Harmondsworth: Penguin.

Weatherford, J. M. 1975 'Anthropology and nannies'. Man, 10: 308–10.

Weber, Max 1972 'Politics as a vocation'. In H. Gerth and C. Mills (eds), *From Max Weber*, 129–56. New York: Oxford Unversity Press.

Weber, Max 1978 *Economy and Society.* 2 vols. Berkeley: University of California Press.

Weeks, Jeffrey 1985 *Sexuality and its Discontents.* London: Routledge & Kegan Paul.

Weiner, Annette 1976 *Women of Value, Men of Renown.* Austin: University of Texas Press.

Weiner, Annette 1979 'Trobriand kinship from another view: the reproductive power of women and men'. *Man*, 14 (2): 328–48.

West, Jackie 1978 'Women, sex and class'. In A. Kuhn and A.-M. Wolpe (eds), *Feminism and Materialism*, 220–53. London: Routledge & Kegan Paul.

Westwood, Sallie 1984 'Fear woman: property and modes of production in urban Ghana'. In R. Hirschon (ed.), *Women and Property, Women as Property*, 140–57. London: Croom Helm.

Whitehead, Ann 1977 'Review of Jack Goody's *Production and Reproduction*'. *Critique of Anthropology*, 3 (9–10): 151–9.

Whitehead, Ann 1981 'I'm hungry, Mum: the politics of domestic budgeting'. In K. Young et al. (eds), *Of Marriage and the Market*, 88–111. London: CSE Books.

Whitehead, Ann 1984 'Men and women, kinship and property: some general issues'. In R. Hirschon (ed.), *Women and Property, Women as Property*, 176–92. London: Croom Helm.

Whyte, Martin King 1984 'Sexual inequality under socialism: the Chinese case in perspective'. In J. Watson (ed.), *Class and Social Stratification in Post-Revolution China*, 198–238. Cambridge: Cambridge University Press.

Wilk, Richard 1984 'Households in process: agricultural change and domestic transformation among the Kekchi Maya of Belize'. In R. Netting et al. (eds), *Households: Comparative and Historical Studies of the Domestic Group*, 217–44. Berkeley: University of California Press.

Wilk, Richard R. and Netting, Robert 1984 'Households: changing forms and functions'. In R. Netting et al. (eds), *Households: Comparative and Historical Studies of the Domestic group*, 1–28. Berkeley: University of California Press.

Wilson, Elizabeth 1977 *Women and the Welfare State*. London: Tavistock.

Wipper, Audrey 1971 'The politics of sex'. *African Studies Review*, 14 (3): 463–82.

Wipper, Audrey 1975 'The Madaleo ya Wanawake movement: some paradoxes and contradictions'. *African Studies Review*, 18 (3): 99–120.

Wolf, Margery 1972 *Women and the Family in Rural Taiwan*. Stanford: Stanford University Press.

Wolpe, Harold 1972 'Capitalism and cheap labour power in South Africa: from segregation to apartheid'. *Economy and Society* 1: 425–56.

Wong, Aline 1981 'Planned development, social stratification, and the sexual division of labour in Singapore'. *Signs*, 7 (2): 434–52.

Wright, Marcia 1983 'Technology, marriage and women's work in the history of maize-growers in Mazabuka, Zambia: a reconnaissance'. *Journal of Southern African Studies*, 10 (1): 71–85.

Yanagisako, Sylvia Junko 1979 'Family and household: the analysis of domestic groups'. *Annual Review of Anthropology*, 8: 161–205.

Yeatman, Anna 1984 'Despotism and civil society: the limits of patriarchal citizenship'. In J. Stiehm (ed.), *Women's Views of the Political World of Men*, 151–76. Epping: Bowker.

Young, Iris 1980 'Socialist feminism and the limits of dual systems theory'. *Socialist Review*, 50–1: 169–88.

Young, M. and Willmott, P. 1962 *Family and Kinship in East London*. Harmondsworth: Penguin.

Young, Kate, Wolkowitz, Carol and McCullagh, Roslyn (eds) 1981 *Of Marriage and the Market*. London: CSE Books.

Youssef, Nadia 1976 *Women and Work in Developing Societies*. Westport, Conn.: Greenwood Press.

Youssef, Nadia 1978 'The status and fertility patterns of Muslim women'. In L. Beck and N. Keddie (eds), *Women in the Muslim World*, 69–99. Cambridge, Mass.: Harvard University Press.

Youssef, Nadia and Hefler, Carol 1983 'Establishing the economic condition of woman-headed households in the third world: a new approach'. In M. Buvinic et al. (eds), *Women and Poverty in the Third World*, 216–43. Baltimore: Johns Hopkins University Press.

INDEX

Africa 28–9, 34, 37–8, 44–6, 55–9, 60–2, 63–4, 70–1, 74–7, 80–1, 85–9, 91–3, 95–7, 101–2, 104, 111–12, 119–23, 125, 130–1, 133, 153, 155–64, 166–7, 169–70, 181–2
agriculture
  commercialization of 57–8, 74–82, 93, 152–3
  extension services 76, 153
  feminization of 75–80
  wages 93–4
  women's contribution to 43–4, 56–9, 66, 74–82
  see also labour; rural production systems; women; work
Altorki, Soraya 116–17
anthropology
  and development 151–2
  feminist see feminist anthropology
  and political elites 150–1
  and the state 130–1
  and the writing of ethnography 193–5
  see also ethnocentrism; feminism; fieldwork; state
apartheid 70–1, 86–9, 172
  see also ethnocentrism; race; racism; South Africa
Arab States 99, 103–8
Ardener, Edwin 1, 3–4, 14
Aries, Philip 26
Arizpe, Lourdes 90–1
Australian Aborigines 1, 23, 28–9, 32–3

Bamileke 130
Barnes, John 24
Bemba 60
betrothal gifts 65–7
biology
  as culturally constructed 14–16
  differences between the sexes 7, 190
  and motherhood 25–30
Bledsoe, Caroline 166
Boon, James 27–8
Boserup, Esther 43–6, 74
Brazil 101–2
bride-service 36
bridewealth 45, 70–2
Bryceson, Deborah 95–6
Buckley, Mary 141–3
Bujra, Janet 166, 170
Bukh, Jette 76–7
Burman, Sandra 70–1

capital
  accumulation of 80, 89–92
  relation to family form 90–1, 116–27

  and women's employment 112–16
  see also capitalism; family; labour; state
capitalism
  articulation with pre-capitalist modes of production 73–4
  and cottage industries 83–5
  differential effects on women 74–82
  and domestic labour 85–9
  and industrialization 97–112
  and marriage 119–27
  theories of women's employment 112–16
  see also capital; family; feminism; labour; rural production systems; wage labour; work
Caplan, Patricia 55–6, 168–9
Caribbean 62–3, 94, 123, 154
childbirth 16–17, 25
  payments for 70
childcare 52, 61, 63, 96–7, 108, 140
  state provision of 128, 139–40, 142–3
children
  and childhood 26
  custody of 70–1
  and the domestic 15, 25–6
  and nannies 26–7
China 65–7, 145–7, 148
Chonyi 70
Christianity and Western gender ideologies 83–4, 119–23, 126–7
civil rights 151
class
  definition of 209
  differences between women 9–10, 51, 79–82, 89, 90–1, 166, 168–70, 176, 209–12
  and the informal economy 90–3
  intersections with gender 10–11, 79–82, 85–9, 95–7
  intersections with race 9–10, 85–9
  and wage labour 103–6
  see also capitalism; women
Cock, Jacklyn 86–9
Collier, Jane 36
colonialism
  effects on marriage 119–23, 125
  effects on women 31–3, 44, 74–5, 133
  and history of anthropology 7, 193
  see also capitalism; ethnocentrism; rural production systems; women
couvade 29–30
  see also men; menstruation
Coward, Rosalind 47
Croll, Elizabeth 65–7, 139–43
Cuba 139–43